Anti-Catholicism in America, 1620–1860

Using fears of Catholicism as a mechanism through which to explore the contours of Anglo-American understandings of freedom, *Anti-Catholicism in America, 1620–1860* reveals the ironic role that anti-Catholicism played in defining and sustaining some of the core values of American identity, values that continue to animate our religious and political discussions today. Farrelly explains how that bias helped to shape colonial and antebellum cultural understandings of God, the individual, salvation, society, government, law, national identity, and freedom. In so doing, *Anti-Catholicism in America, 1620–1860* provides contemporary observers with a framework for understanding what is at stake in the debate over the place of Muslims and other non-Christian groups in American society.

Maura Jane Farrelly is Associate Professor of American Studies at Brandeis University, Massachusetts.

Cambridge Essential Histories

Cambridge Essential Histories is devoted to introducing critical events, periods, or individuals in history to students. Volumes in this series emphasize narrative as a means of familiarizing students with historical analysis. In this series, leading scholars focus on topics in European, American, Asian, Latin American, Middle Eastern, African, and World History through thesis-driven, concise volumes designed for survey and upper-division undergraduate history courses. The books contain an introduction that acquaints readers with the historical event and reveals the book's thesis; narrative chapters that cover the chronology of the event or problem; and a concluding summary that provides the historical interpretation and analysis.

Editors

General Editor: Donald T. Critchlow, Arizona State University

Other Books in the Series

Edward D. Berkowitz, *Mass Appeal: The Formative Age of the Movies, Radio, and TV*
Howard Brick and Christopher Phelps, *Radicals in America: The U.S. Left since the Second World War*
Sean P. Cunningham, *American Politics in the Postwar Sunbelt*
Ian Dowbiggin, *The Quest for Mental Health: A Tale of Science, Medicine, Scandal, Sorrow, and Mass Society*
John Earl Haynes and Harvey Klehr, *Early Cold War Spies: The Espionage Trials That Shaped American Politics*
James H. Hutson, *Church and State in America: The First Two Centuries*
Maury Klein, *The Genesis of Industrial America, 1870–1920*
Michael G. Kort, *The Vietnam War Reexamined*
John Lauritz Larson, *The Market Revolution in America: Liberty, Ambition, and the Eclipse of the Common Good*
Wilson D. Miscamble, *The Most Controversial Decision: Truman, the Atomic Bombs, and the Defeat of Japan*
Mark E. Neely Jr., *Lincoln and the Democrats: The Politics of Opposition in the Civil War*
Charles H. Parker, *Global Interactions in the Early Modern Age, 1400–1800*
Stanley G. Payne, *The Spanish Civil War*
W. J. Rorabaugh, *American Hippies*
Jason Scott Smith, *A Concise History of the New Deal*
David M. Wrobel, *America's West: A History, 1890–1950*

Anti-Catholicism in America, 1620–1860

MAURA JANE FARRELLY
Brandeis University, Waltham, Massachusetts

CAMBRIDGE
UNIVERSITY PRESS

CAMBRIDGE
UNIVERSITY PRESS

University Printing House, Cambridge CB2 8BS, United Kingdom

One Liberty Plaza, 20th Floor, New York, NY 10006, USA

477 Williamstown Road, Port Melbourne, VIC 3207, Australia

314-321, 3rd Floor, Plot 3, Splendor Forum, Jasola District Centre, New Delhi - 110025, India

79 Anson Road, #06-04/06, Singapore 079906

Cambridge University Press is part of the University of Cambridge.

It furthers the University's mission by disseminating knowledge in the pursuit of education, learning and research at the highest international levels of excellence.

www.cambridge.org
Information on this title: www.cambridge.org/9781107164505
DOI: 10.1017/9781316690932

© Maura Jane Farrelly 2018

First published 2018

A catalogue record for this publication is available from the British Library

Library of Congress Cataloging in Publication data
NAMES: Farrelly, Maura Jane, author.
TITLE: Anti-Catholicism in America, 1620–1860 / Maura Jane Farrelly, Brandeis University, Waltham, Massachusetts.
DESCRIPTION: New York : Cambridge University Press, 2018. | Series: Cambridge essential histories | Includes bibliographical references and index.
IDENTIFIERS: LCCN 2017030745 | ISBN 9781107164505 (alk. paper)
SUBJECTS: LCSH: Anti-Catholicism – United States. | United States – Church history.
CLASSIFICATION: LCC BX1770 .F37 2017 | DDC 305.6/8273–dc23
LC record available at https://lccn.loc.gov/2017030745

ISBN 978-1-107-16450-5 Hardback
ISBN 978-1-316-61636-9 Paperback

In memory of *Laurence D. Nee*

1970–2013

Contents

Figures

Preface

When GOP presidential candidate Mitt Romney announced that he had chosen Wisconsin Congressman Paul Ryan to be his running mate, the 2012 presidential election officially became historic. Not even four years had passed since Americans sent their first African-American to the White House, and already the Democratic and Republican parties were both offering up tickets that did not include a single White Anglo-Saxon Protestant.

Journalists and a handful of evangelical leaders did their best to explore the contours of Romney's Mormon faith. Stories about a "Mormon Moment" or "The Mormon in Mitt" snagged the covers of *Newsweek* and *Time* magazines, while conservative Christians who had not hesitated to use the word "cult" in the lead-up to the Republican National Convention found themselves scrambling in the months after that convention to convince their co-religionists that Romney was a "man for whom a faith with which we don't agree manifests itself in terms of values with which we *absolutely do* agree."[1]

With the exception of a few, untelevised testimonies from key members of Mitt Romney's temple in Belmont, Massachusetts, the Romney campaign said very little about the Church of Jesus Christ of Latter Day Saints. Americans may have reached a point where they were willing, finally, to cast their ballots for a Mormon, but the evangelical blogosphere made it clear that many of them would be doing so with heavy hearts. Romney's people wanted to make sure those hearts did not become so heavy that voters could not carry them all the way to the polls.

Such concerns did not animate Paul Ryan and Joe Biden, both of whom were more than happy to talk about the Catholic faith they had each been born into. Voters got a primer on the Catholic concept of "subsidiarity" from Ryan, who pointed to his Church's preference for "local solutions" when recommending that Medicare be turned into a voucher program. Biden spoke freely of his Catholic education when explaining his support for the president's overhaul of the country's healthcare system, pointing specifically to the "dignity in every man and woman" that he'd learned about from the priests and nuns who had helped to form him.[2]

Put simply, Catholic identity was not a problem for the two men who were looking to be second-in-command at the White House in 2012. Four years later, it wasn't a problem for Jeb Bush, Marco Rubio, Rick Santorum, or Chris Christie either, as they sought the Republican Party's nomination for president, or for Tim Kaine, as he accepted Hillary Clinton's request that he be her running mate. In 2004, John Kerry's Catholicism raised no red flags in his bid to unseat George W. Bush – except, ironically, among Catholic voters themselves. Kerry lost that election in part because more than half of the Catholics who voted in 2004 cast their ballots for the evangelical incumbent from Texas, rather than the Catholic senator from Massachusetts. Those voters – some of whom took their cues from bishops such as Raymond Burke of St. Louis, Michael Sheridan of Colorado Springs, John Myers of Newark, and Charles Chaput of Denver – were put off by Kerry's decision to part ways with his Church and vote against a national ban on late-term abortions.[3]

But no prominent, non-Catholic political, intellectual, cultural, or religious leader mentioned John Kerry's faith as a reason to vote against him. It is questionable, therefore, whether anti-Catholicism really is "the last acceptable prejudice," as some scholars and religious leaders have recently asserted.[4] That there is still much ignorance among non-Catholic Americans about the Church's beliefs and practices is undeniable. And certainly, the Catholic Church has proven to be a reliable, if easy punching bag in contemporary American popular culture, ranging from Andres Serrano's photograph, "Piss Christ" (1987), to Kevin Smith's film, *Dogma* (1999), to Dan Brown's novel, *The Da Vinci Code* (2003). My own experience with writing an article in 2015 for *Aeon* magazine proved to me that hostility toward the Catholic Church is still alive and well. The article was about anti-Catholicism, and several readers – possessing no sense of irony – wrote to me about the "well-beaten path" that connects Washington to Rome and is utilized by the Catholics who've been sent to Congress by the pope.[5]

It is no longer "acceptable," however (except among paranoid internet trolls), to point to Catholic identity as a threat to American democracy, even if an implicit openness to the existence of that threat may be what has given Dan Brown's novels their entertainment value. It is highly unlikely, for instance, that any Yale professor today would ever say about Catholicism what Harold Bloom said about Mormonism in 2011. Bloom is a Sterling Professor of Humanities – the highest rank given to any faculty member at Yale. His editorial in the *New York Times*, published about a year before the 2012 presidential election, suggested that Mitt Romney was unfit to lead the United States because his church was secretive and "not even monotheistic, let alone democratic."[6] Educated people who hold prestigious positions at elite universities simply don't say things like that about Catholics anymore.

But this trust in the democratic bona fides of American Catholics is a radical departure from the trajectory that American culture's understanding of Catholicism was on for most of the last four centuries. Long before the United States even was the "United States," voters, religious leaders, and politicians viewed Catholicism as a threat to national identity, individual liberty, personal salvation, and the stability of free government. Their fears continued up through the 1960 election campaign of John F. Kennedy, who famously met with the Greater Houston Ministerial Association to assure nervous Protestant voters that "I believe in an America where the separation between church and state is absolute . . . [and] no public official either requests or accepts instructions on public policy from the pope."[7]

Why American voters are, for the most part, no longer concerned about the prospect of a Catholic in the White House – even as they gobble up fictional narratives about Vatican conspiracies to hide murder, sexual hypocrisy, and historical truth – is an incredibly complex question. Without a doubt, Kennedy's election itself (if not his too-short presidency) played a role. So, too, did the decision of the Second Vatican Council (1962–1965) to call liberty of conscience a "right" grounded in the "dignity of the human person" nearly 175 years after the United States adopted the First Amendment to the Constitution. The political alliance that was crafted between Catholic leaders and conservative evangelical Christians in the 1970s and 1980s, as both groups worked to oppose the effects of second- and third-wave feminism and the rise of the gay rights movement, has also been important.[8]

But before we can understand why Catholicism is not a hurdle for ambitious politicians today, we first have to appreciate the significance of that very question. We must grapple, in other words, with the origins and meaning of what the noted twentieth-century Harvard historian

Arthur Schlesinger Sr. once called "the deepest-held bias in the history of the American people."⁹

In saying this, I feel I should stipulate that I don't think Schlesinger was correct when he characterized anti-Catholicism in this way. He was born in 1888. Even though he saw the start of the Civil Rights movement before he died, Schlesinger didn't live in an age when video technology was able to capture the implicit racial biases we all carry within us. There were no social media sites challenging him to confront the irrefutable evidence of this racial bias and its sometimes deadly consequences. In this age of Philando Castile and Walter Scott and John Crawford and Tamir Rice – not to mention the police officers who've been assassinated in retaliation for their deaths – I think it's undeniable that a bias against black people is actually the deepest-held bias in the history of the American people. *All* American people.

That being said, the history of anti-Catholicism in the United States does challenge us to confront some of the forces that animate our contemporary racial, ethnic, and religious biases, even if those biases have nothing to do with Catholicism. It does this by providing us with a window into the meaning of American identity and the values we stake a claim to when we assert that identity.

The Catholic Church represented different threats to different Americans at different points in time; and yet, over the course of the two and a half centuries that this book explores, one characteristic of the threat remained constant: Catholicism was at all times seen as antithetical to freedom. Freedom, in turn, was seen as the foundation of "American" identity – whether that identity belonged to the Puritans in the seventeenth century, the Patriots in the eighteenth century, or the Unitarians and Nativists in the nineteenth century.

Any understanding of anti-Catholicism, then, requires us to interrogate the meaning of American freedom and, by extension, the promise of American identity. The history of anti-Catholicism asks us to consider why, as a culture, we have sometimes built fences around the promise of American identity, thereby excluding some people from that promise even as we have clung to the idea that the freedom at the core of American identity is a universally "human" right, available to everyone.

The history of anti-Catholicism asks us to take fear seriously – to consider what anxieties people were actually expressing when they fretted about "popish plots" and "Romish conspiracies" and to explore how those anxieties were finally alleviated or eliminated, creating the conditions that allowed people to abandon their bigotry. If the history of anti-Catholicism teaches us anything, it is that bigotry can be highly complex. There is a real, if perverse logic that sustains it. And appreciating the complexity of that logic is an important first step toward eliminating the fear that fuels it.

This book is organized into two parts. The first three chapters deal with anti-Catholicism in British colonial America – or what became the United States in 1783, at the close of the American Revolution. The second three chapters consider anti-Catholicism in the new republic, before the Civil War.

It's impossible to understand the history of anti-Catholicism without an understanding of what it was that Protestants feared about the Church of Rome. To understand the early history of anti-Catholicism in the United States specifically, one needs to know what British Protestants feared, since anti-Catholicism in America was initially a British import. To understand what British Protestants feared about Catholicism, then, one needs to know who, exactly, these people were – what they believed, why they believed it, and how they differed from one another on important theological points.

Chapter 1, therefore – subtitled "Anti-Catholicism in Old England and New" – provides readers with the English political and religious context that influenced the settlement and development of colonial New England. It takes readers through a brief history of the Protestant Reformation, exploring the theological stakes behind the Catholic Church's "corruption" and how and why Protestant theologians responded to that corruption the way they did.

The chapter informs readers that of all the Protestant responses to the corruption of the sixteenth-century Catholic Church, the two that had the greatest influence on the early history of America were the Calvinist response and the Anglican response. The chapter explores what made these two Protestant theologies different from one another, how the adherents of one theology viewed the adherents of the other, and when and why anti-Catholicism became a bridge between the two, uniting Calvinists and Anglicans in the Old World and the New under the aegis of a single "Protestant" and "English" identity.

Chapter 2 continues with the connections between England and its colonies in North America. Subtitled "Anti-Catholicism and Colonial Catholics in the Seventeenth Century," the chapter considers the limits of anti-Catholicism, even in the English-speaking world, and explores the reality that Catholicism did not disappear from the English landscape after the Catholic Church was outlawed in England. Indeed, there was a small, but wealthy group of people in England who remained committed to their Catholic faith, and these families formed the foundation of the Catholic community in British North America.

That community was small and concentrated – mostly in Maryland, though there were Catholics living in New York and Pennsylvania, as well. All three colonies extended religious toleration to Catholics in the seventeenth century, and the chapter explores the contours of that toleration in Maryland, where it had the greatest impact on Catholic lives. The chapter informs readers from the get-go that this toleration was short-lived; in the 1690s, the connection between "Protestant" and "English" identity spoken about in Chapter 1 ensured that the era of religious toleration for most British colonial Catholics came to an end. Nevertheless, the experience of toleration (and its loss) reverberated into the eighteenth century, having an impact on the kind of Catholic identity that developed in the new United States.

Chapter 3 is subtitled "Anti-Catholicism and the American Revolution." It is here that readers begin to move beyond England and into a more thoroughly "American" context. Fears of Catholicism animated much of the rhetoric leading up to the American Revolution. The chapter explores these fears, explaining that they were grounded in a distinctly Protestant understanding of freedom and the sense, then, that Catholics could not grasp or accept this understanding of freedom because they were Catholic.

The chapter examines how the Catholic Church's approach to freedom *was* different from the Protestant approach – but notes that the experiences Catholics had in British colonial America made their understanding of freedom different from the one advocated by the leadership of their Church. American Catholics, in fact, had an approach to freedom that was more like that of their Protestant countrymen than many of the Patriots were willing to allow, at least at first. Among the experiences that shaped American Catholics' understanding of freedom in the decades leading up to the American Revolution, the experience of being legally, politically, and culturally marginalized was, ironically, the most salient.

In Chapter 4, readers get a bit of a break from anti-Catholicism – but not from religious disagreements. Subtitled "Anti-Catholicism and the New Republic," the chapter considers the surprising *lack* of anti-Catholicism in the early decades of America's existence as a free and independent nation. It also considers the impact that the absence of religious animosity had on the Catholic Church in the United States.

America's first generation of independent citizens seemed to take the commitments they made in the Declaration of Independence pretty seriously (at least when it came to religion); they understood that Catholics, too, had "unalienable rights." The chapter examines the theory of government that animated the American Founding and explains why a collective commitment to religious liberty naturally evolved out of that theory. It also looks at how Catholics in America responded to the environment created by this commitment to religious liberty: they reacted by turning inward and disagreeing with each other. Because they didn't need to fight Protestants anymore for basic civil rights, Catholics (who shared their Protestant neighbors' fiercely republican approach to freedom) were able to fight with one another as they worked to grow and expand their Church's presence on the American landscape.

Chapters 5 and 6, then, are complements to one another; they each tell the story of anti-Catholicism's resurrection in America at a time when thousands – indeed, millions – of Catholic immigrants started pouring into the country from Germany and Ireland. Chapter 5 is subtitled "Anti-Catholicism in the Age of Immigration," and it examines the demographic and cultural changes that provoked the anxiety that led to the re-emergence of anti-Catholicism in the mid-nineteenth century. The immigrants who came to the United States in the thirty-year period between 1820 and 1850 were radically different from the ones who'd come before that time; the chapter explores what made these immigrants different, and it explains why these differences made many native-born Americans uncomfortable.

The chapter notes that immigrants were not the only forces of anxiety-inducing change in the mid-nineteenth century. Traditional Protestant theologies were also losing their grip on America's collective soul. Many people still considered themselves to be deeply religious, but a growing number of them were turning their backs on the arbitrary and immoveable God found in orthodox Calvinism – the theology that had dominated New England and served as an intellectual foundation for the United States for nearly 200 years by that point. In this environment of "softening" religious commitment, traditional Protestants leaders determined that the country was morally vulnerable – and they believed that this vulnerability heightened the threat represented by Catholic immigration.

Chapter 6 is subtitled "Anti-Catholicism and American Politics." It looks more specifically at what Americans feared in the nineteenth century and why those fears led them to join societies (the American Home Missionary Society), form political parties (the Native American or "Know Nothing" Party), and even fight in a war (the Mexican War) in order to contain or eliminate Catholicism's influence on the United States.

Some Americans feared that the uptick in Catholic immigration was part of a papal plot to destroy the United States and the freedom that it represented. To this way of thinking, immigrants were an army of soldiers with two powerful weapons: their slavish habits and their ability to vote. The fear was that Catholic citizens would do as their priests told them to do and elect leaders who would work to eliminate freedom.

Other Americans had more specific and slightly less paranoid concerns – though their concerns, ultimately, brought them to the same place. They worried that the failure of the Catholic Church to loudly condemn the institution of slavery meant that Catholic voters could not be relied upon to fight slavery at the polls. These abolitionists worked, therefore, to deny Catholics the ability to vote.

In the end, the effort to turn anti-Catholicism into a solid and legitimate political movement failed. Chapter 6 informs readers that the Know Nothing Party was undermined by regional differences, the outbreak of the Civil War, and the voting power of immigrants themselves.

Anti-Catholicism continued to be culturally powerful after the Civil War, however – and it manifested, politically, in some surprising ways. Much of our modern-day understanding of Church–State separation, for instance, is indebted to late-nineteenth-century fears of Catholic influence on American children. But fears of Catholicism in the twentieth century never had the rhetorical, political, or foundational power that they had in the seventeenth, eighteenth, and nineteenth centuries. Americans may have refused to send Al Smith to the White House when he became the first Catholic to seek the presidency in 1928 – but New Yorkers sent him to the governor's mansion in Albany four times.

NOTES

1. Walter Kirn, "The Mormon Moment," *Newsweek*, June 5, 2011; Jon Meacham, "The Mormon in Mitt Romney," *Time*, October 8, 2012; Charles Mitchell, "Gov. Romney and 'Traditionally Mormon' Traits," May 21, 2012, *Evangelicals for Mitt*: http://evangelicalsformitt.org/2012/05/gov-romney-and-traditionally-mormon-traits/, accessed January 27, 2015.

2. David Gibson, "Paul Ryan's Subsidiarity," *Commonweal*, April 10, 2012; "Vice President Joe Biden: Catholics for Obama," political ad published on October 29, 2012, accessed on July 8, 2016: www.youtube.com/watch?v=qP5H64VYBpc.

3. "The Catholic 'Swing' Vote," Pew Research Center for Religion and Public Life, October 11, 2012, accessed on July 8, 2016: www.pewforum.org/2012/10/11/the-catholic-swing-vote/; David D. Kirkpatrick and Laurie Goodstein, "Group of Bishops Using Influence to Oppose Kerry," *New York Times*, October 12, 2004.

4. Philip Jenkins, *The New Anti-Catholicism: The Last Acceptable Prejudice* (New York, 2004); James Martin, "The Last Acceptable Prejudice," *America*, March 25, 2000; Joel Connelly, "Anti-Catholicism: The Last Acceptable Prejudice," *Seattle Post Intelligencer*, March 15, 2013.

5. Maura Jane Farrelly, "The War on Rome," *Aeon*, May 22, 2015, accessed on July 8, 2016: https://aeon.co/essays/why-it-has-become-ok-to-be-american-and-catholic.

6. Harold Bloom, "Will This Election Be a Mormon Breakthrough," *New York Times*, November 12, 2011.

7. John F. Kennedy, "Speech of Senator John F. Kennedy, Greater Houston Ministerial Association." Rice Hotel, Houston, TX. September 12, 1960. Available at The American Presidency Project, accessed on July 8, 2016: www.presidency.ucsb.edu/ws/?pid=25773.

8. Randall Balmer, *Thy Kingdom Come: An Evangelical's Lament* (New York, 2006), 1–34.

9. Quoted in John Tracy Ellis, *American Catholicism* (Chicago, 1969), 151.

Acknowledgments

I would like to begin by thanking Don Critchlow of Arizona State University and Lew Bateman of Cambridge University Press for asking me to write this book – and then sticking with me and giving me the space that I ended up needing to complete the project. Thank you, too, to Deborah Gershenowitz at Cambridge for assuming the editorial reins (no easy task). And to Kris Deusch, Helen Cooper, Robert Judkins, and Anubam Vijayakrishnan, for their assistance, as well.

I would like to thank my family – my parents, Eugene and Kathleen Farrelly; my siblings, Gene and Meg Farrelly; and my in-laws, Amber Farrelly and Peter Vinick – along with my friends, Terrell Austin, Gabe Bartlett, Deanna Devaney, Pamela Edwards, Dustin Gish, Peggy Lemieux, Rafe and Robin Major, Eileen McNamara, Eileen, Mary, and Marianne Nee, Amy Nendza, and Ann Rindone, for supporting me while I navigated the difficult space that delayed this book's completion.

In addition to my family and Terrell Austin, I would like to thank the following friends and colleagues for providing me with valuable feedback and/or volunteering to help copy-edit this book: Bryan Barks, Peggy Bendroth, Chris Beneke, Tom Burke, Moira Davenport, Alison Donohue Harding, Kerith Harding, Cliff Putney, Jon Roberts, and, as always, Charley Simmons.

"It Hath Been Found Inconsistent with the Safety and Welfare of this Protestant Kingdom"

Anti-Catholicism in Old England and New

John Winthrop had to work to convince his fellow Puritans to join him on a voyage that would lead to the founding of the Massachusetts Bay Colony in 1630. Journeys across the Atlantic were extraordinarily dangerous in the seventeenth century, and many of the people who subscribed to the Calvinist theology that influenced Winthrop simply didn't think that such a journey was necessary. They shared the lawyer's disdain for the Church of England, believing that that Church's ministers failed to provide the kind of leadership that God demanded. But they were uncomfortable with the idea of moving to the New World, where they would have to occupy land that they knew had "of long time been possessed of others of Adam."[1] They also weren't convinced that the Church of England's problems had gotten so bad that true followers of Christ needed to leave.

Winthrop had the same response to both concerns: Remember that there are menacing Catholics on the horizon. With regard to the natives who'd been living on land in North America for centuries, he advised his fellow Calvinists that those natives were already being dispossessed of their lands by Europeans; the Europeans, however, were nasty Frenchmen – many of them priests. Migration to the New World under these circumstances would be a "service to the church of great consequence," as the Puritans would be able to "raise a bulwark against the kingdom of Antichrist, which the Jesuits labor to rear up in those parts."[2]

As far as English society and the condition of the Church of England were concerned, Calvinists needed to understand just how bad things really were. "The fountains of learning and religion are so corrupted," the future governor of Massachusetts maintained, that "most children (even the best wits and fairest hopes) are perverted, corrupted, and utterly

overthrown by the multitude of evil examples of the licentious government of those seminaries." The problem was that the leader of the Church
of England, King Charles I, had expressed his admiration for some of the
key elements of Catholic theology. He'd also taken a full-blown Catholic
as his wife and tolerated all sorts of "popish ceremonies" within England's
nominally Protestant church.[3] All good Puritans understood why this was
a problem; John Winthrop wanted them to understand that it was not a
problem that could be fixed by staying in England. To reform Christianity
in their country, the "purifiers" needed to leave. They needed to go some-
place new where they'd be able to build a model society for the people
back home to witness, learn from, and eventually replicate.

CHAPTER OVERVIEW

The idea that the Puritans came to the New World in the name of "religious
freedom" is a myth. The truth is that in the seventeenth-century English-
speaking world, no single group was more religiously intolerant than the
Congregationalists who made up the bulk of the Puritan settlements in early
colonial America. Nevertheless, there's a reason that the "religious freedom"
story persists. The Puritans may have been religiously intolerant, but they
also held it as an article of faith that every person had an obligation to "read
and judge for himself" the meaning and import of the Word of God.[4] People
needed to be free to recognize truth on their own, without any guidance or
interference from a priest or bishop; this is why the idea of freedom is so
strongly associated with the Puritans. The Puritan understanding of freedom, however, did not mean that it was acceptable for people to be wrong.

   Outside the State House in Boston, there's a large statue that testifies to
the real religious history of New England (Figure 1.1). For nearly sixty
years now, Massachusetts lawmakers have been passing a bronze rendering of Mary Dyer as they walk to work each morning. Dyer was one of
three Quakers who were hanged on Boston Common in the 1660s because
they refused to leave Massachusetts Bay and take their crazy ideas about
the "inner light" of God with them. Authorities in nearby Dorchester,
Dedham, and Roxbury never went to the extreme of actually killing anyone for being a Quaker, but they did flog and run countless "Friends" out
of town rather than tolerate Quakers' unorthodox ideas about God. Like
their co-religionists in Boston, they also banished more than a few of their
fellow Calvinists for expressing ideas about the governance of the church
that were considered to be "new and dangerous."[5]

FIGURE 1.1 This statue of Mary Dyer was designed by the Quaker sculptor Sylvia Shaw Judson. It was placed outside the Massachusetts Statehouse in 1959 to commemorate the 300th anniversary of Dyer's execution.
Photo credit: Charles B. Simmons.

Native American Indians, too, experienced the religious intolerance of the Puritans. Indeed, one of the many "dangerous" ideas that got Roger Williams banished from Massachusetts was his belief that it was wrong for his Calvinist neighbors to refer to the Narragansett and Wampanoag Indians as "heathens." The members of these local tribes, Williams insisted, were "intelligent, many very ingenuous, plain-hearted, inquisitive, and (as I said before) prepared with many convictions." They were not a people without faith, as the word "heathen" would imply. It was a distinction too subtle for many of the people living in Boston and Salem to compute, however. Williams' approach to the Indians seemed to them to be at odds with the mission of the Massachusetts Bay Company, which was "to win and incite the natives of the country to the knowledge and Obedience of the only true God and Savior of Mankind, and the Christian Faith."[6] The outspoken Baptist, therefore, had to go.

But Roger Williams was not a religious relativist. The committee that banished him may not have understood it, but he definitely wanted the Indians to convert to Christianity – and because of that, he didn't hesitate in some of his personal correspondences to refer to them as "wild, barbarous wretches." The future founder of Rhode Island firmly believed that "the followers of Jesus are now the only people of God." He simply didn't think that the Puritans would be able to convert anyone to their faith so long as they failed to take native religious beliefs seriously.[7]

Such patience and understanding, however, were not something Williams was willing to extend to people who worshipped within the Church of Rome. Like all the other Calvinists in New England, Williams had come to North America to get away from the "popish relics" within the Church of England's theology and liturgy. Granted, he didn't want to see papists hanged – in part because he believed that persecution only caused Catholics to "tumble into the ditch of hell after their blind leaders with more inflamed zeal."[8] He also didn't think it was ever the job of a civil magistrate to enforce matters of religious belief (another of the "new and dangerous" ideas that got him kicked out of Massachusetts).

But Roger Williams had no patience for Catholics, and he certainly wasn't willing to accord them any intelligence, inquisitiveness, or legitimate "convictions." The Indians may have been "wretches," but Williams reserved the word "*Antichristian*" for the "worship in life and death" that had characterized his native country "when *England* was all *Popish* under Henry the seventh." He praised the turn toward "absolute Protestantism" that England had taken "under Queen Elizabeth," even if that turn had retained too much of the pomp and hierarchy of the Church of Rome. And he insisted – almost immediately after praising the religious convictions of the Narragansett – that "if Antichrist be [Catholics'] false head (as most true it is), their body, faith, baptism & hope are all false also."[9]

The Puritans came to North America in the name of *their* religious freedom, and in many of the communities they established – not just in modern-day Massachusetts, but in New York, Maryland, and Virginia, as well – they proved to be more than capable of exhibiting a vast degree of intolerance when it came to ideas about God and humanity's duties to God that conflicted with those of the sixteenth-century Protestant theologian, John Calvin. Of all of the people who got under the Puritans' collars, however, no one got under there more than a Catholic, as the observations of even unusually tolerant Calvinists like Roger Williams proved.

Opposition to Catholicism was the primary reason English Calvinists came to the New World in the 1620s and 1630s. As time marched on, however, and the seventeenth century gradually became the eighteenth century, anti-Catholic sentiment became more than just a motive for emigration; it became a tool that settlers in North America used to maintain their sense of "English" identity, even as they lived 3,000 miles away from England and a growing number of them were living their entire lives never once having set foot on the British isle.

Maintaining their English identity was important to America's early British colonists. It's a reality that we forget sometimes, knowing as we do that the colonies ultimately broke away from England and became their own country. But the Puritans did not travel to the New World so that they could become Americans. They saw themselves as Englishmen and women who happened to be living in North America. For several generations after the initial founding of those settlements along Massachusetts and Cape Cod Bays, the colonists worked hard to teach their children (and remind themselves) that they were English. They read English books, drank English tea, wore English cloth, built English houses, and furnished those houses with English cabinets, tables, and chairs.[10] After 1689, when an anti-Catholic coup in England known as the "Glorious Revolution" firmly established that to be "English" was to be "Protestant," the Puritans in North America also used their long-standing animosity toward the Catholic Church to assert their English identity to each other and to their countrymen on the other side of the Atlantic.

This association between "English" and "Protestant" identity that solidified after the Glorious Revolution actually took a long time to develop. King Henry VIII had broken with the Catholic Church and formed the Church of England (also known as the Anglican Church) more than 150 years earlier, in 1534; that did not mean, however, that England immediately became a Protestant nation. For many years, there were few theological differences between the Anglican and Catholic Churches, and Henry was not very good about forcing people to adhere to the new Anglican faith. Roger Williams himself noted in 1644 that England had moved from "half-Protestantism, half-Popery under *Henry the eighth* to absolute Protestantism under *Edward* the sixth ... to absolute Popery under *Queen Mary*," before Elizabeth I finally assumed the throne in 1558.[11]

Good Queen Bess quickly issued the Acts of Uniformity and Supremacy and the Thirty-Nine Articles of Religion, which did create some solid theological distinctions between the Church of England and the Church of Rome (Puritans never felt those distinctions went far enough...). The Acts and Articles required all of England's residents to attend Anglican church services, redefined the Sacraments to exclude several that were important to the Catholic Church (such as Marriage and Confession), switched the liturgy from Latin to English, and made the Book of Common Prayer (which was written by an English theologian named Thomas Cranmer) the official source of liturgical worship in all of England.[12]

Even then, though, the issue of England's Protestant identity was still far from settled. Elizabeth's successor, King James I, issued a number of harsh laws in the early seventeenth century that required England's minority Catholics to swear their allegiance to him and pay heavy fines whenever they failed to attend Anglican worship services. Those fines, however, were implemented only sporadically; James' wife, Anne, was a secret Catholic convert (a fact that her husband knew – and tolerated – so long as she practiced her faith quietly); and James was himself friendly enough with some of the country's leading Catholics to elevate several of them to the peerage, more than doubling the number of Catholic noblemen in England during his reign.[13]

King James' son proved to be even more accepting of Catholicism than his father had been. Charles I became England's king in 1625, five years before the Puritans sailed to Massachusetts. He was married to a Catholic – Queen Henrietta Maria, who'd been born and raised in France. Her older brother, Louis XIII, was the king of that Catholic country, and her mother, Marie de Medici, belonged to one of the wealthiest and most politically powerful Catholic families in all of Europe. Several popes, in fact, had been members of the Medici family, including Pope Leo X, whose abuses had launched the Protestant Reformation roughly one hundred years before Charles and Henrietta Maria were married.

During his reign, King Charles I worked to reconcile the Anglican and Roman Catholic Churches. He publicly expressed regret that the Reformation had ever happened, and, at one point, he outlined a "middle way" between Anglicanism and Catholicism that included having the Catholic Mass said in English and allowing priests to marry, provided they did not become bishops. Charles I also appointed William Laud as the Archbishop of Canterbury. Puritans hated Bishop Laud, and following his appointment in 1633, many Calvinists who'd been unwilling to join John Winthrop three years earlier hopped on ships and eagerly traveled to the New World. Laud used the word "heretical" to describe many of the beliefs embraced by England's Calvinists, and his efforts to install stained-glass windows in several Anglican churches seemed to the Puritans to smack of popery.[14]

The cozy relationship that Charles I had with Catholicism made even some Anglicans uncomfortable; it goes without saying, therefore, that Calvinists were nearly apoplectic. They rose up against their king in the 1640s and launched a civil war that led to a dour but solidly Protestant period in England's history known as the *Interregnum* – in Latin, "the period between the kings." From 1649 to 1660, England had no ruling monarch because the Puritans in Parliament had executed King Charles I. His two teenaged sons, Charles and James, had fled to France.

During the Interregnum, the country was led by what was known as a "Lord Protector" – an intensely religious Calvinist military commander named Oliver Cromwell. Together with Parliament, Cromwell implemented dozens of policies that reflected his Calvinist understanding of piety and government – among them the banning of Christmas and Easter, which Calvinists considered to be "heathenish customs and pagan rites" that the Catholic Church had co-opted as part of its effort to convert people to a perverted form of Christianity. Cromwell also sent his army into Ireland, which had a predominantly Catholic population, and launched a war there that killed more than 40 percent of the civilian population in just four years through conflict, disease, and artificial famine, brought on by the army's policy of burning crops and slaughtering livestock.[15]

Cromwell's laws during the Interregnum did not always sit well with Anglicans, who shared his dislike of Catholicism, but also enjoyed yule logs and mince pies and believed that regardless of what the Catholic Church may have done with the Christmas holiday, Christians were still obliged to "keep diligently the feast days, and truly in the first place the day of Christ's birth."[16] Anglicans were not the only Protestants in

England who found Cromwell's rules to be a bit problematic. Even some of the Presbyterians who'd helped to launch the English Civil War had some concerns.

As Calvinists, Britain's Presbyterian leaders shared Cromwell's theological outlook and his attitude toward Catholicism; they were disappointed, however, in his failure to turn the Church of England into solidly Calvinist Church. Cromwell had a zero-tolerance policy on Catholicism, but he proved to be surprisingly ecumenical when it came to the numerous Protestant theologies that flourished in England – including theologies that seemed to suggest people might have more control over their salvation than John Calvin and his Congregationalist and Presbyterian followers allowed.

Presbyterians wanted the country to be far more uniform in its approach to religion, and they felt that a monarchy – especially one where the king had been humbled by the execution of his father – would be the best way to achieve that uniformity. When Cromwell died, therefore, they joined with the more traditional Anglicans in Parliament and issued an invitation in 1660 to King Charles I's older son, Charles, to return to England and assume the throne.

This invitation, however, soon put Catholicism front and center in the country again. Charles II died with no legitimate children after twenty-five years on the throne; this meant that his younger brother, James, became the King of England in 1685, and James was a Catholic. He'd converted in 1668, at the age of 34, after spending his teens and twenties in exile in Catholic France following his father's execution at the hands of fanatical Calvinists.

James II did enjoy a loyal following among some people – especially in Scotland, where rebels worked to defend his legacy for many years after he was deposed in 1689. But no one in Parliament wanted a king who was Catholic. When James' Catholic wife, Mary of Modena, gave birth to a baby boy in 1688, therefore, many members of Parliament felt that they had to act fast, or else be subject to another lifetime's worth of Catholic rule.

They invited James' daughter from his first marriage, Mary – who'd been raised as an Anglican – and her Dutch Calvinist husband, William of Orange, to take the throne. In what became known as the "Glorious Revolution," Parliament officially declared that "it hath been found inconsistent with the safety and welfare of this Protestant kingdom to be governed by a popish prince." James II was summarily overthrown, and thanks to the Act of Settlement passed by Parliament a little more than a decade after the Glorious Revolution, England hasn't had a Catholic ruler since. Indeed, the Act of Settlement still bars Roman Catholics from assuming the throne in England; since 2015, however, future monarchs have been permitted to marry people who subscribe to the Roman Catholic faith.[17]

Because the cementing of "English" and "Protestant" identity that was accomplished by the Glorious Revolution involved a deliberate denial of Catholicism's religious and political legitimacy, anti-Catholicism became an expression of "Englishness" in the decades that followed William and Mary's coup. This reality helps to explain why New England became such a hotbed of anti-Catholic sentiment in the eighteenth century, even though Catholics in the region – according to native son, John Adams – were "as rare as a comet or an earthquake."[18]

That's not to say that New Englanders' fears about Catholics and Catholicism were entirely unfounded. Their region bordered Quebec, after all, which was a French and Catholic colony. Between 1688 and 1763, England and France went to war with one another four different times, and during the intervening years, the countries' New World colonists often skirmished over territory and trade, frequently using native Indians as their proxies.

But when they railed against the "tyranny" and "abominable super-stitions" of the Catholic Church, New Englanders were not making statements about any actual Catholics among them. Rather, they were telling the world – and more particularly, themselves and their country-men on the other side of the Atlantic – that they were just as "English" as anyone who'd been born and raised in London or Leeds. And, as Englishmen, the residents of Massachusetts, Rhode Island, Connecticut, and New Hampshire believed they were entitled to a host of individual rights – rights that would one day launch a revolution and lead to the creation of a whole new country in North America.[19]

THE REFORMATION, BRIEFLY CONSIDERED

Protestantism was a reaction against the Catholic Church, a theological "protest" against doctrines and hierarchies that – certainly in the sixteenth century – had become tools of political and economic intrigue, rather than expressions of genuine piety or the fulfillment of God's wishes for human-ity. Dozens of theologians wrote treatises that criticized the Catholic Church's pollution of Christ's message. Martin Luther was by no means the only one, and indeed he was not even the first. Thanks to the invention of the printing press, however – and the support of some very powerful secular authorities, such as Frederick III, the Elector of Saxony – Luther was able to succeed where others before him had failed.[20]

Among the practices that Luther questioned was the Church's distribution of "indulgences," which were intercessions that living Christians could make – *only* with the help of the Church – on behalf of themselves or anyone, really, who had died with the stain of venial sin on his or her soul. According to Church teaching, just about everyone died in a state of venial sin.*

A "venial" sin was one that God had already forgiven out of love. That did not mean it was a sin that had not engendered a penalty, however. Unlike mortal sins, venial sins didn't condemn a soul to Hell, but they did prevent that soul from immediately entering Heaven, requiring the soul instead to spend time in a kind of middling realm known as "purgatory." There, souls would contemplate the damage that sins such as lying, cheating, and laziness did to one's relationship with God, doing penance in purgatory for that damage before moving on to Heaven.[21]

According to Catholic doctrine, an indulgence could shorten the amount of time that a soul spent in purgatory by drawing upon a "treasury of merits" that had been created, sustained, and made available to sinners by the prayers and sacrifices of Jesus and the saints. The Church granted – and indeed still grants – indulgences to Catholics who have engaged in certain prayer exercises, such as the Rosary Novena or the Stations of the Cross, or performed good works for humanity, the Church, and God with devotion and sincerity. The Church no longer grants indulgences in exchange for cash payments, however, which is what many bishops were doing in the sixteenth century when a young Augustinian friar from Wittenberg, Germany, started questioning the doctrine of indulgences – and then many other teachings of the Roman Catholic Church.[22]

In 1513, Giovani de Medici became Pope Leo X. In just a few years, he managed to bring the Vatican to the brink of bankruptcy, hosting elaborate parties that included musicians, dwarves, elephants, and – according to Martin Luther, at least (whose authority on the subject is admittedly

---

* Mary, the mother of Jesus, was the one exception to this rule. She was thought to have been conceived without sin and to have spent her entire life free of sin – though this belief did not have dogmatic distinction at the time of the Protestant Reformation. It was not until 1854 that Mary's "Immaculate Conception" became dogma (i.e., something all Catholics must believe in order to be Catholic).

suspect) – young boys who participated in sexual liaisons. Under Leo X's leadership, the Vatican quickly went broke, and so the young pope turned to what had been a common fund-raising technique under his predecessor: He appointed thirty-one new cardinals and charged each of them a large sum of money for the privilege of assuming his new office.[23]

The new cardinals raised the money they needed by giving indulgences to wealthy laypeople who "donated" money to the Church. It was a practice that Martin Luther believed was misleading and dangerous. "I grieve over the wholly false impressions which the people have conceived from it," he wrote to his bishop, Albrecht von Brandenburg (who happened to be one of the cardinals raising money in this way). "To wit – the unhappy souls believe that if they have purchased letters of indulgence, they are sure of their salvation."

Luther warned his bishop that if he and the other new cardinals didn't stop selling indulgences, someone might "publish writings in which he will confute [the cardinals] ... to the shame of your Most Illustrious Sublimity." Claiming to "shrink very much from thinking that this will be done," Luther nevertheless provided his bishop with a taste of what the Vatican might have to deal with if its officials did not make it clear to the laity that indulgences were not tickets into Heaven. He included with his letter a list of ninety-five observations about Christianity – many of them quite critical of the Church – all the while imploring the bishop to accept the observations "with the greatest clemency, as I offer them out of a faithful heart."[24]

It's not clear that Luther ever actually nailed his theses to the door of All Saint's Church in Wittenberg, as legend maintains. It does seem, however, that the 34-year-old friar fully intended for his points to find a greater audience. Three months after he sent his letter to the Bishop of Mainz in the spring of 1517, Martin Luther arranged for his ninety-five theses to be translated from Latin into German and then printed and distributed throughout the several German principalities. Within two months, those German copies were translated again into English, French, and Dutch and dispersed across central and Western Europe.[25]

The 95 Theses were harbingers – signs of greater criticisms to come. In the years that followed, Luther called for Christians to pay more attention to the words of Scripture than to the extensive body of teachings and instruction – known as "doctrine" – that Catholic theologians had created, debated, and handed down throughout the centuries. It was doctrine, after all – not Scripture – that was responsible for the entire idea of "indulgences." It was doctrine, more than anything else, that had led to the pollution of Christ's message that Christians were now witnessing in the Church. *Sola scriptura* – "by Scripture alone" – became the rallying cry of those who followed Luther, eventually breaking with the Catholic Church and forming their own ecclesiastical tradition within Christianity, known today as "Lutheranism."

PROTESTANTISM, BRIEFLY CONSIDERED

When he pointed to Scripture to justify what his followers came to call a "priesthood of all believers," saying that "a cobbler, a smith, a farmer … are all alike consecrated priests" and that "if we are all priests, why should we not also test and judge what is correct or incorrect in matters of faith," Martin Luther opened a theological can of worms.[26] The Vatican may have been corrupt in the sixteenth century, but it had been doing a pretty good job up of keeping Christianity on-message up until that point – with the exceptions of the "Great Schism" of 1054, which had led to the east–west split between Orthodoxy and Catholicism, and the brief 39-year period at the end of the fourteenth century when, inconveniently, three different men had claimed to be pope.

Now, though, everyone in Western Europe was being told that he had the power to access and understand the will of God on his own – through "Scripture alone." And in the decades that followed, many people did just exactly that.

The most fervent concern of the Protestant theologians who wrote during and after Luther's historic campaign was that God's wishes for humanity be understood and embraced. The second most fervent concern, especially among the first two generations to follow Luther's excommunication in 1521, was that the Catholic Church's corruption be avoided – that the theologies these Christian thinkers shared with the world not fall victim to the same disease that had infected Rome.

That disease, people such as Ulrich Zwingli, Martin Bucer, Menno Simons, John Calvin, and Jacob Arminius all believed, was human frailty. The reason the Catholic Church had become corrupt was that its doctrines had mistakenly taught people, who were unavoidably flawed, that there was something they could to do to influence the will of God – that their divine punishment for sin (and perhaps even their salvation) was theirs to determine through words and deeds. Such a slippery slope, Protestant theologians believed, led inevitably to the kind of corruption that Martin Luther had decried. Even if the Catholic clergy had made it clear to people that indulgences were not tickets into Heaven (and make no mistake, many of the bishops selling indulgences in the fifteenth and sixteenth centuries had *not* made that clear – because they, too, were flawed), it was still inevitable that some people would come to view indulgences in this way. If people were allowed to believe they had power – particularly power over God – that belief would eventually corrupt them.

These theologians, therefore, joined Luther in articulating an understanding of God's wishes for humanity that completely divorced the idea of salvation from the power of human action. Nothing you did – and, just as important, no Church you belonged to – could determine the destiny of your immortal soul. Those who were saved were saved through the power of Christ's sacrifice and the love of God, which God chose to bestow upon human beings freely, according to His will alone and not according to the merits of the lives those human beings led. It was *grace*, not works that saved a soul. You could buy an indulgence or not buy an indulgence; it mattered not as far as your soul's salvation was concerned.

Such a theological premise raised an obvious question – namely, why should anyone bother to be good, if human action had nothing to do with salvation? Here, then, was one of the issues that caused some Protestant theologians to part ways with one another. Most insisted that good works were a natural consequence of the decision to accept God's love – and not the actual *cause* of anything, least of all salvation. But some theologians allowed that good works could provide comfort to people (the idea being that the mere ability to perform good works was probably a sign of one's salvation), while others cautioned against trying to "penetrate the hidden recesses of the divine wisdom" in this way. Some taught that good works helped people to retain the salvation that God had chosen to give them, ensuring that God didn't change His mind some time before they died; others insisted that such reasoning was no different from the "doctrine of works" that had led to the Catholic Church's original corruption. These disagreements – and countless others – sparked the development of numerous and distinct theological traditions that continue to dot the religious landscape in the United States and around the world today: Anabaptist, Adventist, Anglican, Dispensational, Pentecostal, Pietist, Reformed, Unitarian, Wesleyan – the list goes on.[27]

Two theological traditions played particularly important roles in the early development of anti-Catholicism in America – the Anglican tradition and the Reformed tradition. Anglicanism is the theological posture adopted by the Church of England; its tenets were defined in the sixteenth century by Thomas Cranmer, the Archbishop of Canterbury. Reformed theology is more commonly known today as "Calvinism," because although John Calvin was not the only theologian who contributed to this tradition, his ideas were extraordinarily influential in the development of a theology that went on to serve as the foundation of dozens of denominations that differed from one another in terms of polity, history, ritual, or ethnic identity, but shared a common understanding of who God is and what God wants.

Anglicans and Calvinists didn't get along with one another; indeed, the English Civil War in the 1640s had primarily been a battle between adherents of these two theological traditions. Yet, Anglicans and Calvinists had two things in common: They both saw the Church of Rome as the "Anti-Christ": and they both left their mark on the intellectual, political, and cultural landscape of what became the United States.

ENGLISH PROTESTANTISM, BRIEFLY CONSIDERED

The Puritans weren't the only people who believed the Church of England had gotten it wrong (or at least not quite gotten it right) when it broke away from Rome. England was home to quite a few dissenting groups in the seventeenth century. A census that the Archbishop of Canterbury ordered in 1669 estimated that 123,000 people – or roughly 6 percent of the country's entire population – was made up of Protestants whose dissent from the official teachings of the Church of England was strong enough to prompt them to avoid Anglican Church services. The Catholic population at the time may have been equally as large; some historians have estimated it was as high as 120,000. In the mid-seventeenth century, in other words, more than 10 percent of the British population actively disagreed with the country's established Church.[28]

Some of these dissenting groups were quite small, and their beliefs deviated considerably from those of the bishops who guided the Church of England. The Philadelphians, for instance, rejected the authority of Scripture, and they were accused of promoting pantheism because they insisted that the Holy Spirit existed in everyone's soul. The Fifth Monarchists believed that England's break with Rome meant that Jesus would soon be returning to earth – probably some time around the year 1666. The Muggletonians took their name from Lodowick Muggleton, a London tailor who claimed in 1651 to be one of two "witnesses" spoken of in the Book of Revelation who would be empowered by God to "prophecy for 1,260 days" before the coming of the Anti-Christ (Revelation 11:3). The Muggletonians believed that souls were not immortal, challenging one of the great promises of the Christian faith.[29]

Most dissenters were not quite so eccentric. Catholic or Protestant, they embraced basic, Christian beliefs about the divinity of Christ and the immortality of the soul, and they were unconcerned with predicting the exact time and place of Christ's return to Earth. The largest group of Protestant dissenters in the seventeenth and eighteenth centuries was the Calvinists. They adhered to a predestinarian theology that emphasized the inherent depravity of human nature and insisted that God's "uncompromised sovereignty" (the very thing that the Catholic doctrine of indulgences had challenged) meant that eternal salvation was not available to everyone. Salvation came only to those souls that God had chosen, and human behavior had no influence on God's decision to save or damn a soul.[30]

In spite of this shared commitment to predestination, England's Calvinists were by no means a monolith. For starters, some of them believed it was possible to fix the Church of England and convince its leaders to abandon the theological, liturgical, and episcopal elements[†] within it that were reminiscent of Catholicism; others felt the Church of England would never abandon its Catholic ways. The Calvinists who believed the Church of England could be reformed are known to us today as "Puritans." The ones who believed the Church of England was beyond redemption are known to us today as "Pilgrims."

Calvinists also disagreed with one another about how church membership should be determined, how and if individual congregations should relate to one another, and when and why a person should be baptized.[31] These differences led to the formation of several denominations within Calvinism. The three largest Calvinist denominations in Great Britain were the Presbyterians, the Congregationalists, and the Baptists. Presbyterians outnumbered the other two groups by a large margin. According to the 1669 census, there were three times as many of them in the country as there were Congregationalists, and four times as many as there were Baptists.[32]

Presbyterians were the ones who'd had a strong enough presence in Parliament in 1642 to lead the charge against Charles I, launching the Civil War that led to the king's execution and the rise of Oliver Cromwell. They were also the ones who invited Charles' son to come back to England from France in 1660 and become King Charles II. They were not,

[†] "Theology" has to do with what a religious group believes. "Liturgy" has to do with how a religious group engages in worship – its rites and rituals. And "episcopacy" has to do with how a religious group is organized or governed; more specifically, it is a form of governance that relies on bishops. The Puritans felt the Church of England got it wrong in all three areas, but they particularly abhorred the Church's bishop-based system of governance.

however, a majority of the Calvinists who migrated to North America – at least not in the seventeenth century. Congregationalists like John Winthrop made up the bulk of those early immigrants. They differed from the Presbyterians, in that they believed that each individual congregation, with its minister and its members, stood entirely on its own and did not need to be grouped with other congregations that would report to a higher assembly of elders known as a "presbyter." They differed from the Baptists – who had a strong, but minority presence in early New England – in that they believed in infant baptism. Baptists such as Roger Williams felt that human beings needed to reach the age of reason first; they needed to be able to choose to participate in the sacramental rite that marked a person's reception into the community of Christ.[33]

Most of the Congregationalists and Baptists who came to North America were Puritans, which in the seventeenth century was a pejorative term, used by Anglicans to dismiss the people who wanted the Church of England to change. But not all Congregationalists were Puritans. The Pilgrims who migrated to Plymouth in 1620, for instance – and are remembered in the United States each year at Thanksgiving – were known to their detractors as "Independents" or "Separatists," not "Puritans." Theologically, they agreed with John Winthrop and the people who founded the city of Boston in 1630 on many points. The Pilgrims, however, weren't looking to purify the Church of England or create a "city upon a hill" for the people back home to learn from. They wanted nothing to do with the Church of England, and they'd come to North America to get as far away as possible from the Archbishop of Canterbury.

The people who arrived on the *Mayflower* were followers of an English minister named Robert Browne, who – having given up on the idea that the Church of England would ever abandon its episcopal hierarchy – insisted that any church that was legitimate had to be independent from the state. "We hold all those preachers and teachers accursed," Browne asserted, "which say the time has not yet come to build the Lord's house; they must tarry for magistrates and for the parliament to do it." The reason such preachers were "accursed" was that they put their faith in government, rather than in God – even going so far as to "make the magistrates more than gods, yet also worse than beasts." The entire idea of an "established" church – one mandated by the state, with the monarch as its head – was a mockery of God's wishes for humanity because it reversed the direction that "discipline" was supposed to follow. "The Lord's spiritual government" was supposed to "bind the kings in chains and the nobles in fetters" – not the other way around.[34]

On this point, Robert Browne and his followers actually had something in common with Catholics – though certainly they'd have been shocked and appalled to hear their theology described in such a way. Catholicism, too, insisted that kings and nobles had to be bound by the Lord's spiritual government. The difference was that for a Catholic, the "Lord's spiritual government" was embodied not merely in Scripture, but also in the doctrines and hierarchy of the Roman Catholic Church. Secular authorities were obliged, in the words of the sixteenth-century Jesuit, Roberto Bellarmino, to submit to "the authority of legitimate pastors and above all ... that of the one Vicar of Christ on earth, the Roman Pontiff."[35]

But Robert Browne and his Calvinist followers believed that no human being could be Christ's "vicar" on earth. The only spiritual authority with any legitimacy was the will of God, and that will was plainly revealed to human beings through Scripture, "which governs us wholly to do all things wisely, and his words doth bind us." People who allowed themselves to be spiritually bound by anything other than Scripture were "servile and slavish," according to Robert Browne – easily recognized by "the carelessness and dullness [that] be spied in them." Catholics had allowed themselves to be "mastered" when they placed themselves "under one chief Antichrist, the Pope," who "forceth his religion by civil power or by binding their consciences." They became "vile and nothing [of] worth" because "they are made, handled, and led by others" and "limited by others which rule them."[36]

CALVINISM AND LIBERTY

When Robert Browne described Catholics as "mastered" in 1582, he helped to create a template that would be utilized by Protestants in the Anglo-American world for many centuries to come. As late as the 1870s, the American political cartoonist Thomas Nast was carefully depicting the "dullness" that Browne had insisted could be easily "spied" in all Catholics nearly three hundred years earlier. The characters Nast created for *Harper's* magazine had eyes that reflected no light and faces that revealed no curiosity. Their posture was hunched and submissive, and their gait was more characteristic of an ape's or a service animal's than a human being's (Figure 1.2). Nast's Catholics were ignorant and ignoble, and the reason for their drabness was perfectly clear: their natures had been rendered dull and their intelligence unremarkable by generations of deference to the whims of their clergy.[37]

THE USUAL IRISH WAY OF DOING THINGS.

FIGURE 1.2 This cartoon by Thomas Nast appeared in *Harper's Weekly* on September 2, 1871. Nast typically portrayed Irishmen as dumb, drunk, violent, and ape-like.

Robert Browne's sixteenth-century characterization of Catholics also touched upon a theme that would prove to be extremely important to his fellow Calvinists – and indeed, to all English-speaking Protestants – in the centuries to come: *liberty*. It was something that Catholics simply did not have, or at least Protestants didn't think they had it. The reason Catholics were "vile," after all, was that they were "led by others" when it came to their understanding of God; they were not free to apply their own reason to the words of Scripture. That subservience left them vulnerable to precisely the corruption that Rome had been perpetuating.

The Protestant emphasis on *sola scriptura* obliged people to read their Bibles and use their reason to construct a personal piety that began with God's Word and the undeniable reality of their sinfulness. Liberty, in this Protestant way of thinking, was something given to human beings by God so that they might choose to receive God's grace. Christians were obliged to "stand fast in the liberty wherewith Christ hath made them free," the Calvinist Separatist Leonard Busher wrote in 1614. Jesus' sacrifice on the cross meant that God no longer expected His children to be "tangled with the yoke of bondage. No, not with circumcision, much less with the discipline and doctrine of the Church of Rome."[38] God did expect His children to engage the revelations of Scripture, however. And to that end, God had given human beings the ability to think and the freedom to do so.

A true Church was not one in which doctrines were handed down from on high to an ignorant and complacent laity; it was, rather, a community in which all members "disputed [and] inquired" about the "extraordinary revelations and infallible assistances" found in the Bible. A true Church, according to Connecticut's Congregational founder, Thomas Hooker, was one in which "each man had allowed liberty to propound his thoughts, had recourse to the Scriptures, and reasoned out of them."[39] Any institution, then – such as the Catholic Church – that denied individuals the freedom to apply their own reason to Scripture was, by its very nature, an ungodly institution.

The word "liberty" made its way into the titles of hundreds of sermons and tracts that Calvinists delivered in the seventeenth and eighteenth centuries. George Gillespie's *Wholesome Severity Reconciled with Christian Liberty* (1645), John Saltmarsh's *Groanes for Liberty* (1646), and Charles Wolseley's *Liberty of Conscience: The Magistrate's Interest* (1668) are just a few of the titles published by Calvinists in Britain. In America, Jonathan Edwards delivered his sermon, *Christian Liberty*, in 1721, just one year after graduating from Yale College in Connecticut. In Massachusetts, Harvard graduate Samuel Mather, who came from a long line of Puritan ministers, published his *Apology for the Liberty of the Churches in New England*‡ in 1738, using a local printer in Boston, Daniel Henchman, to do it.[40]

This obsession with liberty is the reason the Puritans have been portrayed in America's "creation myth" as having come to North

---

‡ In the eighteenth century, an "apology" was a defense or justification, not an atonement or admission of fault.

America in the name of religious freedom, even though they hanged Quakers, banished Baptists, railed against Catholics, and removed Indian children from their tribes in an effort to convert them to Christianity. Many English Calvinists pointed to liberty as essential to the realization of God's wishes for humanity, even as they were also quite unwilling to tolerate "false religion" in the name of securing that liberty for everyone.

This disconnect does not mean that the Puritans' dedication to the idea of liberty was not real or impassioned. Human beings are many things, after all, but "consistent" is rarely one of them. A few leaders did take the time to justify their religious intolerance, distinguishing between liberty and license and insisting that a commitment to liberty ought not to become an excuse for anarchy. Thomas Case, for instance, insisted in 1647 that it could be danger-ous if civil authorities "doth not indeed the *punishing* and *suppressing* of *Spiritual Whoredoms* against God – *Idolotry, Heresie, Blasphemie* and the rest." As a Presbyterian, Case was committed to the idea that individuals needed to be able to use their own reason to confront the reality of their sinfulness; it was not enough for the Church merely to identify and condemn people's sins for them. Nevertheless, Case insisted that his fellow Calvinists were reckless whenever they published declarations that "let the people of *England* know that it is the *right* and *liberty*, to which the subjects of England are born, that every man may *hold* what he *please*, and *publish* and *preach* what he holds."

Such blanket declarations could easily be interpreted as endorsements of a theological and political "catch that catch can," in Case's words. If people were allowed to believe whatever they wanted – even and especially things that were blasphemous – a whole host of traditional hierarchies that brought order to society could soon crumble. "Liberty of conscience may in good time improve itself into liberty of estates [i.e., social classes] ... liberty of wives, and in a word, liberty of perdi-tion, of souls and bodies." Unfettered freedom, Thomas Case argued prophetically, could even one day cause some of England's citizens to conclude "that it is their *birth-right* to be freed from the Power of Parliaments." And if that ever happened, civilization would be lost.[41]

Most Calvinists didn't feel obliged to follow Thomas Case's lead and explain the disconnect between their principles and their behavior when they insisted upon the theological importance of liberty, even as they punished or denigrated those whose consciences had led them to different conclusions. *Liberty*, nevertheless, remained central to the way Calvinists understood their obligations before God. Indeed, as Case's own words suggest, liberty was starting to become central to the way at least some English Protestants in the mid-seventeenth century understood themselves not just as people of God, but as people of England, as well. The freedom to use one's reason to form an understanding was more than just a *human* right, after all; Calvinists were presenting it as a right "to which the subjects of England are born."

During the second half of the seventeenth century, this association – between Christianity and liberty, liberty and Protestantism, and Protestantism and English identity – became increasingly diffuse in the Anglo-American world, spreading beyond the Calvinists who'd emphasized the association early on and into the greater Anglican community, culminating in the Glorious Revolution in 1689. When they ousted their Catholic king and ignored the traditional line of monarchical succession so that they wouldn't have to place his Catholic son on the throne, the predominantly Anglican members of Parliament set themselves up as global defenders of what they called "the Protestant Interest."[42] This "interest," they believed – just like their Calvinist countrymen – was a commitment to individual freedom.

In the years that followed the Glorious Revolution, New England's Calvinists were anxious to assert their own role in the British defense of the Protestant Interest, in spite of their decades of opposition to the Church of England. "What Hearty Friends, the vast Body of Non Conformists [i.e., Calvinist dissenters] are to the English liberties," Increase Mather wrote to Richard Coote ten years after William and Mary had assumed the throne. Mather was the leader of a group of Congregational ministers from Boston, and Coote was an Anglican who'd recently been sent to Massachusetts by King William III to serve as the colony's governor.

Mather wanted Coote to know that even though most of New England's residents were opposed to the Church of England – so opposed, in fact, that they'd refused for decades to allow Anglican ministers to practice in Massachusetts – they were all, ultimately, on the same page with their new governor when it came to the problem of popery and the importance of English liberty. Coote should rest easy, Mather insisted, in the knowledge that "all Good Men, whether Conformists or Nonconformists, will contribute unto the strength of the Protestant Interest."[43] Indeed, Mather implied, no people may have better understood the need for vigilance when it came to the Protestant interest than the Calvinists of New England.

THE DOMINION OF NEW ENGLAND AND THE PROTESTANT INTEREST

It was not without reason that Protestants in Old and New England used the word "tyrannical" to describe their converted Catholic king. In the brief, three-and-a-half-year period that constituted his reign, James II managed to suspend Parliament indefinitely and quadruple the size of England's army – an expansion that flew in the face of a long-standing English tradition of not maintaining career soldiers during times of peace.[44] More galling to his subjects in North America, James also revoked the charters and disbanded the locally elected assemblies of every colony north and east of Pennsylvania, creating one massive British colony that, had it lasted, would have resembled the French colony of Quebec in terms of the amount of control that the king and his advisors had over colonists' lives.

What came to be known as the "Dominion of New England" encompassed present-day New Jersey, New York, Connecticut, Rhode Island, Massachusetts, New Hampshire, Vermont, and Maine. The idea for the colonial administrative unit didn't actually originate with James; it originated with his older brother, King Charles II, who was unhappy about the fact that settlers in New England had been flagrantly violating laws that prohibited them from trading directly with other countries or even other British colonies. From the Crown's perspective, New World colonies existed so that they could make money for the parent country – and every time merchants in Boston bought molasses from the French or tobacco from planters in Maryland, the merchants, ship captains, port masters, and excise tax collectors in England who might have made money off of the deal were denied their cut.

Charles made plans in 1684, shortly before he died, to revoke the charters and disband the locally elected assemblies for the Massachusetts Bay and Plymouth Colonies and place both communities under the authority of a single, crown-appointed governor; that governor's jurisdiction was to extend into settlements in Rhode Island, New Hampshire, and Maine, as well. It was a controversial idea, made more audacious by the fact that Charles had just dissolved Parliament three years earlier, following a political battle known as the "Exclusion Crisis." Several prominent members of Parliament, eyeing their aging and technically childless king,[§] had

---

[§] Charles II did have a son, James Crofts, the Duke of Monmouth. Crofts had been born out of wedlock, however, to a mistress that Charles had while he was living in Continental Europe during the Interregnum. Because he was illegitimate, Crofts was not entitled to the throne.

attempted to pass a bill that would have denied Charles' brother access to the throne because he was Catholic.

The MPs were concerned that James would implement an autocratic, top-down style of rule that resembled the absolutism of the pope and France's King Louis XIV, whom James had grown up under during the Interregnum. Neither the "Sun King" nor Innocent XI had much use for something so pedestrian as a popularly elected parliament – raising obvious concerns among England's MPs.

King James II's decision, therefore, to continue with his brother's plan of revoking the charters to Plymouth and Massachusetts Bay – even expanding that plan to include Connecticut, East and West Jersey, and his own proprietary colony of New York, which he'd received as a gift from his brother in 1664 – seemed only to confirm the worst fears of the members of Parliament. His decision to create the Dominion of New England also confirmed the fears of Calvinists in North America, who'd been making their own laws and selecting their own governors for more than fifty years by the time James took that right away from them.

Puritans in Massachusetts were convinced they saw what they called a "popish plot" in the policies of Edmund Andros, who'd been serving as James' hand-picked governor in New York for more than a decade by the time the king chose him to be the governor of the Dominion in 1685. Andros quickly invalidated dozens of laws that had been passed by local "town meetings" across New England, including laws that pertained to property ownership and taxation. He mandated that Congregational ministers no longer receive their salaries from the colonies' tax revenues; that tax money was instead to be used to pay for Anglican priests, whom Governor Andros hoped would now come to New England since they were guaranteed salaries. Andros also enforced the "navigation acts" that had been designed to ensure that the colonists traded with England and not with each other or some other country. To that end, he stationed several military officers in the port of Boston, at least one of whom – Anthony Brockholes – was a Catholic.[45]

Brockholes was able to serve in the military because King James II had relaxed many of the laws that inhibited Catholics' participation in public life in Great Britain, among them a law that required all office holders to swear an oath in which they denied the Doctrine of Transubstantiation. That doctrine, which states that the bread and wine used in the Eucharist are transformed into the body and blood of Christ, was and still is an essential teaching of Catholicism – and something that set Catholics apart from even the most traditional Anglicans, who believed the bread and wine were only symbols of Christ's body and blood. James' decision to allow Catholics to join the military and serve in positions of rank was one of the violations of liberty that Parliament specifically pointed to in 1689, when its members made William and Mary their new king and queen.[46]

When word of William and Mary's coup reached the shores of Boston in April of 1689, people in the town revolted, arresting Governor Andros and his military advisors. The revolt's leaders then climbed to the top of Beacon Hill, waived an orange flag (in honor of William, the Prince of Orange), and read a declaration that they later published, in which they claimed to have thwarted a "horrid popish plot." King James II, the rioters alleged, had exercised "absolute and arbitrary authority" and planned to establish "papal tyranny" throughout New England, a region that had been "so remarkable for the true Profession and pure Exercise of the Protestant Religion."[47]

When they spoke of "the Protestant Religion," the rioters staked a claim to the common ground that Calvinists and Anglicans now shared. Just forty years earlier, Calvinists in England had launched a civil war against the Anglican establishment in their country, rounding up and executing dozens of Anglicans, including even the king. But now, in a classic diplomatic move, whereby the "enemy of my enemy" becomes "my friend," Calvinists in England and North America were proclaiming their solidarity with the Church of England. It didn't matter anymore whether a person adhered to the theology of Thomas Cranmer – as Queen Mary did – or the theology of John Calvin, as her Dutch Calvinist husband did. What mattered now was whether a person defended "the Protestant religion" by opposing Catholicism.

The alliance between Anglicanism and Calvinism that followed the Glorious Revolution was not immediate, and it was far from easy. In Great Britain, many Anglicans remained suspicious of the Calvinists in their midst. They resurrected a law from 1673 that had been suspended by James II; that law required anyone holding office in the country to receive Communion within the Church of England. A number of MPs felt that the law did not go far enough, however, since it was not uncommon for Calvinists to receive Communion in the Church of England just so that they could hold office, even as they continued to condemn many of the rites and beliefs that animated the Anglican Church. The MPs tried several times, therefore, to pass an "Act for Preventing Occasional Conformity." Had they succeeded, the act would have made it illegal for any office-holder, no matter how minor, to "*knowingly* or *willingly* resort to or be present at any Conventicle, Assembly, or Meeting, under Colour or Pretence of any exercise of Religion, in other manner than according to the Liturgy and Practice of the Church of England."[48]

In New England, Congregational ministers were still advising people as late as 1729 not to imitate Anglicans by celebrating Christmas. That was the year the Reverend John Barnard of Marblehead, Massachusetts, preached a sermon in which he reminded his congregants that the Christmas holiday was "firstly introduced by the Roman Church." It was part of that church's campaign to "oblige the *Pagans*" and "there was no such custom in the primitive Church as the keeping the Birth Day of *Christ*." Additionally, the holiday had become an excuse in some circles for "Revelling and Debauchery." That fact, Barnard insisted, "should make a considerate person very cautious, how he embraced a custom that is so vilely abused when there is no plain Institution for it."[49]

Some people took Barnard's words so seriously that they started harassing the Anglicans in Marblehead who were celebrating the "twelve days of Christmas," the period between December 25 and the Epiphany, when the Magi are said to have arrived in Bethlehem with their gifts. According to George Pigot, the rector of St. Michael's Anglican Church in Marblehead, some of Barnard's "credulous Hearers" had interpreted his sermon as "an unanswerable Argument against the *Church* of *England*," and they "did frequently and loudly unbraid the Members of my Church ... with such Tauntings as these: What is to become of your Christmas-Day now, for Mr. B – d has proved it to be Nothing else but an Heathenish rioting? Will you never have done with your Popish Ceremonies, that you must have four or five days running to observe what Mr. B – d has made out to be no such thing as you pretend?"[50]

But tussles such as these aside, many political and cultural leaders in New England recognized in the years following the Glorious Revolution that some kind of détente would have to be achieved between Calvinists and Anglicans, if for no other reason than that the colonists who'd lost their charters when the Dominion of New England was formed wanted them back – and William and Mary's ascension, in and of itself, did not guarantee that that would happen. The government back home in England would have to feel that the colonists could be trusted with the freedom and autonomy that came with a colonial charter if the charters were to be restored and – just as important – retained.

THE POWER OF PRINT AND THE PROTESTANT INTEREST

To gain the trust of Parliament and the king, New England's leaders worked to cultivate a kind of "pan-Protestant" identity among all of the region's residents and between the residents of Old England and New. To do this, they relied upon the indigenous print culture that began to take off in Massachusetts, Rhode Island, and Connecticut in the early eighteenth century, made possible by the tools and talents of printers like James Franklin, older brother to Ben, and bookbinders like Daniel Henchman, who helped to establish the first paper mill in New England in 1731 and published Samuel Mather's "Apology" for the liberty of New England's churches seven years later.[51]

Newspapers, almanacs, sermons, and "chapbooks," i.e., cheaply printed booklets that contained poetry, nursery rhymes, short stories, and folksy "words of wisdom," helped to cement New England's Protestant identity in the eighteenth century. They did so by questioning Catholicism's legitimacy as a "Christian" faith, emphasizing the violence that Catholics sometimes inflicted upon Protestants, and insisting upon the foreign, bizarre, and/or dishonest nature of Catholicism.[52]

The print culture focused heavily on Catholicism's connection to France, a country that was frequently at war with England during the eighteenth century. It also highlighted the Catholic practice of "clerical celibacy," which most Protestants refused to believe was real or even possible, seeing the tradition instead as a cloak for lewd and lascivious behavior. New England's newspapers informed readers of the threats that Protestants faced around the world from priests and governmental authorities who were enslaved to Catholicism. They also lamented the damage that was being done to Christianity by the Jesuits, an order of priests that had been founded in the sixteenth century specifically to evangelize – and that, interestingly enough, was having more success at converting the Indians in North America to Christianity than either the Anglicans or the Congregationalists.[53]

Newspaper editors in British North America found no shortage of stories about the violence, duplicity, and all-out tyranny of Catholics in Continental Europe. Often, these stories came to the editors' attention via reports that had been made to newspapers in London by "correspondents" who were by no means the equivalent of a modern-day reporter – and were held by no one (most especially themselves) to the standards that animate modern journalism in the Western world. Nevertheless, sometimes the stories these correspondents told were actually true.

Readers in New England learned about the "Massacre at Thorn," a riot that broke out between Lutherans and Catholics in the Polish part of Prussia in 1724; more than a dozen Protestants were executed following that riot, including the mayor of Thorn, whose head was chopped off and displayed on a stake. New Englanders were horrified, but fascinated to learn of the execution of two young sisters from Vienna who'd had their hands and heads cut off after they threw a crucifix on the ground. And they were dismayed by the "manifest injuries" that Catholic authorities inflicted upon Reformed Protestants in Germany, such as "making them pay double Taxes" and "taking their children from the Protestant schools, and obliging them to put them in Popish schools."[54]

The plight of the Huguenots in France particularly captured readers' attentions. Like the Congregationalists and Baptists living in New England, the Huguenots were Calvinists. They had always been a minority in France, but toward the end of the sixteenth century, their numbers had been large enough – and the violence between them and the Catholic majority had been heinous enough – to compel King Henry IV to extend a modicum of toleration to them. The Edict of Nantes, which Henry issued in 1598, allowed the Huguenots living in specified regions of France to worship openly and even hold office, provided they continued to pay a tithe to the Catholic Church. The Edict also committed France's military to protecting Huguenots who traveled abroad from the interrogation and punishment of the Catholic Church's Inquisition.[55]

But after 1685, all that quasi-toleration in France was gone. The same year England's King James II created the Dominion of New England, the king he had grown up under, King Louis XIV of France, revoked the Edict of Nantes. Not only was Protestantism illegal in France, but a cohort of specially commissioned soldiers known as "Dragoons" now had the responsibility of harassing and torturing Protestants in the country in order to get them to convert to Catholicism. Estimates of the number of Protestants who fled France over the course of the next four decades vary widely – ranging from 400,000 to nearly one million.[56] Regardless of the number, the fact remains that it became extremely unpleasant to be Protestant in France after 1685.

Calvinists in New England eagerly read and discussed the misfortunes of their co-religionists in France, not because they took pleasure in the bloodshed, per se, but because stories about the atrocities of "Soul-Destroying Popery" confirmed for them the moral superiority of their Protestant way of doing things – even as the stories also emphasized how vulnerable that superior morality was to destruction. "Our ministers are not Banished . . . nor Dragoons let in upon us, to torture us a thousand ways" the Reverend John Danforth observed to his congregants in Dorchester, Massachusetts, in 1716. "Do we escape the Woeful day because of our Godliness and Righteousness, that is greater than [the Huegenots']? No verily."[57]

Protestants in New England were just as vulnerable as Protestants everywhere else in the world to the "Nasty Dungeons and Holes full of Mire and Dirt" that "Blood thirsty Papists" liked to use in their campaign against "the Church of God."[58] It was important, therefore, that Calvinists in North America put aside their differences with the Anglicans who were controlling things in London and increasingly leaving their mark on the New England landscape. Only together would Great Britain's Protestants secure, protect, and advance Protestant morality throughout the English-speaking world.

New Englanders learned about the "Holes full of Mire and Dirt" supposedly used by Catholic persecutors from an account of the Huguenots' condition that was appended to a popular chapbook in England and America some time around 1719. The name of that chapbook was *The French Convert*. It was a completely fictional rendering of a young girl's conversion experience, though it's not clear that everyone who read the book actually understood it wasn't real. The story was first published in London in 1696; by 1725, it was being re-issued by printers in Boston, Philadelphia, and New York. Indeed, *The French Convert* was so popular that it went through twenty-one different printings in North America and twenty-five in England – with the last copy coming off the presses in 1897, more than 200 years after the chapbook's initial release.[59]

The theme of *The French Convert* was one that would become far more popular with Protestant readers in the nineteenth century, but which clearly found an audience in the eighteenth century, even among the most puritanical of bookworms. That theme – to quote a pamphlet that circulated in Boston in the 1740s – was the idea that "the Popish doctrine, forbidding [clergy] to marry is a devilish and wicked Doctrine" that "leads to much Lewdness and Villany [sic.], as Fornication, Adultery, Incest, Sodomy, Murder, &c."[60]

Protestants simply could not believe that clerical celibacy was real. It had to have been a cover for something far more nefarious – such as the seduction efforts of the priest Antonio, who "burns with Lustful desires to enjoy the tender Beauties" of *The French Convert*'s main character, Deidamia. She is a Catholic by birth who converts to Protestantism after experiencing the unadulterated piety of her Huguenot gardener, Bernard. Deidamia retains her virtue; the lecherous Antonio fails in his endeavor to corrupt her. But in emphasizing the priest's effort to use his clerical authority to corrupt an innocent girl, *The French Convert* reminded readers of what the Church's authority had been able to do to Christianity in the age before the Reformation. The book also drew readers' attention to Catholicism's alien qualities, exemplified most starkly by the bizarre "fiction" of clerical celibacy.

Antonio was a caricature – a stand-in for every priest who had ever existed or ever would. Nevertheless, the author of *The French Convert* identified him as a "Fryar of the Order of St. Francis," indicating that the leaders of the movement to unite England's citizens under the banner of one common, Protestant identity did know that there were differences between and among particular orders of priests.[61] They probably didn't understand what made a Franciscan different from a Dominican, an Augustinian, or a Carmelite. But they knew that not all priests were the same – and they also knew that the worst priests in the world were the Jesuits.

The Society of Jesus was an order founded in the mid-sixteenth century by Ignatius of Loyola, a Basque soldier who became a priest after he was injured in battle and spent his recovery time reading about the lives of the saints. The Jesuits were so bad in the minds of most English-speaking Protestants that they could make even some Catholics seem worthy of sympathy. New England's newspapers regularly published stories about the Jansenists, whom the Jesuits opposed. These were members of a Catholic theological movement in France and the Netherlands that, like Calvinism, espoused predestination.[62]

New Englanders liked the Jansenists – sort of. These Catholics seemed to them to be a little bit Protestant, and, of course, they seemed that way to the Jesuits, too, which was precisely the problem. Newspaper editors in Boston published numerous stories about the Jesuits' persecution of the Jansenists. Readers learned that in the Netherlands in the summer of 1706, a group of "*Roman Catholicks*, who idolize the Jesuits ... assaulted and wounded one of the Priests suspected of Jansenism." They also learned that the Jesuits had convinced the pope's representative at The Hague to issue an order that "required the Romish Priests in this Country to Subscribe to a certain Paper against the Doctrine of Jansenius."[63] That paper, *Vineam Domini*, was a papal decree that said it was not enough for priests merely to remain silent on the issue of Jansenism; they had to actively condemn the movement as heretical and encourage their laity to fight it.

New England's Calvinists also learned that the Jesuits were so unscrupulous that they'd arranged for the arrest of an innocent young girl in southern France in order to "re-establish the Reputations of these Fathers in the Province."[64] The Society's reputation, it seems, had been sullied by the antics of one of its own – a notorious Jesuit named Jean-Baptist Girard who had seduced several young women in Provence. One of the women he seduced was Marie Catherine Cadière, an eccentric teenaged girl who claimed to receive mystical visions from God.

The Jesuits seized upon this admission and used it to discredit Cadière, arranging for her to be arrested and charged with witchcraft. She was convicted in 1731, though that conviction was later overturned. Forty years after Calvinists in New England had executed nineteen people for being witches, the editor of the *Boston Weekly-Rehearsal* wrote with no sense of irony that charging young girls like Cadière with witchcraft was "an odd way to bully a Country into Affections; but all the World knows that the Drifts of these Sons of Ignatius are not easily discovered."[65]

CHAPTER CONCLUSION

New Englanders did get their charters back, and they kept them until they didn't want them anymore in 1776. The effort to establish a trans-Atlantic "English" identity that was rooted in a generic version of Protestantism had worked – perhaps a little too well. In the decades that followed the Glorious Revolution, New England's residents became so invested in this generic Protestantism – defined more by an opposition to Catholicism and a commitment to liberty than by a Calvinist understanding of the reality of human depravity and unconditional election – that some ministers started to worry New Englanders had forgotten why they were all there in the region in the first place.

Jonathan Edwards' sermon, *Sinners in the Hands of an Angry God*, which he delivered several times throughout Massachusetts and Connecticut in the 1740s, was designed to shock people out of this generic complacency and get them to confront a core belief of Calvinism – namely, that Hell was a very real place, and that most people's souls were going to end up there, no matter how often they called the pope the "AntiChrist" or defended the "Protestant Interest." Edwards' sermon worked, and a Calvinist revival that emphasized the individual's obligation to confront the reality of sin was "awakened" in New England in the 1740s and 1750s. Today, we call that revival the "First Great Awakening."[66]

The cementing of "English" and "Protestant" identity that happened in the wake of the Glorious Revolution, however, failed to stamp out one very curious animal in the early modern British world: The English Catholic. No matter how hard they tried, Great Britain's monarchs and MPs never did manage to eradicate Catholicism from the land. "New" England may not have had any papists, but Old England did – and so did a handful of colonies south of Connecticut.

The experience of being English and Catholic in the colonies was very different from the experience of being English and Catholic in the parent country, largely because Calvinists weren't the only people who got colonial charters. Cecilius Calvert (Maryland), William Penn (Pennsylvania), and James, the Duke of York (New York) all got charters, too. Calvert and James were Catholic, and Penn, a Quaker, believed that religious toleration was a mandate from God. The charters these men received allowed them to found colonies where Catholicism was tolerated. While the charters never succeeded in completely insulating English Catholics from the realities of anti-Catholicism, they did afford those Catholics rights and privileges that they had nowhere else in the English-speaking world. Those rights became an important component of the identity that English-speaking Catholics created for themselves in the New World.

NOTES

1. John Winthrop, "General Considerations for the Plantations in New England, with an Answer to Several Objections," 1629, in *The John Winthrop Papers*, Allyn Bailey Forbes, ed. (Boston, 1931), 2:120.
2. John Winthrop, "Reasons to be Considered for Justifying the Undertakers of the Intended Plantation in New England and for Encouraging Such as Whose Hearts God Shall Move to Join with Them in It," 1629, in *The Puritans in America: A Narrative Anthology*, Alan Heimert and Andrew Delbanco, eds. (Cambridge, MA, 1985), 71.
3. Ibid., 72.
4. George William Curtis, "The Puritan Spirit: An Oration Delivered at the Unveiling of the Puritan Statue by the New England Society in the City of New York," in *Orations and Addresses of George William Curtis*, Charles Eliot Norton, ed. (New York, 1894), 1: 379.
5. Nathaniel B. Shurtleff, ed., *Records of the Governor and Company of the Massachusetts Bay in New England, 1628–1686* (Boston, 1853), 1: 160.
6. Roger Williams, "Christenings Make Not Christians" (1645), in *Rhode Island Historical Tracts*, Henry Martyn Dexter, ed. (Providence, 1881), 14: 2,10; Gustav Warnek, *Outline of the History of Protestant Missions, from the Reformation to Present Time*, George Robson, trans. (New York, 1903), 47.

7. Roger Williams to John Withrop Jr., December 6, 1659, in *Memoir or Roger Williams, Founder of the State of Rhode Island*, James D. Knowles, ed. (Boston, 1834), 310; "Christenings Make Not Christians," 3, 14.

8. Williams, *The Bloudy Tenent of Persecution for Cause of Conscience* (1644), Richard Groves, ed. (Macon, GA, 2001), 81.

9. Williams, "Christenings Make Not Christians," 10–12.

10. Jack P. Greene, *Pursuits of Happiness: The Social Development of Early Modern British Colonies and the Formation of American Culture* (Chapel Hill, 1988), 70, 175.

11. Ibid., 12.

12. F. Procter and W.H. Frere, *A New History of the Book of Common Prayer* (New York, 1965), 94; "Thirty-Nine Articles of Religion," 1571, 1662, and 1801 in Anglicans Online, Articles XI and XVIII, accessed on July 29, 2011: www.anglicansonline.org/basics/thirty-nine_articles.html.

13. J.C.H. Aveling, *The Handle and the Axe: The Catholic Recusants in England from Reformation to Emancipation* (London, 1976), 123–125; Pauline Croft, *King James* (New York, 2003), 24–25.

14. Oskar Meyer, "Charles I and Rome," *American Historical Review* 19 (1913): 13–26; Nicholas Tyacke, "Puritanism, Arminianism, and Counter Revolution," in *Reformation to Revolution: Politics and Religion in Early Modern England*, Margo Todd, ed. (New York, 1995), 53–70; Samuel Eliot Morison, *Builders of the Bay Colony*, rtp. (Boston, 1982), 82; Nigel Kelly, Jane Shuter, and Rosemary Rees, *The Making of the United Kingdom* (Oxford, UK, 1998), 45.

15. Thomas Mockett, "Christmas, the Christians Grand Feast (1651)," in *The English Civil War: Papists, Gentlewomen, Soldiers, and Witchfinders in the Birth of Modern Britain*, Diane Purkiss, ed. (New York, 2006), 240; David Keen, "The Political Economy of War," in *War and Underdevelopment: The Economic and Social Consequences of Conflict*, Frances Stewart and Valpy Fitzgerald, eds. (New York, 2001), 1:51; Michael St. John Parker, *The Civil War: 1642–1651* (Stroud, UK, 1993), 24.

16. Allan Blayney, *Festorum Metropolis* (1652), 14.

17. "Catholics Still Barred from Throne Despite Law Change," *The Scotsman*, October 29, 2011), accessed June 29, 2017: www.scotsman.com/news/uk /catholics_still_barred_from_throne_despite_law_change_1_1937348.

18. John Adams, "A Dissertation on Canon and Feudal Law," in *The Works of John Adams, Second President of the United States*, Charles Francis Adams, ed. (New York, 2008, rtp.), 3:456.

19. Will of John Paul Dudley (1751), quoted in "Address for Rev. Francis B. Hornbrooke," *Annual Meeting of the Governor Thomas Dudley Family*, Sanford H. Dudley, ed. (Boston, 1893), 37.

20. Diarmaid MacCulloch, *Reformation: Europe's House Divided, 1490–1700* (New York, 2004), 132.

21. Alan Spence, *Justification: A Guide for the Perplexed* (New York, 2012), 60–61.

22. William Kent, "Indulgences," *The Catholic Encyclopedia*, 7 (New York, 1910), accessed July 13, 2015: www.newadvent.org/cathen/07783a.htm; Ane Bysted, *The Crusade Indulgence: Spiritual Rewards and the Theology of the Crusades* (London, 2014), 132–139; Romanus Cessario, "St. Thomas

Aquinas on Satisfaction, Indulgences, and Crusades," *Medieval Philosophy and Theology*, 2 (1992), 74–78.

23. Charles A. Coulombe, *Vicars of Christ: A History of the Popes* (New York, 2003), 337–342; Silvio A. Bedini, "The Papal Pachyderms," *Proceedings of the American Philosophical Society* 125 (1981), 75–90; Derek Wilson, *The Life and Legacy of Martin Luther* (New York, 2007), 282. Luther alleged in 1531 that Pope Leo X encouraged, protected, and promoted "sodomites" in the Church.

24. Martin Luther, "Letter to the Archbishop Albrecht of Mainz," in *Works of Martin Luther with Introductions and Notes*, Adolph Spaeth, ed. (Philadelphia, 1910), 26–28.

25. Martin Brecht, *Martin Luther: His Road to Reformation, 1483–1521* (Minneapolis, 1985), 201.

26. Martin Luther, "Open Letter to the Christian Nobility of the German Nation" (1520) in *Luther Primer*, Albert T.W. Steinhaeuser, ed. (Columbia, SC, 1917), 20, 27.

27. John Calvin, *The Institutes of Christian Religion* (1581), rpt., John T. McNeill, ed. and Ford Lewis Battles, tr. (Louisville, KY, 1960), 968; Sydney E. Ahlstrom, *A Religious History of the American People* (New Haven, 1972).

28. Richard L. Greeves, *Enemies Under His Feet: Radicals and Nonconformists in Britain, 1664–1677* (Stanford, CA, 1990), 151–152; John Bossy, *The English Catholic Community, 1570–1850* (New York, 1976), chapter 8.

29. John Morrill, "The Puritan Revolution," in *The Cambridge Companion to Puritanism*, John Coffey and Paul C.H. Lim, eds. (New York, 2008), 67; Charles William Heckthorn, *The Secret Societies of All Ages and Countries* (London, 1875), 14–15; Louise Fargo Brown, *The Political Activities of the Baptists and Fifth Monarchy Men* (Washington, DC, 1912), 22–27; William Lamont, *Last Witnesses: The Muggletonian History: 1652–1979* (Burlington, VT, 2006), 13–85.

30. Susan Schreiner, "Predestination and Providence," *Ad Fontes* (Princeton Theological Seminary), accessed July 29, 2015: www3.ptsem.edu/offices/cone d/adfontes/second.aspx?reflect=16&title=2&detail=±Predestination±and± Providence.

31. A.S.P. Woodhouse, *Puritanism and Liberty, Being the Army Debates (1647–9), from the Clarke Manuscripts with Supplementary Documents* (Chicago, 1951), 29–30.

32. Greeves, *Enemies Under His Feet*, 152.

33. Morrill, "The Puritan Revolution," 67–88; Walter L. Lingle and John W. Kuykendall, *Presbyterians: Their History and Beliefs* (Louisville, KY, 1944); Geoffrey Nuttall, *The Congregational Way, 1640–1660* (New York, 1957); William Thomas Whitley, "Debate on Infant Baptism, 1643," *Transactions of the Baptist Historical Society* 1 (1910), 237–245.

34. Robert Browne, *A Treatise of Reformation Without Tarrying for Anie* (1582), rpt. (Whitefish, MT, 2007), 2–3.

35. Roberto Bellarmine, *The Controversies* (1586), quoted in Gerald O'Collins and Mario Farrugia, *Catholicism: The Story of Catholic Christianity* (New York, 2015), 327.

36. Robert Browne, *A Book which sheweth the life and manners of all true Christians, and how unlike they are unto Turkes and Papists and Heathen Folke* (1582), 2, 5, 7, 25, 27, 3.

37. Niall Whelehan, *The Dynamiters: Irish Nationalism and Political Violence in the Wider World, 1867–1900* (New York, 2012), 225–226.

38. Leonard Busher, *Religions Peace; or a Plea for Liberty of Conscience* (1614), in *Tracts on Liberty of Conscience and Persecution, 1614–1661*, Edward Bean Underhill, ed. (London, 1846), 21, 15, 17.

39. Edward Hopkins and William Goodwin, "To the Reader, Especially the Congregation of the Church of Jesus Christ in Hartford, Upon Connecticut," in Thomas Hooker, *A Survey of the Summe of Church-Discipline* (London, 1648), iii; Thomas Hooker, "Part IV: Concerning Synods," in ibid., 4.

40. Morrill, "The Puritan Revolution," 67; John Coffey, "Puritanism and Liberty Revisited: The Case for Toleration in the English Revolution," *The Historical Journal* 4 (1998), 961–985; Jonathan Edwards, "Christian Liberty," in *The Works of Jonathan Edwards, Sermons and Discourses, 1720–1723*, Volume 10, Wilson H. Kimnach, ed. (New Haven, 1992), 627–628; Samuel Mather, "An Apology for the Liberty of the Churches in New England," 1738, Mather Family Papers, 1613–1819, American Antiquarian Society, Box 6, Folder 12.

41. Thomas Case, *Spirituall Whoredom discovered in a Sermon preach'd before the Honourable House of Commons* (1647), 33–34.

42. Thomas S. Kidd, *The Protestant Interest: New England After Puritanism* (New Haven, 2004).

43. Increase Mather, *To His Excellency, Richard, Earl of Bellomont ...* (Boston, 1699), 2.

44. John Childs, *The Army, James II, and the Glorious Revolution* (Manchester, UK, 1980), 1–3; Tim Harris, *Revolution: The Great Crisis of the British Monarchy, 1685–1720* (New York, 2008), 95–100.

45. David S. Lovejoy, *The Glorious Revolution in America* (Hanover, NH, 1987), 180–181; Stephen Saunders Webb, *Lord Churchill's Coup: The Anglo-American Empire and the Glorious Revolution Reconsidered* (New York, 1995), 183–184; Dennis E. Owen, "Spectral Evidence: The Witchcraft Cosmology of Salem Village, 1692," in *Essays on the Sociology of Perception*, Mary Douglas, ed. (New York, 1982), 286; Martin I.J. Griffin, "Anthony Brockholes, Commander-in-Chief at New York, 1674–1689," in *Catholic Historical Researches*, A.A. Lambing, ed. (Pittsburg, 1886), 94–97.

46. "English Bill of Rights, 1689," *The Avalon Project: Documents in Law, History and Diplomacy*, Lillian Goldman Law Library, Yale University, accessed on August 13, 2015: http://avalon.law.yale.edu/17th_century/england.asp.

47. Quoted in Webb, *Lord Churchill's Coup*, 191.

48. *The Bill Entitled An Act for Preventing Occasional Conformity ... and the Proceedings Thereupon* (London, 1702), 7; A Layman, *The Right of Protestant Dissenters to a Compleat Toleration Asserted* (London, 1789), 23–25.

49. John Barnard, *The Certainty, Time, and End of the Birth of Our Lord and Savior Jesus Christ* (Boston, 1731), 31, 30, 29, 33; Kidd, *Protestant Interest*, 115.

50. George Pigot, *A Vindication of the Practice of the Ancient Christian; as well as the Church of England, and Other Reformed Churches in the Observation of Christmas-Day* (Boston, 1731), 6; Kidd, *Protestant Interest*.

51. William T. Baxter, "Daniel Henchman, a Colonial Bookseller," *Essex Institute Historical Collections* 70 (1934), 1–30.

52. Thomas S. Kidd, "Recovering 'The French Convert': Views of the French and Uses of Anti-Catholicism in Early America," *Book History* 7 (2004), 98.

53. James Axtell, *The Invasion Within: The Contest of Cultures in Colonial North America* (New York, 1986), 72.

54. Kidd, *Protestant Interest*, 68, 60; *Boston News-Letter*, June 27–July 4, 1720.

55. George A. Rothrock, "Some Aspects of Early Bourbon Policy Towards the Huguenots," *Church History*, 1 (1960), 17–24.

56. José M. Magone, *Contemporary European Politics: An Introduction* (New York, 2011), 31.

57. Kidd, Protestant Interest, 60–63; John Danforth, *Judgement Begun at the House of God* (Boston, 1716), 42–43.

58. "A Brief Account of the Present Persecutions Against the French Protestants," in "A. d'Auborn," *The French Convert*, 6th edition (London, 1719), 111, 109.

59. Kidd, "Recovering 'The French Convert'," 101.

60. Unknown, *A Protestant's Resolution* (Boston, 1746), 18–19; Frank D. Cogliano, *No King, No Popery: Anti-Catholicism in Revolutionary New England* (Westport, CT, 1996), 10–11.

61. "A. d'Auborn," *The French Convert*, 9.

62. William Doyle, *Jansenism* (New York, 2000), 1–5, 14.

63. *Boston News-Letter*, January 7–4, 1706.

64. *A Compleat Translation of the Whole Case of Mary Catherine Cadière Against the Jesuit Father John Baptist Girard* (London, 1732); *Boston Weekly-Rehearsal*, October 1, 1733.

65. Ibid.

66. Harry Stout, "Edwards as Revivalist," in *The Cambridge Companion to Jonathan Edwards*, Stephen J. Stein, ed. (New York, 2007), 125–143.

2

"This Province is God be Thanked very Peaceable and Quiet"

Anti-Catholicism and Colonial Catholics in the Seventeenth Century

New Englanders such as Increase Mather weren't the only settlers in British North America who spoke of "the Protestant Interest" in the years that followed the Glorious Revolution. In 1691, eight years before Mather wrote to his new crown-appointed governor about the willingness of New England's Puritans to "contribute unto the strength of the Protestant Interest," Jacob Leisler urged his fellow New Yorkers to advance "the Glory of the protestant interest" by uniting against the Catholics (whom he called "a Common enemy") who lurked within their colony. Mather, presumably, wrote his words while sitting in the comforts of his living room or library on Hanover Street in Boston. Leisler, however, who'd come to the New World thirty years earlier to make his fortune, shouted his words from a scaffold in lower Manhattan. Moments later, he was hanged.[1]

CHAPTER OVERVIEW

Jacob Leisler was put to death because following the Glorious Revolution he launched a rebellion in New York, where a small but powerful group of Catholics and Catholic sympathizers were serving in the administration of the colony's Catholic proprietor, King James II of England. New York was one of two colonies where Catholics held positions of power prior to 1689. Maryland was the other colony – and Catholics there were actually far more numerous and far more integrated into the colony's political infrastructure than they were in New York.

Both colonies experienced anti-Catholic rebellions after King James II was overthrown, and in both colonies the Catholics in power were given the boot, just like their king. Leisler's executioners, in other words, were not the Catholics he'd rebelled against following the Glorious Revolution; someone else had reason to believe he was dangerous enough to be put to death – someone who, unlike the colony's recently ousted leaders, had the power to do it.

Jacob Leisler's execution revealed that there were limits to what even anti-Catholicism could accomplish in the Anglo-American world. Leisler insisted that his rebellion, much like the Puritans' rebellion against Governor Andros' rule in Massachusetts, had been designed to ensure that everyone in New York accepted and celebrated William and Mary's take-over of the British throne. The Anglican governor who sentenced Leisler to death disagreed with this interpretation of events, however. Indeed, Henry Sloughter had been sent to the colony by King William III specifically to deal with Jacob Leisler because a number of prominent people in New York – all them Protestants – were complaining about him. The fact that William and Mary repudiated Leisler, even as his rebellion was animated by the same spirit of anti-Catholicism that Parliament had used to launch the Glorious Revolution, suggests that it was possible, even in the seventeenth century, to take fears of Catholicism a little too far.

The problem with Jacob Leisler was that his animosity toward Catholics was almost pathological. He hated Catholicism even more than the Puritans in Massachusetts did, and he didn't seem to know how to shut this hatred off once he'd turned it on, or how to confine it to targets that were "appropriate" according to the social and cultural logic of colonial New York. This inability to be discriminating in his discrimination made Jacob Leisler a loose cannon. His rebellion created a great deal of social discord in New York in the years that followed the Glorious Revolution; that discord was the primary reason Leisler was sentenced to death.

It's not clear why Jacob Leisler became such a staunch supporter of the "Protestant Interest" after word of William and Mary's coup reached New York. He was a German-born Huguenot who'd immigrated to New Amsterdam in 1660, four years before the British navy took possession of that Dutch settlement. Like many of the people living in New Amsterdam, Leisler had had no particular loyalties to either the British or the Dutch at the time of the naval invasion; he'd come to the New World to make money, and so long as no one got in the way of that, Leisler and most of the other European settlers on Manhattan Island didn't much care who was in charge – even if that person were a Catholic like James, the Duke of York.[2]

The colony that England's King Charles II took from the Dutch and then gave to his brother was ethnically and religiously diverse – more diverse, even, than the country in Europe that had founded it as a trading post in 1614. The Republic of the United Netherlands was a voluntary union of seven autonomous provinces in northern Europe, each with its own history and government. A variety of languages – French, German, Dutch, and Frisian– were spoken by the residents of the provinces. While most of the people in the United Netherlands practiced some version of Reformed Christianity, there were quite a few Lutherans, Mennonites, Jews, and Catholics living in the region, as well. Indeed, the provinces had been brought together primarily by a shared opposition to Spain and the Holy Roman Empire, rather than a shared commitment to the teachings of John Calvin.

Officials in the Netherlands dealt with the diversity that characterized both their country and their North American colony by simply accepting it, albeit grudgingly. Lawmakers did formally establish the Reformed Church in the Netherlands, but local leaders often turned a blind eye to the Catholic and Jewish practices that they knew people were engaging in privately in their own homes. They also allowed the public expression of a wide variety of Protestant beliefs, including even Arminianism, which was similar to Calvinism but dismissed the idea that salvation was limited, i.e., not available to all Christians. Some Calvinists were deeply offended by Arminianism – among them, the English Pilgrims who'd migrated to the Netherlands in 1608 to get away from the Church of England. The Pilgrims eventually left the Netherlands in 1620 and migrated to the New World to avoid the "manifold temptations" that the Dutch approach to religious diversity presented.[3]

Because Dutch officials had a de facto policy of religious toleration in both Europe and North America, New Amsterdam attracted settlers from all over the world. The colony already had a small, but solid population of Catholics living within it when the English took possession of the city in 1664. Because the king of England gave the colony to his Catholic brother, the number of Catholics living in New York grew over the course of the next two decades. Indeed, some of these Catholics were even able to assume positions of political power in New York under the proprietorship of the Catholic Duke of York; Thomas Dongun, for example, a Catholic from Kildare, Ireland, moved to New York in 1683 after the Duke of York asked him to become New York's governor.[4]

It probably wasn't any personal or familial connection to the reality of Catholic persecution that provoked Jacob Leisler's hatred of Catholicism.

His Huguenot father had left France decades before the revocation of the Edict of Nantes. Nevertheless, Leisler, like the Puritans, would have read accounts of the Dragoons' atrocities against the Huguenots in New York's newspapers. It makes sense to think that he might have been angered and horrified by the treatment of his co-religionists in Europe. This anger may have been the reason he was "especially anxious to allow no Papist to remain in any office" in New York following the Glorious Revolution, according to one of his critics.[5]

In 1688, less than a year before he seized control of Fort James in Manhattan and declared himself the new lieutenant governor of New York, Leisler helped a group of thirty-three Huguenot families secure a patent to land that was north and east of New York City. The families named their settlement "New Rochelle" after the town in France from which they had fled. Leisler's involvement in the founding of this community lends itself to the idea that his Huguenot identity was one of the reasons he fueled his rebellion against King James' administrators in New York with anti-Catholicism.[6]

The other reason, no doubt, was that Jacob Leisler recognized just how efficient and effective a fuel like anti-Catholicism could be. He wanted power, and he believed a campaign to root out Catholics was the best way to get it. When he targeted Catholics in his effort to move people to rebellion, Jacob Leisler tapped into an evocative tradition in the English-speaking world that had already proven itself on more than one occasion to be powerful enough to oust a king. In that sense, his strategy to assume political control of the English colony he lived in was brilliant – made all the more remarkable by the fact that Leisler himself was not even English.

The problem for Jacob Leisler was that his hatred of Catholicism didn't recognize any logical boundaries. It was one thing when the German-born Huguenot directed his rage against the small number of Catholics who held positions of authority in New York, thanks to the religious identity of the colony's former proprietor. Few people felt compelled to defend Matthew Plowman, for example, when Leisler told him in 1689 that he could no longer keep his job collecting fees for the port of New York because "he was no protestant," and Leisler fully intended to enforce a royal proclamation that required "all Justices of the Peace, Sheriffs, Collectors, etc." to be Protestants.[7]

Few people seemed to care, either, when Leisler went after non-Catholics who'd held prominent positions in the Dominion of New England, an administrative unit that many New Yorkers abhorred almost as much as the Puritans in Massachusetts did. Leisler accused Francis

Nicholson, the Dominion's Anglican lieutenant governor, of being merely a "pretended protestant" who secretly supported the "Popish party." Not only did no one in New York defend Nicholson against this charge, but two brothers actually testified in court that they'd seen Nicholson "upon his knees before the Altar in the papist Chappel" that was located within Fort James. Nicholson eventually fled New York and returned to London.[8]

When Jacob Leisler started slinging anti-Catholic insults at people like Phillip French, however – a prominent, well-liked, and *Calvinist* merchant who eventually became the mayor of New York City – that was when some people in New York started to question Leisler's intentions, even hinting that the man may have been insane. Colonel Nicholas Bayard, for instance, accused Leisler of "insolent conduct" in the summer of 1689, after he learned that "Mr. French with several other English gentlemen ... without any cause given were assaulted by Jacob Leisler, who in a great passion, threatened to kane [Mr. French], calling him all the Popish Doggs and Divells imaginable." A year later, William Nickolls wrote to Leisler directly, following the arrest of Phillip French and his colleague, Jacobus de Key. "It May reasonably be suspected that you intend to murder them or impose some other villany [that] your frantick brain may urge you to," Nickolls wrote, before threatening to use "poisone, pistoll, or other sure meanes" against Leisler if "so much as the least haire of their heads" was injured during their time in prison.[9]

Word of the local opposition to Jacob Leisler eventually reached England, and when Henry Sloughter arrived in New York City in March of 1691 to be the new crown-appointed governor of New York and Massachusetts, one of the first things he did was arrest Leisler and his key advisors and charge them all with treason. Opposition to Catholicism had proven to be strong enough in New York to oust Francis Nicholson and the Catholic officials who had enjoyed some degree of authority in the colony so long as James had been in charge. It had also been strong enough to cause many of the colony's Catholic residents to flee, lowering the number of Catholics in New York City from about 5 percent of the European population in 1685 to 2 percent by 1700, with none of those Catholics being served by priests.[10] Clearly, however, there were limits to the power of anti-Catholicism, at least in New York. Fears of Catholic influence in the colony were not strong enough to save the life of Jacob Leisler, who was found guilty of treason and subsequently executed on May 16, 1691.

Nehemiah Blakiston's experiences in Maryland were quite different. Like Leisler, Blakiston led a rebellion against the ruling authorities in his colony after he learned of William and Mary's ascension in 1689. He, too, managed to gain temporary, if unauthorized control of his colony as a consequence of this rebellion. Unlike Jacob Leisler, however, Nehemiah Blakiston was not executed once authorities arrived from London to take over the situation and represent the king's interests. Indeed, following the arrival in 1692 of Lionel Copley, the man King William III had chosen to be Maryland's new governor, Nehemiah Blakiston was made a justice in the Provincial Court in St. Mary's City. He held that position until his death by natural causes a year later.[11]

Like New York, Maryland had been a proprietary colony. Proprietary colonies were "gifts" that the king gave to his friends and political allies. The charters associated with proprietary colonies were issued to individuals, rather than to joint-stock companies, and while that meant that the individuals who received the charters assumed much of the financial risk that came with setting up a New World colony, it also meant that the proprietors reaped most of the financial rewards.

Virginia, Plymouth, and Massachusetts were not proprietary colonies; they'd all been founded by joint-stock companies. People gave the companies money in exchange for membership, and the companies used that money to finance the costs of settlement once they had received a colonial charter from the king. Some of the members of these companies actually migrated to the New World, but many of them stayed home in England. They hoped that their investment would pay off and that they'd soon be making money off of the natural resources that the colonists in the New World were hunting and harvesting.[12]

New York, of course, had been the personal possession of the Duke of York, who became King James II in 1685. Maryland, when it was founded in 1634, was the personal possession of Cecilius Calvert, whose father, George, had campaigned heavily for the charter that led to the creation of a colony along the shores of the upper Chesapeake Bay. Cecilius rather than George received the charter because George Calvert died shortly before King Charles I signed and sealed the document that made the charter legitimate. George had had great plans for his colony, however – which was to be called *Terra Mariae*, or "Maryland," after King Charles I's wife, Henrietta Maria of France. Those plans involved the creation of a haven for English-speaking people who subscribed to the same faith that Queen Henrietta Maria and George and Cecilius Calvert all subscribed to. That faith was Roman Catholicism.[13]

When he received the charter, Cecilius Calvert fully intended to honor his father's wishes; there were political and financial limits, however, to what he was able to do. Maryland could not become a Catholic colony – meaning it could not become a colony where the Catholic Church was formally "established" or supported financially by the government. Charles I may have had Catholic sympathies; certainly the Puritans who killed him thought he did. But England's Protestant king would never allow the Catholic Church to be established anywhere in the English world.

Maryland also couldn't become a colony that had a majority-Catholic population. The number of Catholics living in England (which was where most of Maryland's future residents would be found) was too small to supply a majority-Catholic colony. Cecilius Calvert knew he was going to have to recruit Protestants to settle in Maryland if the colony were to have any hope of ever turning a profit– and Calvert really needed Maryland to be profitable. His father had accumulated quite a bit of debt during an earlier – and failed – effort at establishing a colony in what is now Newfoundland, and under seventeenth-century England's rules of inheritance, Cecilius Calvert was responsible for a large chunk of that debt.[14]

Still, although Maryland's Catholic population never came close to being a majority, it did prove to be a much larger percentage of the entire population than the Catholic population in England had ever been – 2 to 10 times larger, at least during the early decades of settlement. Not only that, but Maryland's Catholics tended to be wealthier than their Protestant counterparts, and they augmented that wealth by bringing poor indentured servants to the colony and receiving land from the proprietor as a reward for populating Maryland with laborers who would increase the colony's potential to generate revenue. Many of these servants were Protestants who grew to resent their former masters' wealth after they'd served their 5–9-year terms of indenture and found that all of the good land in the colony already belonged to wealthy planters like the Catholic men who had once been their masters.[15]

Not only were Catholics in Maryland wealthy, they also held prominent positions in the colony's local government; indeed, there were far more Catholics in Maryland's government than there had ever been in the government of New York under King James I. In Maryland, the governor, the colonial secretary, and a majority of the members of the governor's council were all Catholics who'd been appointed to their positions by the colony's Catholic proprietor. In England, Catholics were not allowed to serve in government. In Maryland, however, the colonial charter gave

Cecilius Calvert a great deal of autonomy. From the very beginning, Calvert believed it was important to use that autonomy to create a political landscape that gave Maryland's minority Catholics some degree of power. That meant, though, that the colony's Protestants had to answer to a kind of authority that they had never had to answer to while they lived in England.[16]

Cecilius Calvert was gone by the time Nehemiah Blakiston and his supporters rose up against their proprietor in 1689 and assumed control of Maryland. Cecilius died in November of 1675; when the Protestant Associators launched their rebellion, therefore, it was against Calvert's only surviving son, Charles, who had been the owner of Maryland for fourteen years by that point. Charles, too, was Catholic – and he was even more committed than his father had been to a policy of giving Catholics disproportionate political control of the colony.

The Protestant Associators' rebellion brought the era of Catholic rule in colonial Maryland to an end. King William revoked the charter that gave Charles Calvert proprietary control of the colony, and that charter was not restored to the Calvert family until 1715 – after Charles had died and his grandson and all of that grandson's children had converted to Anglicanism.

No openly Catholic man would serve again in Maryland's government until 1779, three years after the colonies had declared their independence from England. That was when residents of the free state of Maryland elected Thomas Sim Lee, a Catholic convert, as their governor. Lee's political ascendance testifies to the fact that Catholics continued to be prominent members of Maryland's society, even after their faith was effectively outlawed in the colony in 1703. It also testifies to the complicated nature of anti-Catholicism in a colony where Catholics and Protestants worked together, lived near one another, and – often – were related to one another by blood and marriage.[17]

THE ENGLISH ORIGINS OF COLONIAL AMERICA'S CATHOLICS

Whether they settled in New York or Maryland, the vast majority of Catholics living in British North America in the seventeenth century came from England. Ireland, the country typically associated with American Catholicism prior to the twentieth century, would not start supplying large numbers of Catholic immigrants to the North American population until the 1840s and 1850s.

The phrase that many historians use to describe the trajectory of Catholicism's development in early modern England is "from monopoly to minority."[18] The Catholic Church, in other words, went from being the only game in town in 1533, the year King Henry VIII formally severed ties with the pope and made himself the arbiter of all things religious in England, to being the faith of just a tiny and politically impotent slice of the British population by the time King James I assumed the throne in 1603.

There's a debate about how committed people in England were to Catholicism when their king decided that the country's residents ought not to be Catholic anymore – a debate that exists primarily because the surviving evidence from the period is so scant. For many years, scholars insisted that people in England did not have a solid understanding of the teachings of the Catholic Church at the time of the Henrician Reformation. Eighty percent of them, according to one historian, were "simple illiterates" who "flourished" on mindless recitations of the rosary, augmented their devotions with a wide variety of occult practices, had little or no understanding of the Latin liturgy, and showed "no coherent reaction at all" to Henry's denial of the pope's authority, his dissolution of the country's Catholic monasteries and convents, and his confiscation of those orders' buildings, land, and finances.[19]

The Catholicism adhered to by early modern England's residents, according to this reading, was rooted in superstition as much as it was in faith, and this made it easy for Catholics to jump ship as soon as the waters around them got a little rough. Certainly some of the priests serving in England at the time of the country's Reformation agreed with this reading and considered the lay Catholics they served to be fickle and unreliable. "People of this kind come into the Church without difficulty," John Gerard observed in 1609, a few years after he'd escaped from the Tower of London, having been sent there for being a Jesuit who secretly said Mass in people's homes. "But they fall away the moment persecution blows up."[20]

Some historians have challenged this reading as unfair, suggesting that religious understanding and commitment among early modern England's Catholics may have been deeper and more complicated than someone like John Gerard (who had obvious reasons to complain whenever the laity failed to defend their priests) could ever recognize or admit. Yes, there were many Catholics who didn't understand Latin and whose devotion to particular saints smacked of superstition rather than reasoned faith. And certainly there were many people who weren't willing to pay heavy fines or be imprisoned in the Tower of London – and who agreed to attend weekly services in an Anglican church in order to avoid having to do that. But it would be a mistake, according to these scholars, to see such people as mindless and fickle, or as having "fallen away" from the Catholic Church. Many attended Catholic Masses secretly and had their marriages blessed and their children baptized by Catholic priests, even as they went to Anglican services each week and subscribed to oaths that denied the right of the pope to depose England's monarch. Indeed, such people were so commonplace that Anglican and Catholic leaders alike each had derogatory names for them; Catholics called them "schismatics" and Anglicans called them "church papists."[21]

When church papists – or people who were probably church papists – are counted along with those individuals who flagrantly violated the law and lived openly as Catholics, the estimated number of Catholics in England in the first half of the seventeenth century rises to 120,000. That number is three times higher than the estimates that confine themselves just to what were known as "recusant rolls" – that is, formal lists that county authorities kept in early modern England of people who failed to attend Anglican church services, as they were required to do by law.[22] Still, even at three times higher, this estimate reveals a population that was a mere shadow of what it had been a century earlier, regardless of whether that earlier population understood Latin – or whether that question even matters.

During the reigns of the Stuart kings (James I, Charles I, Charles II, and James II), England's overall population was between 2.5 and 3 million. That means that at most, Catholics made up just 5 percent of the entire population in Stuart England, and the number of people who lived openly as Catholics, refusing to attend Anglican church services and paying the fines that were a consequence of that decision, may have been as low as 1 percent.[23]

In contrast, the earliest surviving census records from colonial Maryland reveal that nearly 10 percent of that colony's white population was Catholic, and in some counties – such as St. Mary's County, home to the colony's first capital, St. Mary's City – a full third of the white residents subscribed to the Catholic faith.[24] These Catholics also didn't have to pay fines or risk jail time when they attended Mass with a Catholic priest instead of an Anglican minister. In early colonial Maryland, all Catholics lived openly, which is part of the reason Maryland is mistakenly seen by some people today as having been a "Catholic colony," even though the Catholic

Church never enjoyed any financial support from the government there and Catholics themselves were always a minority.[25]

England's Catholic population was undeniably small by the time the "virgin queen" Elizabeth died in 1603 and her Scottish cousin, James, took over the throne. However, it was also wealthier, better educated, and more committed to its faith than it had been seventy years earlier, the debate about occult practices and mindless recitations of the rosary aside. This was because being and remaining Catholic in England had become more of a challenge than it used to be. Catholic identity was no longer something someone merely inherited or blindly fell into; it was a conscious choice, as one convert explained to his father when he insisted that he needed the help of the "great Clerks and Holy Fathers" of the Catholic Church in order to understand "the Incarnation, Resurrection, and Ascension of Christ" which "do involve great and hidden mysteries and profound difficulties."[26]

This anonymous convert's decision to seek the help of the Catholic Church led to his imprisonment – as indicated by the title given to his letter when it was illegally published by a Catholic printer in London in 1623, *An Epistle of a Catholicke young gentleman (being for religion imprisoned). To his Father, a Protestant.* Indeed, prison time was not the only penalty that early modern English Catholics faced when they chose to live their faith openly. There were also heavy fines, deliberately designed in some cases to bankrupt people, and as ninety-one Catholic clergy and twenty-six Catholic laypeople discovered between 1586 and 1681, the decision to live as a Catholic could result in one's execution, as well.[27]

For the most part, only people who had the resources to pay the heavy recusancy fines could afford to remain Catholic after King James I assumed the throne in 1603. This was why Maryland's Catholics tended to be wealthy; they came from a population of English men and women who were still Catholic because they could afford to be. The Jesuits' policy of targeting elite families and living among them, then – a strategy that was cultivated by the order's founder, Ignatius of Loyola – increased the likelihood that a Catholic in seventeenth-century England or Maryland would come from a wealthy family.[28]

Technically speaking, it was a capital offense after 1585 for any Roman Catholic priest to set foot on English soil. For that reason, many Catholic gentry had secret rooms – or "priest holes" – in their houses that clergy could hide in, should they find themselves in trouble with the local authorities. Indeed, one of the jobs that George Calvert had before he converted to Catholicism and resigned from public life involved keeping track of all of the priests who were illegally in the country. The men were not supposed to be there, but the government couldn't always be bothered to arrest them and put them on trial; sometimes it was enough simply to know where the priests were and what they were doing, without necessarily issuing a warrant for their arrest.[29]

While the Jesuits were not the only priests who risked their lives to serve England's tiny Catholic population, they were the largest single group of Catholic clergy to do so. Their chosen tactics, therefore, ended up having a strong influence on the demographic character of England's and Maryland's Catholic population. The best way to "go about making converts," the Jesuit John Gerard advised his colleagues, was to "bring the gentry over first and then their servants, for Catholic gentlefolk must have Catholic servants."[30] It was a strategy that made sense; many gentry, in fact, did try to ensure that most of their servants either were or became Catholic, because they feared that having a large number of Protestants in the house could draw attention to their recusancy.

After 1605, the risks that came with being Catholic in England got bigger. In the fall of that year, a plot to blow up the House of Lords on November 5 was discovered by one of the chamber's members and subsequently thwarted. The so-called "Gunpowder Plot" involved a handful of Catholic priests and at least twelve Catholic laymen who planned to kill James I in the explosion and then kidnap his nine-year-old daughter, Elizabeth (Figure 2.1). The idea was that Elizabeth would be forced to convert to Catholicism – a task that the conspirators did not expect would be too difficult, since she was young and impressionable, and her mother, Anne, was already a Catholic convert. The newly converted Elizabeth would then become England's queen.[31]

One of the conspirators was a mercenary soldier from Yorkshire named Guy Fawkes who had himself converted to Catholicism as a child. Fawkes spent several years fighting for the Spanish in that country's war to bring the Netherlands under Catholic control. When he returned home to England, he used the knowledge of explosives that he'd gained from that wartime experience to rig thirty-six barrels of gun powder to explode in a basement room of the Palace of Westminster.[32]

Fawkes was hanged for his troubles – and got off easy, actually, since he managed to jump from the scaffold and break his neck instantly before anything else could be done to him. His co-conspirators were not so lucky. They were each cut down from the gallows before they'd had a chance to suffocate from the pressure of the nooses around their necks; while still

FIGURE 2.1 This engraving of the Gunpowder Plot Conspirators was done by Crispijn de Passe the Elder in 1605, not long after the Plot's discovery. Guy Fawkes is third from the right. Detail credit: National Portrait Gallery, UK.

conscious, the men were castrated, disemboweled, and quartered. Additionally, the bodies of two other conspirators who had been shot and killed before they could be captured were exhumed and decapitated, and their heads were placed on spikes outside the Parliament building.[33]

For the next three centuries, people in England and the colonies would "remember, remember the fifth of November" by lighting bonfires and hanging effigies of the pope, the devil, and Guy Fawkes. These celebrations were designed to remind English-speaking Protestants of the violence that was thought to be endemic to Catholicism. In America, the celebration of "Pope's Day" was eventually condemned by General George Washington, who worried in 1775 that the effigies would alienate Catholics in Canada and stymie the efforts of the Continental Congress to get the Canadians to join the Americans in their bid for independence. In England, the annual hanging of effigies – or what came to be known as "guys" – on November 5 continued well into the nineteenth century. The anti-Catholic tenor of the celebrations did die down a bit during the reign of Queen Victoria (1837–1901), however, as the queen made it clear that she sympathized with her Catholic subjects who found the celebrations insulting.[34]

In the late nineteenth and early twentieth centuries, some writers of what were known as "penny dreadfuls" – a cheap and sensational genre

FIGURE 2.2 On July 17, 2016, the computer hacking group "Anonymous" released a video, saying they would target ISIS in the wake of the Bastille Day attack on Nice, France. Note the Guy Fawkes mask the announcer wears – made ironic, perhaps, by the context.

of illustrated fiction that, among other things, introduced the world to Sweeny Todd, the "demon barber of Fleet Street" – challenged the negative view of Guy Fawkes by depicting him as a hero, instead of a villain. R.J. Lambe's *The Boyhood Days of Guy Fawkes*, published in 1895, described the mercenary soldier as "hot-headed" and "rebellious," but insisted that he had "a kind heart" and a "most generous disposition" and was "one of the bravest youths to be met with."[35]

Thus began the reimaging of one of England's most notorious traitors and terrorists – a transformation that was complete by the late 1980s, when Alan Moore and David Lloyd used the image of Guy Fawkes in their graphic novel, *V for Vendetta*, which was turned into a Hollywood film starring Natalie Portman in 2006. The anarchist hero of that dystopian story disguises himself with a Guy Fawkes mask as he challenges the fascists who have taken over England's government. Today, Fawkes' visage is associated with the computer hacking group "Anonymous" and anyone, really, who claims to fight injustice by exposing political corruption and economic exploitation(Figure 2.2).[36] The executed Catholic's face is *not* associated with a group of religious extremists who sought to advance a political and religious agenda through bloodshed and fear.

THE CATHOLIC CALVERTS AND THE PUZZLE
OF ANTI-CATHOLICISM

George Calvert converted to Catholicism nineteen years after the discovery of the Gunpowder Plot, when fears of popery were still running high in England. He'd actually been born into a Catholic family; his parents lived on a small but respectable estate in Yorkshire, a rural county far from London where religious dissenters were able to live fairly peacefully. However, in 1592, when George was thirteen years old, Anglican authorities discovered that his parents had been sending him and his brother to a tutor who used a "popish primer" in the classroom. The Calverts were ordered to send their sons to a Protestant tutor in a neighboring town, and not long after that George and Christopher Calvert both converted to the Church of England, convinced to do so by that tutor.[37]

It was a conversion that George seems to have taken seriously, as evidenced by the fact that he married his first wife, Anne Mynne, within the Church of England. Anglicans were not required to have church weddings, since marriage wasn't a sacrament for them the way it was for Catholics. Many church papists, therefore, who considered themselves to be secretly Catholic avoided being married in the Anglican Church, because legally they could. The fact that Calvert's first marriage was performed by an Anglican minister suggests strongly that he was not a church papist; he was – for a time, at least – an honest and true Anglican.[38]

It may have been his wife's death that prompted his conversion back to Catholicism. According to letters that Calvert sent to his friends, he was quite devastated when Anne died giving birth to the couple's tenth child in 1622. Perhaps it was questions about the purpose of life and the immortality of the soul that brought him back to the faith he had been born into. Certainly, a conversion to Catholicism was not something Calvert ever could have done had he still been interested in maintaining his position in the court of King James. Calvert was an elected Member of Parliament, and he'd worked as a translator for King James for many years before becoming one of the king's two principal secretaries of state in 1619.

By 1625, however, Calvert was tired of public life. He was being ridiculed by many of his colleagues, thanks to his involvement in a failed diplomatic effort to marry Prince Charles to the youngest daughter of King Philip III of Spain. In February of 1625, therefore, at the age of 46, George Calvert resigned from all of his government positions. He'd secretly converted to Catholicism three months earlier, and following his resignation he made no effort to hide that conversion.[39]

In his retirement, George turned his attention to North America – convincing his friend, the king, to give him a charter that would allow him to found a colony called "Avalon" in what is now Newfoundland. That colony ended up being a financial disaster; the winters were too harsh and the growing season in Canada was too short for money to be made from anything but fishing. And so in 1629, after he'd spent a miserable year living in Avalon with his second wife and several of his children, George Calvert petitioned King James' successor, Charles I, for a colonial charter just like the one James had given him – only this time Calvert wanted land much farther south, in a warmer climate.[40]

Writing from Canada, Calvert made it clear to Charles that it was very important to him that the new charter have all of the same "provisions as the king, your father, my most gracious master, was pleased to give me here."[41] The reason the new charter needed to be like the old one was that the charter for Avalon contained some very special language that was entirely unique in 1629, and essential to the success of Calvert's plans in the New World.

England's king had given out eight North American charters by that point. Only one of them – Calvert's for Avalon – referenced the province of Durham, a remote and sparsely populated area in northeast England, far removed from the centers of power in London. Local authorities in Durham enjoyed a great deal of autonomy. Since at least the fourteenth century, they'd had the power to create courts and appoint judges, which everywhere else in England was the purview of the Crown. They'd also had the power to indict or pardon anyone for any crime – including even the capital offense of treason.

The reason Durham's officials had been given this much power was that the territory's precarious position near the Scottish borderlands – an area populated with people who'd resisted England's efforts to annex Scotland for centuries – required that local leaders there have the flexibility to respond quickly and successfully to the tenuous and often volatile local conditions. Durham's officials ruled a unique community within England that several kings and queens had recognized could not always be governed by the same principles that animated life in the rest of the country. The area was home to a cadre of people who had their own traditions and were inclined sometimes not to recognize the legitimacy of their local leaders' rule. Those leaders, therefore, needed to have the freedom to construct a legal system that reflected the unique needs of the population living in their province – even if that meant that some of the laws and traditions that governed life in the rest of England weren't always followed.[42]

George Calvert's charter to Avalon gave him the same "Jurisdictions, Privileges, Prerogatives, Royalties, Liberties, Immunities, and royal Rights ... as any Bishop of Durham ... ever heretofore hath had, held, used, or enjoyed." It was a stunningly sweeping grant – one that gave Calvert the power to do almost anything he felt was necessary. In the history of British colonialism in North America, only two other charters would give this much power to their grantees. The second charter, granted in 1663 to eight men who had helped to restore King Charles II to the throne following Oliver Cromwell's death, gave Carolina's proprietors the flexibility they needed to plant an English colony on land that was already claimed by the Spanish. The first of the two other charters was granted in 1632. It was given to Cecilius Calvert, five weeks after his father George had died.[43]

George Calvert needed the same autonomy that the bishops of Durham enjoyed because he planned on being the Catholic ruler of an English colony that had a mixed population of Catholics and Protestants – many of whom, he knew, would be loath to submit to the needs, plans, and desires of a papist proprietor. His son Cecilius needed that autonomy, too, because Cecilius, like his father, was Catholic. He and at least three of his younger siblings – Leonard, Anne, and George – had converted around the same time as their father. Indeed, the name "Cecilius" was a mark of the oldest Calvert son's commitment to his chosen faith; the nineteen-year-old graduate of Trinity College, Oxford, had been named "Cecil" at birth, but he changed his name to "Cecilius" after his conversion because it sounded more Roman.[44]

While the reason behind Calvert's desire for autonomy may have been obvious, James' reasons for giving it to him – and Charles' reasons for extending that same autonomy to Cecilius – were less apparent. James, after all, had nearly been killed by a group of angry Catholics just two decades earlier, and if those Catholics had succeeded in implementing their plan, Elizabeth – not Charles – would have succeeded James I as England's sovereign. Why, then, were James and Charles willing to give the Catholic Calverts a colonial charter at all – let alone two charters, each of which gave the Calverts so much power?

The answer to this question points to the complicated difference between Catholicism – an idea and an institution that was deeply feared in England, the British colonies, and eventually the United States of America – and Catholics – that is to say, individual people who were often on quite friendly terms with the Protestants they lived near, worked with, and sometimes even married. Thomas Wentworth, for instance, who was the Lord Deputy of Ireland, used his influence with King Charles I to help his good friend George Calvert secure the charter for Maryland, even as Wentworth worked to confiscate the property of anyone in Ireland who was caught harboring a Catholic priest. The famous diarist John Evelyn was delighted to be able to visit his friend Thomas Arundel in his home just six days after Arundel – a Catholic – was released from prison, having been mistakenly arrested following the discovery of the Gunpowder Plot. Evelyn brought his nineteen-year-old daughter along to sing for Arundel, even though he also worried quite openly that "secret papists" were teaching at University College, Oxford, turning bright young men into thoughtless minions who would "bring in Popery, which God in Mercy prevent!"[45]

One of the ironies of King James I's monarchy was that even as the king cracked down on the practice of Catholicism in England – levying harsh fines against people who failed to attend Anglican services and requiring Catholics to swear that the pope had no authority to "depose the King ... or to authorize any Foreign Prince to invade or annoy him" – he also tolerated his wife's secret conversion to Catholicism, married his oldest surviving son, Charles, off to a French Catholic princess, and elevated ten Catholic men to the British peerage, more than doubling the number of Catholic noble families in England. One of the Catholic men James elevated was his friend and former secretary of state, George Calvert, who received a patent to 2,300 acres of land in the Irish midlands not long after he announced his conversion – making him the first "Lord Baltimore."[46]

British anti-Catholicism, in other words, was complicated. And it became even more complicated in Maryland, thanks to the contingencies of colonial life, which required that people who might have had nothing to do with one another in England come together to clear fields, form businesses, construct buildings, and sometimes even create families.

In Maryland, the fear of Catholicism that animated English life was real – no less real than it was in the Calvinist communities that dotted the Long Island Sound and Massachusetts and Cape Cod Bays. But because Catholics were a 'known quantity' in Lord Baltimore's colony – far better known in Maryland than they were even in James' New York – anti-Catholicism tended not to be a pervasive or perpetual component of the British culture along the northern edge of the Chesapeake. It raised its head there in fits and starts. Indeed, in 1696, just four years after Nehemiah

Blakiston and his men had succeeded in bringing the era of Catholic rule in colonial Maryland to an end, Protestant lawmakers in the colony prevented their new Anglican governor from confiscating Catholics' guns, saying that the action was not necessary because relations between Protestants and Catholics in the colony were so good. "This Province is God be thanked very peaceable and quiet," the lawmakers informed their new governor before rejecting his gun confiscation order and advising him not to antagonize the Catholics in their midst.[47]

But as the very existence of that Anglican governor testified to, things were not always "peaceable and quiet" between Protestants and Catholics in Maryland. In fact, when anti-Catholicism did show its face in the colony (and the Protestant Associators' rebellion in 1689 was certainly not the first time), the effects could be quite ugly – uglier, even, than they were in New England, precisely because Maryland had a sizable Catholic population that could be hurt by the anti-Catholicism and could also fight back.

CALVERT'S EARLY (AND UNSUCCESSFUL) STRATEGY FOR PEACE

Cecilius Calvert's initial strategy for keeping the peace in Maryland was fairly simple. To keep the Catholics in line (and, as his experiences with Maryland's priests soon showed, he did need to govern some of his co-religionists with a heavy hand), he relied upon what he called "the dependency which the Government of Maryland hath upon the State of England."[48] To keep the Protestants in line, he constructed a government that was made up primarily of Catholics.

Even before the first settlers reached the Potomac River, Calvert had his brother, Leonard, remind his co-religionists that they were not setting up a Catholic colony. It was British law – not Church law (or what was known as "canon law") – to which Maryland's English proprietor was ultimately bound. Certainly, the Anglican Church would not be established in Maryland and Catholics there would be allowed to practice their faith openly, which was not the case in England. Nevertheless, the Catholic Church would not enjoy any special privileges in the colony, as it did in the great Catholic countries of Continental Europe.

Reading from a list of instructions that Cecilius Calvert put together some time before the *Ark* and the *Dove* set sail for North America in November of 1633, Leonard Calvert asked that all "Acts of the Roman Catholique Religion" be "done as privately as they may be," both during the journey across the Atlantic, when Catholics and Protestants were obliged to share tight quarters with one another on the boats, and after, when the colony of Maryland had finally been set up. He also instructed his religious brethren to be "silent upon all occasions of discourse concerning matters of Religion," so that "no scandal nor offense" would be "given to any of the Protestants in the colony." Reminding Maryland's first Catholics that the residents of Virginia were already unhappy about the fact that a Catholic had been given permission to found a colony less than fifty miles north of the Rappahannock River, Leonard Calvert insisted that Catholics needed to treat all of the Protestants they encountered with "mildness and favor," so that no "just complaint may hereafter be made by them, in Virginia, or in England."[49]

Cecilius Calvert never lived in Maryland, but he hand-picked many of the men who would be responsible for running the colony. He chose his brother Leonard to be Maryland's first governor. He selected two other Catholics, Jerome Hawley and Thomas Cornwallis, to be the colony's first commissioners. About a year after Maryland was settled, Calvert sent his friend, John Lewger, over to be the colony's first secretary of state; Lewger was a recent Catholic convert. In fact, of the six men Calvert appointed to serve in the Proprietary Assembly of 1638, five were Catholic. The sixth – an Anglican – never attended any of the meetings, for reasons that are unclear.[50]

These proprietary appointees, however, weren't the only people responsible for making and executing Maryland's laws. Lord Baltimore's charter required him to allow the colony's freemen to choose their own legislative representatives, and judging from the men those freemen sent to the first Assembly, the proprietor's penchant for Catholics was not shared by everyone in his colony. Nine men were elected to the Proprietary Assembly of 1638, and of the eight whose religious identities are known, six were Protestants. One of those Protestants, John Gray, was a Calvinist who went on to participate in a violent rebellion against the proprietor's authority seven years later.[51]

Cecilius Calvert's initial strategy for keeping the peace in Maryland did not work – and Protestants like Gray were not the only reason why. Catholics, too, proved to be a thorn in Baltimore's side. Many of them refused to heed his advice about the importance of avoiding contentious religious conversations. They brandished their faith openly in Maryland, not only building a chapel in the heart of St. Mary's City, but also working to convert the children of some of the colony's more prominent Protestant residents and occasionally denying their Protestant servants the right to read religious books that were authored by Calvinists.[52]

The Jesuits proved to be particularly egregious offenders, refusing to pay their property taxes and insisting that they were not obliged to do so since they were clergy (and deserving, therefore, of special privileges). It was galling enough, according to the Jesuits' leader in Maryland, Thomas Copley, that the priests had had to pay for their own passage to the colony and were serving Catholics there "gratis," meaning without any salary. "One would think that even out of gratitude, they might free us of such kind of taxation," he wrote to the proprietor in 1638, after Maryland's lawmakers had forced the Jesuits to contribute funds toward the construction of a new fort.

Copley didn't like that Cecilius Calvert had made no effort to "provide or show any favor to Eccelsiastical persons or to preserve for the [Catholic] Church the Immunity and privileges which she enjoyeth elsewhere," by which the priest meant countries such as Spain and France. He urged the proprietor to review Maryland's laws and to change them so that priests would be exempt from the taxes, duties, and restrictions that applied to all of the other landowners in the colony. "I beseech your Lordship," Copley warned, "before you do anything about these laws, that you would be pleased to read over and ponder well the *Bulla Coenae*." It was a thoroughly unveiled threat, a reminder to Lord Baltimore that in 1627 Pope Urban VIII had issued a bull that prohibited Catholic rulers from imposing taxes on Church properties without the pope's permission. Any leader who ignored the directive risked excommunication.[53]

Cecilius Calvert was enraged by Copley's letter. He fired off his own letter to the Jesuits' supervisor in London. Asserting that the laws of Maryland "do bind all persons whatsoever as well spiritual and lay," Baltimore reminded that supervisor that although Maryland's proprietor was Catholic, and although the free practice of Catholicism was certainly to be maintained in Maryland, the colony was still English. Its laws, therefore, had to conform as near as possible to the laws of England. Baltimore and his colonial officers, "although they be Roman Catholics," were not "obliged in conscience" to give any special consideration to the Catholic clergy or the mandates of the pope. They could treat the priests as they would any other citizens "without committing any sin or incurring the censure of Bull Coenae for so doing."[54]

The proprietor's fight with the Jesuits made a number of Maryland's Catholics uncomfortable. Thomas Cornwallis warned Baltimore that he might have to leave Maryland if the proprietor didn't settle the dispute peaceably. "I shall with as much Convenient speed as I can with draw myself, and what is left of that which I brought with me," he wrote to

Calvert, "out of Danger of being involved in the spiritual ruin" that the proprietor was courting. Baltimore's sister, Anne, and her husband, William Peasley, joined Leonard Calvert in asking Cecilius to make good with the Society of Jesus. Cecilius responded by telling Leonard – who was, of course, in Maryland – that the Jesuits in London had been saying nasty things about him. "Whatsoever you may conceive of [the Jesuits]," he wrote to his brother in 1642, "you have no reason upon my knowledge to love them very much if you knew as much as I do concerning their speeches and actions here toward you."[55]

In the end, Baltimore and the Jesuits did make peace with one another – but it wasn't because they came to an agreement about the pope's jurisdiction in Maryland. It was because Protestants in the colony rose up against Cecilius Calvert, his representatives, and all of the Catholics living in Maryland. In a pattern that would repeat itself later in the century, after the Glorious Revolution, political unrest in England spilled over into Maryland in the 1640s, to the detriment of the colony's Catholics.

Responding to the anti-Catholic tenor of the English Civil War, two Calvinists fomented a rebellion against Maryland's government in 1644: Richard Ingle, a ship's captain based in England who didn't reside in the colony but visited it often in order to trade with its residents; and William Claiborne, an eccentric fur-trader and land-surveyor who lived on a remote island in the middle of the Chesapeake and whose descents would ultimately include a governor (William C.C. Claiborne of Louisiana), a fashion designer (Liz Claiborne), a journalist (ABC's Cokie Roberts), and, ironically, a United States' ambassador to the Vatican (Corinne "Lindy" Claiborne Boggs, Cokie's mother, who served as US Ambassador to the Holy See from 1997–2001).[56]

The Ingle–Claiborne Rebellion lasted for two years, during which time the rebels targeted and destroyed numerous Catholic properties. The plantation that Giles Brent shared with his sister, Margaret, was plundered by William Claiborne's forces, who slaughtered the Brent family's cattle and sheep, stole their tobacco, and burned their fields. Fr. Thomas Copley reported that the rebels burned the Jesuits' entire library to the ground. Valued at £150, the collection of books was worth more than three-quarters of the estates in St. Mary's County.[57]

The rebellion was eventually crushed – but not until after 80 percent of the settlers in St. Mary's County had either fled or been killed. Leonard Calvert retreated to Virginia shortly after Richard Ingle launched his assault in February of 1645. There, Calvert raised an army and re-crossed the Potomac, taking his brother's colony back in December of 1646. His enjoyment of the victory was brief, however. Just seven months after re-establishing his authority in Maryland, Governor Leonard Calvert was bitten by a snake and died.[58]

THE ANTI-CATHOLIC ORIGINS OF RELIGIOUS TOLERATION

Cecilius Calvert now faced a number of problems. First and foremost, he had to re-populate his colony. Yes, Maryland was a religious experiment – but it was also a money-making endeavor. And the rebels had done a very good job of undoing a decade's worth of financial progress in Lord Baltimore's colony.

Calvert also had to find a new governor, since his brother was dead. He was astute enough to recognize that his policy of relying almost exclusively on Catholic leaders had failed to keep the peace in Maryland; indeed, the policy had only exacerbated Protestants' distrust of people who subscribed to the Catholic faith. He was, therefore, more ecumenical when choosing his second governor, asking a Calvinist, rather than a Catholic to be his representative.

Needless to say, it was a risky move. William Stone wasn't even living in Maryland at the time that Calvert asked him to be his colony's next governor; he was living in Virginia, along what is now known as the Delmarva Peninsula (because the states of Delaware, Maryland, and Virginia all claim territory there). Stone, however, had something that Cecilius Calvert needed. He'd promised Lord Baltimore that he would bring 500 Calvinist settlers from Virginia to Maryland with him if the proprietor made him governor. These settlers would be ready to start working right away, since they'd been living in North America for years and would not have to go through the "seasoning process" that weakened and killed so many European migrants when they first arrived in the New World and encountered the microbes there. Calvert knew how devastating the seasoning process could be; his own brother, George, had become ill shortly after arriving in the Chesapeake in 1634 and died at the age of twenty-one.[59]

Stone insisted that the Calvinists would be eager to come, since they were living in a colony that had formally established the Anglican Church and refused to recognize the legitimacy of the Puritans' take-over of the government in England. He didn't pretend that his co-religionists would be pleased to learn that Maryland's proprietor was Catholic; he promised, however, that they would rather live in a colony with no religious

establishment than in one that form.
as Virginia did.

Cecilius Calvert could not afford to refuse Stone
Claiborne rebellion had resulted in more than £10,000 in land,
damage to his colony, which was half of what he himself had invested in
the initial process of settlement.[60] Lord Baltimore needed these Virginians
more than they needed him. He was not naïve, however. To protect
himself and his fellow Catholics from the religious intolerance that seemed
to be almost endemic in Calvinist thought and behavior, Cecilius Calvert
sent his friend Thomas Hatton to Maryland shortly after appointing Stone
as governor. Hatton came with a very important document. It was the
draft of what eventually became the first act of religious toleration in the
English-speaking world.

The "Act Concerning Religion" is frequently referred to by historians as the
"Toleration Act" – although modern-day readers, steeped as they are in our
contemporary understanding of religious pluralism, may find it difficult to
find much "toleration" in the act, given that it calls for people who "deny our
Savior Jesus Christ to bee the sonne of God" to be "punished with death."
Still, in the seventeenth-century British world, the Toleration Act's man-
date that Catholics and Protestants stop destroying one another was
pretty revolutionary – particularly given that the act was issued in
Maryland in 1649, the same year Puritans in England executed their
Anglican king for being a little too "Catholic."

The Act Concerning Religion placed restrictions on Maryland's citizens
as much as it did on Maryland's government. Baltimore's objective when
he proposed the law was to force his colony's residents to be civil toward
one another. To that end, the act did more than simply guarantee that the
government would not interfere in matters of Christian conscience (as
important as that was). It also required Maryland's residents to keep their
religious bigotry to themselves. It forbade the use of a long list of terms,
some of them fairly innocuous today, but all of them designed to insult in
the seventeenth century: "heretic," "schismatic," "idolator," "Puritan,"
"Independent," "Presbyterian," "Popish Priest," "Jesuited Priest,"
"Lutheran," "Calvinist," "Anabaptist," "Antinomian," "Roundhead,"
"Separatist" – the list went on. Under the act, anyone in Maryland who
used "a name or term in a reproachful manner relating to matter[s] of
Religion" was subject to a fine that escalated with each incident. If the fine
got to a point where the guilty party could no longer afford to pay,
imprisonment and/or a public flogging would be the penalty.[61]

...nd his allies in Maryland's colonial assembly recog-
...portant role that civility played in the achievement of religious
...ralism – and the vital role that pluralism played in the achievement of peace and its consequent prosperity. Ideally, the civility that Lord Baltimore knew his colony needed would come naturally; until that day arrived, however, Maryland's proprietor was determined to force it. Every time another generation grew up in Maryland not hearing words like "Puritan" or "Papist," or else seeing the people who used such offensive language flogged and fined for doing so, the goal of achieving genuine civility and real religious pluralism would get a little closer. In the meantime, Calvert hoped the Act Concerning Religion would at the very least shut people up long enough that they could start working together in the colony and making money for themselves – and, of course, for him.

The strategy worked – sort of. The first few decades that followed the Ingle–Claiborne Rebellion were hardly tranquil in Maryland, but, for the most part, the Act Concerning Religion did manage to keep religious animosity at bay, at least until Cecilius Calvert's death in 1675. After that, his son's clumsiness joined forces with people's growing fears about the possibility of a Catholic king to create a tumultuous situation in Maryland that eventually led to the temporary revocation of the colony's charter and the religious conversion of the entire Calvert family.

THE DEMISE OF THE CATHOLIC CALVERTS AND THE RISE OF CONTRACTARIAN GOVERNMENT

Charles Calvert was thoroughly ungifted in matters of diplomacy. Not long after he became Maryland's new proprietor in 1675, he cut the number of delegates who represented Maryland's two most Protestant counties in half. Anne Arundel and Kent Counties were Calvinist strongholds. They were also sparsely populated, which was ostensibly why Calvert reduced their number of delegates. Nevertheless, it was a stupid move – one that could not fail to antagonize Maryland's Calvinists and convince them that their new Catholic proprietor was a tyrant.[62]

Calvert probably should have known better. Unlike his father, he lived in Maryland. He'd arrived in the colony in 1661 at the age of twenty-four and served as Maryland's governor until his father's death. Even after he became proprietor, Charles Calvert continued to reside in Maryland, returning to England just twice during his proprietorship – once, shortly after Cecilius' death, to settle his father's estate, and a second time in 1684, in an attempt to settle a boundary dispute he was having with

William Penn, who'd founded the colony of Pennsylvania two years earlier. That dispute would not actually be settled until 1776, when the surveyors Charles Mason and Jeremiah Dixon were jointly hired by the Calvert and Penn families to fix the boundary between their two colonies.[63]

Although he lived in Maryland, Charles Calvert seemed to have no understanding of how precarious the peace that his father had brokered from London actually was. Upon becoming proprietor in 1675, he stacked the government with Catholics and Catholic sympathizers – a tactic that Cecilius Calvert had learned in the 1640s just did not work. He also increased the property requirements on voting, making it far more difficult for Protestants to vote or hold office, since they were poorer than Catholics.[64]

In neighboring Virginia, Governor William Berkeley learned in 1676 that it was a bad idea to have a bunch of angry freemen running around a colony with no mechanism for expressing themselves politically. That was the year 500 yeoman farmers and un-enfranchised freemen turned their guns on Virginia's House of Burgesses, claiming that the elite members of that body had been ignoring their interests and leaving them vulnerable to Indian attacks. The participants in what became known as "Bacon's Rebellion" had sent a letter to King Charles II before they rebelled, complaining that Governor Berkley was acting like a "fool" and warning the king that something needed to be done. The Virginians, however, were not the only people who signed that letter. A group of men from Maryland had signed it, too.

The letter complained as much about Charles Calvert as it did about William Berkeley. Maryland's proprietor, the petitioners alleged, had filled the colony's assembly with "papists, [his] own creatures, and ignoramuses" who assisted him in his campaign to "overturn England" and "drive us Protestants to Purgatory within ourselves in America."[65] The characterization was not entirely wrong. Politically, Charles Calvert was a bit of a dinosaur – seemingly unaware of the fact that the winds in the English-speaking world were changing and that his philosophies of government were failing to keep up. That cluelessness would ultimately cost him his inheritance.

Charles Calvert ruled Maryland the way James I and Charles I had ruled England; like those early Stuart kings, he believed he was "beholden to no elective power." The idea that "the king or magistrate holds his authority of the people, both originally and naturally for their good" – a notion that was first articulated by the Calvinist poet and philosopher John Milton in 1650 –

was not one that the third Lord Baltimore signed on to.[66] He believed his proprietary authority emanated not from the people, but from his charter, which had been given to him by the king, whose authority, in turn, came from God.

It's unlikely that Calvert had this absolutist approach to government because he was Catholic and belonged, therefore, to a church that stressed the importance of hierarchy and denied the legitimacy of individual authority. His critics, however, certainly saw it that way, largely because the new philosophy of government that people like John Milton were calling for – whereby government came to be seen as a "contract" between the people and their leaders – had its roots in Protestant understandings of freedom. It was no coincidence that Milton was a Calvinist – that he subscribed to a theology that emphasized the individual's obligation to confront the reality of his or her sinfulness and have an unmediated conversation with God about that sinfulness. A contractarian philosophy of government insisted that rulers had an obligation to protect human freedom – and that freedom was about the exercise of certain individual rights. Those rights were the natural outgrowth of the individual obligations that Calvinists insisted all Christians had to confront sin.[67]

Increasingly throughout the seventeenth century, especially during the decades that followed the English Civil War, English-speaking Protestants came to believe that governments that respected an understanding of freedom that began with individual rights were "godly" governments, and all other governments were hopelessly corrupt. By the dawn of the eighteenth century, Englishmen in the Old World and the New no longer believed that their leaders had a "divine right" to rule over them. In a properly organized society, the political philosopher John Locke proclaimed in 1689, everyone – even the king – was "obliged to submit to the determination of the majority."[68]

Of course, 1689 was the year the majority of England's MPs determined they no longer wished to submit to the rule of the Catholic King James II. It was the year Jacob Leisler rebelled against James' administrators in New York. And it was the year Protestants in Maryland brought the rule of the Catholic Calverts – and that brief period of limited, but real religious toleration in Maryland – to an end.

CHAPTER CONCLUSION

Catholics did not disappear from the landscape in Maryland after Nehemiah Blakiston and his men succeeded in marginalizing them; they did not flee, as their co-religionists in New York did. Thanks to their wealth, they continued to be economic leaders in their colony, and because their extensive land and slave holdings were vital to the success of a colony that had committed itself to tobacco (and therefore desperately needed labor and capital), Maryland's Catholics were able to chafe – openly and sometimes even aggressively – against the anti-Catholic legislation that was proposed and sometimes passed in their colony during the decades that followed the Glorious Revolution. They could chafe because they knew Maryland's lawmakers needed them.

Some Catholics did migrate from Maryland to Pennsylvania, which was founded a few years before the Glorious Revolution. Catholicism was legally tolerated there, thanks to the Quaker principles of William Penn, who firmly believed his colony should be a place where "all persons ... who confess one Almighty God to be the creator, ruler, and upholder of the world" could "live peaceably and justly in civil society." Most of the Catholics living in Pennsylvania, however, were not migrants from Maryland. They were European immigrants who came to the colony directly because of its religiously tolerant legal landscape. Many of these immigrants were Germans who found they actually had more in common with the German-speaking Lutherans and freethinkers who also settled in Pennsylvania than they did with the English-speaking Catholics who worked along Philadelphia's docks.[69]

Maryland's Catholics formulated sophisticated ideas about constitutional government as they attempted to fight the anti-Catholic legislation that governed their colony throughout most of the eighteenth century. These ideas – articulated as early as 1718 – would prove to be remarkably similar to the ideas articulated by leaders of the independence movement in Massachusetts and Virginia in the 1760s. It is perhaps not surprising, then, that Maryland's Catholics enthusiastically joined that cause – in spite of the grossly anti-Catholic tenor of the revolutionary rhetoric.

NOTES

1. Increase Mather, *To His Excellency, Richard, Earl of Bellomont...* (Boston, 1699), 2; "Leisler's Speech at the Gallows, May 16th, 1691," in *Ecclesiastic Records, State of New York*, Hugh Hastings, ed. (Albany, 1901), 2:1017.
2. Henry L. Schoolcraft, "The Capture of New Amsterdam," *English Historical Review* (1907), 674–693.
3. Evan Haefeli, *New Netherland and the Dutch Origins of American Religious Liberty* (Philadelphia, 2012), 54–81; William Bradford, *History of Plimouth Plantation* (1630–1651), rpt. (Boston, 1898), 32.

4. Jason K. Duncan, *Citizens or Papists? The Politics of Anti-Catholicism in New York, 1685–1821* (New York, 2005), 1–6.

5. Hastings, *Ecclesiastical Records*, 2:984.

6. J. Thomas Scharf, *History of Westchester County, New York* (Philadelphia, 1886), 685–688.

7. Hastings, *Ecclesiastical Records*, 2:965.

8. Deposition of Andries and Jan Meyer, September 26, 1689, quoted in Duncan, *Citizens or Papists?*, 10; Charles Sommerville, "The Early Career of Francis Nicholson," *Maryland Historical Magazine* 4 (1909), 217.

9. "McCarthy-Welch Exchange, 9 June, 1954," accessed August 27, 2015: www.youtube.com/watch?v=K1eA5bUzVjA; "An Act for Outlawing Phillip French and Thomas Wenham, Mechants, and Enforcing Process of Outlawry," April 30, 1702/03, in *The Colonial Laws of New York, Year 1664 to the Revolution*, Charles Z. Lincoln, William H. Johnson, and A. Judd Northrup, eds. (Albany, 1896), 1:476; Hastings, *Ecclesiastical Records*, 2: 982, 965; William Nickolls to Jacob Leisler, June 24, 1690, in *The Leisler Papers*, Peter R. Christoph, ed. (New York, 2002), 163–164.

10. Duncan, *Citizens or Papists*, 6, 14, 22–23; Joyce D. Goodfriend, *Before the Melting Pot: Society and Culture in Colonial New York, 1664–1730* (Princeton, 1992), 61.

11. Christopher Johnson, "Blakistone Family," *Maryland Historical Magazine* 2 (1907), 57.

12. Samuel Eliot Morison, *Builders of the Bay Colony* (New York, 1958), 34; E. H. Goss, "About Richard Bellingham," *The Magazine of American History With Notes and Queries* 13 (1885), 263; Brendan Wolfe, "Sir Thomas Smythe," *Encyclopedia Virginia* (Virginia Foundation for the Humanities), accessed on Austust 27, 2015: www.encyclopediavirginia.org/Smythe_Sir_Thomas_ca_1558-1625.

13. Maura Jane Farrelly, *Papist Patriots: The Making of an American Catholic Identity* (New York, 2012), 55–61.

14. Ibid., 62–63.

15. Ibid., 27, 68, 118.

16. Ibid., 64–65.

17. Ibid., 145, 255–56.

18. Christopher Haigh, "From Monopoly to Minority: Catholicism in Early Modern England," *Transactions of the Royal Historical Society* 31 (1981): 129–147.

19. J.C.H. Aveling, *The Handle and the Axe: The Catholic Recusants in England from Reformation to Emancipation* (London, 1976), 27; 30–31.

20. John Gerard, *The Autobiography of an Elizabethan* (1609), Philip Caraman, trans. (London, 1951), 32.

21. Lucy E. M. Wooding, *Rethinking Catholicism in Reformation England* (New York, 2000); Alexandra Walsham, *Church Papists: Catholicism, Conformity, and Confessional Polemic in Early Modern England* (Rochester, NY, 1993).

22. John Bossy, *The English Catholic Community, 1570–1850* (New York, 1976), chapter 8; John Coffey, *Persecution and Toleration in Protestant England, 1558–1689* (New York, 2000), 87.

23. Farrelly, *Papist Patriots*, 27.

24. Ibid., 242, n. 48.

25. John Dorsey, "'Maryland: First Catholic Colony' centers on Bishop Carroll," *Baltimore Sun*, October 19, 1990; Bruno Aguilera-Barchet, *A History of Western Public Law: Between Nation and State* (New York, 2015), 337; Keith Lindley, "Review of English and Catholic: The Lords Baltimore in the Seventeenth Century," *English Historical Review* 121 (2006), 307.

26. N.N. *An Epistle of a Catholicke young gentleman (being for religion imprisoned). To his Father a Protestant* (London, 1623), 12–13.

27. Patrick Barry, "The Penal Laws," *L'Osservatore Romano*, November 30, 1987.

28. Haigh, "From Monopoly to Minority," 142.

29. Allan Fea, *Secret Chambers and Hiding Places: The Historic, Romantic & Legendary Stories & Traditions About Hiding Holes, Secret Chambers, etc.* (London, 1904), 17–69; Farrelly, *Papist Patriots*, 60.

30. Gerard, *Autobiography*, 33.

31. Antonia Fraser, *Faith and Treason: The Story of the Gunpowder Plot* (New York, 1996), 140.

32. Ibid., 173.

33. Ibid., 235–236, 279–283; Alan Haynes, *The Gunpowder Plot: Faith and Rebellion* (Stroud, UK, 1994), 115–116.

34. J.A. Sharpe, *Remember, Remember: A Cultural History of Guy Fawkes Day* (Cambridge, MA, 2005), 145; Ronald Hutton, *The Stations of the Sun: A History of the Ritual Year in Britain* (New York, 1996), 401.

35. Louis James, *Fiction for the Common Man, 1830–1850: A Study of the Literature Produced for the Working Classes in Early-Victorian Urban England* (New York, 1974), 136; Sharpe, *Remember, Remember*, 128; R.J. Lambe, *The Boyhood Days of Guy Fawkes; or, The Conspirators of Old London* (London, 1895), 7.

36. Nick Thompson, "Guy Fawkes Mask Inspires Occupy Protests Around the World," *CNN*, November 5, 2001, accessed on September 26, 2015: www.cnn.com/2011/11/04/world/europe/guy-fawkes-mask/.

37. James W. Foster, *George Calvert: The Early Years* (Baltimore, 1983), 27.

38. John D. Krugler, *English and Catholic: The Lords Baltimore in the Seventeenth Century* (Baltimore, 2004), 32.

39. Ibid., 66–69; George Calvert to the 2nd Earl of Salisbury, August 12, 1622, in *Calendar of the Manuscripts of the Most Honorable Marquee of Salisbury, Preserved at Hatfield House, Hertfordshire*, Montague Spencer Giuseppi and Geraint Owen, eds. (London, 1915), 22:328.

40. Farrelly, *Papist Patriots*, 55–58.

41. George Calvert to Charles I, August 19, 1629, in John Thomas Scharf, *History of Maryland, from the Earliest Period to the Present Day* (Baltimore, 1879), 1:105.

42. W.S. Holdsworth, *A History of English Law* (London, 1903), 1:50; Gaillard Thomas Lapsley, *The County Palatine of Durham: A Study of Constitutional History* (London, 1900).

43. Krugler, *English and Catholic*, 122–123; Aaron F. Miller, John D. Krugler, Barry C. Gaulton, and James L. Lyttleton, "'Over Shoes, Over Boots': Lord Baltimore's Final Days in Ferryland, Newfoundland," *Journal of Early*

American History, 1 (2011), 170; "The Charter of Maryland, 1632," *The Avalon Project: Documents in Law, History, and Diplomacy*, Yale Law School, accessed on September 30, 2015: http://avalon.law.yale.edu/17th_cen tury/ma01.asp; "Charter of Carolina, March 24, 1663," ibid., http://avalon .law.yale.edu/17th_century/nc01.asp.

44. Krugler, *English and Catholic*, 130–131.

45. Ibid., 117; Dermot B. Fenlon, "Wentworth and the Parliament of 1634," *Journal of the Royal Society of Antiquaries of Ireland*, 94 (1964), 159–175; John Evelyn, *Memoirs of John Evelyn, Comprising his Diary from 1641 to 1705–06* (London, 1827), 3:208, 127.

46. "An Act for the better discovering and repressing of Popish Recusants," Jac. I, c. 3,4, in *Statues of the Realm*, T.E. Tomlins, John France, William Elias Taunton, and John Raithby, eds. (London, 1810–1828), 4:1071–1074; Robert J. Brugger, *Maryland: A Middle Temperament, 1634–1980* (Baltimore, 1988), 4; Aveling, *The Handle and the Axe*, 123–125; Pauline Croft, *King James* (New York, 2003), 24–25; Fraser, Faith and Treason, 15. Simon Stock, the priest who claimed responsibility for George Calvert's conversion, actually insisted that James' wife Anne "always put off her conversion, and finally died outside the true Church, although in heart a Catholic." See "Stock's Narrative," in *Carmel in England: A History of the English Mission of the Discalced Carmelites, 1615–1849*, Benedict Zimmerman, ed. (New York, 1899), 30.

47. *Archives of Maryland*, William Hande Brown, et al., ed. (Baltimore, 1883–present), *Archives of Maryland Online*, 19:36–37; 389–390, accessed on July 19, 2017: http://aomol.msa.maryland.gov/html/index.html.

48. "Baltimore's Four Point. Submitted to the English Provincial, and to be issued in the name of the latter," 1641, in *History of the Society of Jesus in North America, Colonial and Federal, Documents*, Thomas Hughes, ed. (New York, 1907), 1:167.

49. "Lord Baltimore's Instructions to the Colonists," November 13, 1663, in *The Calvert Papers*, John Wesley Murray Lee, ed. (Baltimore, 1889), 1:134, 136–137.

50. Edward C. Papenfuse, *A Biographical Dictionary of the Maryland Legislature, 1635–1789*, (Baltimore, 1979).

51. Ibid.; *Archives of Maryland Online*, 426: 17, 134, 149, 161, 176, 204, 234, 348, 371, 373, 533, 660, 676, 807, 887.

52. *Archives of Maryland Online*, 10:354–355; 4:35–36, 38–39; Saint Mary's City Men's Career Files, Maryland State Archives (MSA), SC5094.

53. Thomas Copley to Lord Baltimore, April 3, 1638, *Calvert Papers*, 1:162–163, 166; John Prior, "In Coenae Domini," *The Original Catholic Encyclopedia* (New York, 1907–1912), 7:717–718.

54. Lord Baltimore to Edward Knott, 1641, in Thomas Hughes, *History of the Society of Jesus in North America, Colonial and Federal, Text* (New York, 1908), 1:166–167.

55. Thomas Cornwaleys to Lord Baltimore, April 16, 1638, and Lord Baltimore to Leonard Calvert, November 23, 1642, in *Calvert Papers*, 1:171–172; 217–218; William Peasley to Fr. Gervits, S.J., September 30, 1642, and Ann Calvert

Peasley to Fr. Gervits., S.J., October 5, 1642, in "Applications for the Maryland Mission – 1640," *Woodstock Letters* (Woodstock, MD, 1872–1969), 9:91–93.

56. Parke Rouse, "Claiborne Colony's First Entrepreneur," and "For the Record," *Daily Press*, March 2, 1997 and March 7, 1997; Karen Holt, "Louisiana's William Claiborne Has a Designingly Fragrant Legacy," *Examiner*, January 20, 2014; Adam Bernstein, "Liz Claiborne, 78, Fashion Industry Icon," *Washington Post*, June 28, 2007; Stephanie Hanes, "Lindy Boggs Dies; Congresswoman and Democratic Leader," *Washington Post*, July 27, 2013.

57. Timothy B. Riordan, *The Plundering Time: Maryland and the English Civil War, 1645–1646* (Baltimore, 2004), 11, 29, 131–139, 172, 184, 206–211; *Archives of Maryland Online*, 4:4350436; Michael Graham, "Meetinghouse and Chapel: Religion and Community in Seventeenth-Century Maryland," in *Colonial Chesapeake Society*, Lois Green Carr, Philip D. Morgan, and Jean B. Russo, eds. (Chapel Hill, 1988), 268–269.

58. Riordan, *Plundering Time*, 263–267, 296–298.

59. Riordan, *Plundering Time*, 320–323; Farrelly, *Papist Patriots*, 107.

60. Lois Green Carr, "Sources of Political Stability and Upheaval in Seventeenth-Century Maryland," *Maryland Historical Magazine* 79 (1984), 55; Cecilius Calvert, "he Lord Baltemore's Case, Concerning the Province of Maryland, adjoining to Virginia in America, With full and clear Answers to all material Objections, touching his Rights, Jurisdiction, and Proceedings there, And Certaine Reasons of State, why the Parliament should no impeach the same" (1653), in *Narratives of Early Maryland, 1633–1684*, Clayton Colman Hall, ed. (New York, 1946), 167, 169, 175.

61. "An Act Concerning Religion," April 21, 1649, *Archives of Maryland Online*, 1:244–247.

62. Archives of Maryland Online, 7:118; Michael Kammen, "The Causes of the Maryland Revolution in 1689," *Maryland Historical Magazine* 55 (1960), 298.

63. Maria A. Day, "Charles Calvert, Third Lord Baltimore, 1637–1714/15," *Biographical Series*, Maryland State Archives (MSA), SC 3520-193; John H.B. Latrobe, "The History of Mason and Dixon's Line," *Annual Address before the Historical Society of Pennsylvania* (Philadelphia, 1854), 5–9.

64. Farrelly, *Papist Patriots*, 117; Francis Edgar Sparks, *Causes of the Maryland Revolution of 1689* (Baltimore, 1896), 50; Graham, "Meetinghouse and Chapel," 268–269.

65. "A Complaint from Heaven with a Huy and Crye and a petition out of Maryland and Virginia," in *Archives of Maryland Online*, 5:134–139. For more on Bacon's rebellion, see Stephen Saunders Webb, *1676: The End of American Independence* (Syracuse, NY, 1984).

66. James I, The Trew Law of Free Monarchies (1598), in *The Political Worlds of James I*, Charles H. McIlwain , ed. (Cambridge, MA, 1918), 69; John Milton, *The Tenure of Kings and Magistrates* (1650), William Talbot Allison, ed. (New York, 1911), 15, 40, 11.

67. For more on the contractarian theory of government, see Michael Zuckert's *National Rights and the New Republicanism* (Princeton, 1994), 49–118.

68. John Locke, *The Second Treatise of Government* (1689), Joseph Carrig, ed. (New York, 2004), 57.

69. "Laws Agreed on in England, May 5th, 1682, between Penn and Settlers, Law 35," in *The American Catholic Historical Researches*, Martin I.J. Griffin, ed. (Philadelphia, 1901), 64; Maura Jane Farrelly, "Conflict and Community in Early Pennsylvania's Catholic Church," *Pennsylvania Legacies*, 15 (Fall, 2015), 6–11.

3

"The Common Word Then Was: 'No King, No Popery'"

Anti-Catholicism and the American Revolution

Were it not for anti-Catholicism, the map of the United States today might look a bit different. The men who served in the Second Continental Congress – the body that adopted the Declaration of Independence in July of 1776 – had hoped that America's boundaries would extend much farther north, all the way up to the mouth of the St. Lawrence River in what is now the Canadian province of Quebec. That's why they sent Richard Montgomery, Benedict Arnold, and nearly 3,000 American soldiers into Quebec in the fall of 1775, ten months before the Declaration was even signed. Congress hoped the Continental Army would be able to defeat the British troops stationed in Montreal and Quebec City and encourage the French-speaking Quebecois to join the independence movement.

The effort was a colossal failure that cost Montgomery his life.[1] One of the reasons the Americans failed in their bid to take Quebec from the British was that the French Catholic residents of that colony did not trust them. The Americans, therefore, were not able to rely upon the Quebecois for help when they confronted British troops.

Canada's Catholics didn't trust the Americans because roughly a year before Montgomery's invasion, Congress had made diplomatic overtures to the Quebecois that were revealed to be stunningly disingenuous. Congress had written a letter to Canada's French-speaking Catholics, outlining several reasons why the Canadians should join the Americans in their campaign against British tyranny. The spirit of that letter and the truthfulness of its assertions, however, were called into question when the Quebecois learned that the members of Congress had also written to the people of Great Britain, justifying their independence movement by pointing to the Canadians as dangerous and telling England's people that the Americans abhorred the Canadians' Catholic faith.

Fears of Catholicism – or what the colonists called "popery" – played an important role in tipping the scales in America toward independence. Choosing to break away from England was not an easy decision for most people, no matter how angry they were at the government in London. For more than a decade before the colonists declared their intention to separate from Great Britain, political leaders up and down the eastern seaboard criticized Parliament for levying taxes on the colonists without their consent. These criticisms, however, drew an important distinction between "Parliament" and "the king," and that distinction kept most people from embracing the idea of independence.

Before George III called for the passage of the so-called "Intolerable Acts" in 1774, many colonists clung to the belief that the king was still good and that it was corrupt ministers in Parliament who were destroying liberty in the American colonies. Under such circumstances, independence was not the solution; the solution was to clean up Parliament.

After the passage of the Intolerable Acts, however, many colonists changed their opinion of King George III. The argument that "the British government – the *King*, Lords, and Commons have laid a regular plan to enslave America" was asserted "over, and over, and over again," according to one frustrated Loyalist from Connecticut.[2] And one of the things that made the Intolerable Acts so completely "intolerable" to the colonists was the fact that the final act tolerated Catholicism in Quebec.

The "Intolerable Acts," of course, was not the formal name given to the five laws that the British government passed in the months that followed the Boston Tea Party in December of 1773. The term was a deliberately inflammatory nickname that colonial newspaper editors used to describe the laws. Four of the acts were designed to punish the residents of Massachusetts for the massive destruction of property that they'd committed during their "party" in Boston Harbor. The acts shut down Boston's port, dismantled Massachusetts' assembly, obliged the colonists to provide housing to British soldiers, and allowed Massachusetts' new governor, who'd been appointed by the Crown, to protect British soldiers who were accused of committing crimes while stationed in North America. Under the law, the governor had the power to move any soldier's trial from Massachusetts, where he'd be judged by a jury of colonists, to a court in England.[3]

The fifth Intolerable Act actually had nothing to do with Massachusetts – or with life in any of the other twelve colonies that ultimately declared their independence. It applied to the people living in Quebec, a colony that had belonged to France until 1763, when the French were obliged to give it to the English government as a provision of the treaty that ended the Seven Years' War (also known as the "French and Indian War"). The reality that the Quebec Act wasn't about them didn't stop the colonists in the lower thirteen colonies from seeing the law as an example of the king's tyranny, however. That's because the Quebec Act extended religious toleration to a faith that had, for generations, represented the vilest despotism to them.[4]

The Quebec Act told the French-speaking Catholics in Canada (who were the vast majority of people in that colony) that they'd be able to practice their faith freely, even though the colony they lived in was now part of a Protestant country. Many Americans – including many of the men serving in the Continental Congress – saw the act as a clear sign that George III intended to "establish the Romish Religion and IDOLOTRY" throughout North America.[5] Naturally, though, that was not how Congress spoke of the Quebec Act when that body wrote to the Canadians in October of 1774, hoping to convince them to join the independence movement.

Congress made the argument that the Quebec Act was insulting and dangerous to the Canadians because "liberty of conscience in religion" was not something the king or Parliament could ever give. Religious liberty was something "God gave you," the Protestant members of Congress told the Catholic Quebecois. If the British government could give liberty of conscience, after all, the British government could also take it away. And the Quebecois should know that they *would*, in fact, lose their religious freedom to the "arbitrary ... and precarious tenure of [the government's] mere will" if they did not "unite ... with the other Colonies to the south" in a collective action against the government's overreach. This union would be peaceful and easy, Congress assured the Quebecois, in spite of the religious differences that separated the Protestant Americans from the Catholic Canadians. A "mutual devotion to liberty" would elevate everyone "above all low-minded infirmities."[6]

It was an argument that seemed to resonate with the Quebecois at first. Congress' letter was "very Kindly received" by the people of Montreal, according to John Brown, one of the men from Massachusetts who'd been tasked with delivering the message to Canada. An anonymous Englishman who lived in Montreal confirmed Brown's assessment. According to that observer, Congress' letter "attracted the notice of some of the principal *Canadians*" – meaning French-speakers in the city – who were "flattered" by Congress' invitation to join the lower thirteen colonies in their bid for independence.[7]

Unfortunately for the members of Congress, Montreal's French leaders were so flattered by the letter that they hired a translator "to try his hand at that address to the People of *Great Britain*" that Congress had also commissioned.[8] Just five days before he sat down with John Dickinson of Pennsylvania and Thomas Cushing of Massachusetts to write a letter to the Quebecois, Richard Henry Lee of Virginia had penned a similar letter to the British people. That letter justified Congress' complaints against the king and Parliament and assured Britain's citizens that the Americans' gripe was with the government, and not with them.

"Oh, the perfidious double-faced Congress," the residents of Montreal supposedly cried when the translated letter was read out loud to them on the streets. "Let us bless and obey our benevolent Prince [George], whose humanity ... extends to all Religions. Let us abhor all who would reduce us from our loyalty ... and whose Addresses, like their Resolves, are destructive of their own objects."[9]

Congress' letter to the people of Great Britain, it seems, had painted a less-than-flattering picture of Catholics – and the Quebecois in particular. Indeed, King George III's unforgivable sin was identified in the letter not as his effort to usurp the authority of God by giving religious freedom to the Catholics in Canada, but as his willingness to *tolerate* Catholicism, a religion that "disbursed impiety, bigotry, persecution, murder, and rebellions throughout every part of the world."[10]

According to Congress, the Quebec Act had "established" Catholicism in Canada because it gave priests there the authority to collect tithes from their parishioners – even though the act said nothing at all about requiring attendance at Catholic Mass or making people who were not Catholic pay the tithe. Its religious provisions, the Americans insisted, would soon be applied to the lower thirteen colonies – even though the only parts of the Quebec Act that even touched upon the lives of people living in those colonies had nothing to do with religion. The act formalized Quebec's boundaries, drawing them out to include territory north and west of the Ohio River that England ultimately ceded to the United States at the conclusion of the Revolutionary War (Figure 3.1). The formal boundaries placed the Ohio River Valley under the auspices of Quebec's local assembly, effectively making it

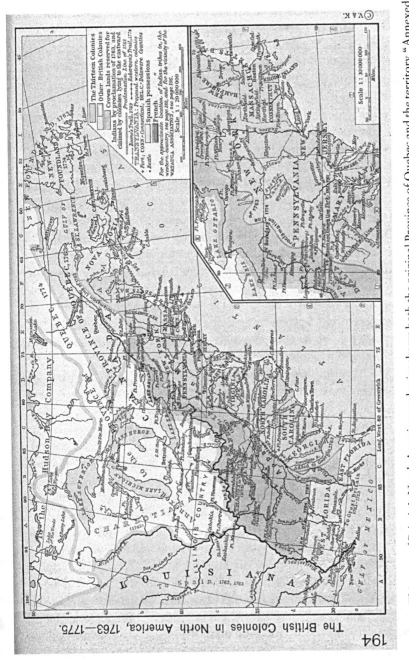

FIGURE 3.1 This map of Britain's North American colonies shows both the original Province of Quebec and the territory "Annexed to the Province of Quebec" by the Quebec Act in 1774. Map credit: University of Texas Libraries.

impossible for land speculators from Virginia to claim territory in the region and make money off the sale of that land. Several prominent Virginians had been interested in doing just that – among them George Washington's half-brothers, Lawrence and Augustine Washington, and Thomas Jefferson's guardian, Thomas Walker, who had cared for the future president after Peter Jefferson died when his son was fourteen years old.[11]

In "establishing" Catholicism, Congress told the people of Great Britain, the Quebec Act made it inevitable that everyone living in Canada would be "deprived of a right to an assembly, trials by jury, and the English laws in civil cases." This development was problematic not because of what it meant for the Quebecois (who, as French Catholics, were used to having no freedom), but because of what it meant for the English-speaking Protestants who had recently migrated to Canada. Under the provisions of the Treaty of Paris of 1763, King George III had agreed to extend the benefits of English law to Canada, "under the faith of which many English subjects settled in that province." If the people of Great Britain and America quietly accepted the legitimacy of the Quebec Act, Congress explained, they would be abandoning "their affectionate, protestant brethren" in Canada to their "enemies . . . whose intrigues, for several years passed, have been wholly exercised in sapping the foundations of civil and religious liberty."[12]

Loyalists in the lower thirteen colonies thoroughly enjoyed the Canadians' reaction to Congress' hypocrisy. The letter that Congress had sent to the Quebecois was "truly Jesuitical," in the deliberately ironic words of Daniel Leonard, a Loyalist whose anonymous letters to the *Boston Gazette* irked John Adams to no end. In New York, John Lind, an opponent of independence, declared that "both Boston and Quebec must be blind indeed, if they do not see . . . [Congress'] double dealing at the very first glance." The British essayist Samuel Johnson – who was famous for his sarcastic and curmudgeonly observations, even by our modern-day 'tweeting' standards of what constitutes celebrity – could not decide "whether our indignation at the Colonies should be more excited by the baseness of their hypocrisy, or the insolence of their presumption." Following the publication of both of Congress' letters in several London newspapers, Johnson lampooned the American "Patriots'" diplomatic clumsiness: "After representing the Canadians as a nation of blood-thirsty bigots, highly dangerous to the freedom of the Protestant province, we see the Congress flattering those bigots as they call them into rebellion."[13]

Why were the members of Congress so obtuse? Their effort to bring the Canadians into their fold, after all, seems to have been sincere; not long after General Montgomery's disastrous military defeat in Quebec, Congress sent a delegation to Montreal to try one last time to convince the Quebecois to join the independence movement. That four-man delegation consisted of two prominent Catholics from Maryland, one of whom, John Carroll, was a priest who eventually became the first bishop of the United States. The diplomatic mission, however, never even got a hearing with Montreal's French leaders.[14]

Part of the answer, no doubt, is that the members of the Second Continental Congress simply didn't think they would get caught. They wanted the Canadians to join them – but they also wanted to garner the sympathies of the British people, and they understood that in the eighteenth century, no fight was more worthy of British sympathy than the fight against Roman Catholicism.

But many people in the lower thirteen colonies also genuinely believed that the Catholic faith could be antagonistic to freedom – and freedom was the foundation that they wanted their new country to be built on. Following the Glorious Revolution, the vast majority of people in the English-speaking world believed it was the job of the state to protect human freedom; the problem with the king and Parliament, according to the Patriots, was that both entities were no longer doing that. And "freedom," for most English-speakers, was defined exclusively in Protestant terms.

Freedom was the absence of mediation or outside restraint. It was the "power of acting as one thinks fit," in the words of the eighteenth-century English jurist William Blackstone, whose legal and philosophical commentaries were consulted by members of the First and Second Continental Congresses and the US Constitutional Convention. Blackstone understood that membership in a society meant that people couldn't *always* act as they thought fit; for the sake of peace, people came together and agreed to laws that restrained their behavior in some way. Such restraints, however, should extend "no farther than is necessary and expedient for the general advantage of the publick," according to Blackstone. Proper societies were ones that defined freedom as the absence of outside restraint, even as they accepted the necessity of certain restraints. Proper societies also understood that some freedoms – the freedom to own property, for instance, or to assemble openly with one's peers – were "a right inherent in us by birth." Such rights could not, therefore, ever be restrained, modified, or forfeited, regardless of what anyone perceived to be necessary.[15]

Proper societies were not run by Catholics, according to William Blackstone. Indeed, England's own history had shown that Catholicism and freedom were incompatible with one another. Writing in 1765, the jurist noted that before Protestantism had taken root in England under Elizabeth I, "particular liberty" and the "personal independence of individuals" had been "little regarded or thought of" in the English world. Until the "popish clergy, detected in their frauds and abuses ... stood trembling for their very existence in England," the English people and their rulers could not "entertain a more just opinion of the dignity and rights of mankind."[16]

Blackstone's political understanding of freedom was an outgrowth of the theological understanding of freedom offered up by Protestantism. For Protestants, freedom was something God gave to individual people so that each person could, on his or her own, read the Scriptures, confront the reality of sin, and choose to receive God's grace. "Every man must give an account of himself to God," the Baptist minister John Leland wrote from his home in Massachusetts in the late eighteenth century. "Therefore every man ought to be at Liberty to serve God in that way that he can best reconcile it to his conscience."[17]

Freedom, for Protestants, was not something to be realized by human beings only with the help of others – that is to say, within a proper, communal context. That way of thinking reflected the Vatican's belief that truth was something too complex for any one person to access on his own; it therefore smacked of popery. The Bible was not "so intricate and high, that none but the letter learned ... can read it," John Leland insisted. The idea that "the ignorant part of the community are not capacitated to judge for themselves supports the Popish hierarchy."[18]

On this point, Leland's assessment of late-eighteenth-century Catholicism was actually quite accurate. For a Catholic – and particularly a Catholic who lived and worshipped before the Second Vatican Council brought changes* to Catholicism in the 1960s – freedom was something to be sought and realized only through the body of the Church. It was the fulfillment of God's wishes for humanity. Only when a man or woman finally understood and realized the will of God could true freedom be

---

* Some theologians and scholars, among them Avery Cardinal Dulles and Pope Benedict XVI, insist that the Second Vatican Council did not "change" the Catholic Church, but merely "renewed" the Church's traditional teachings in a modern context. I, however, subscribe to the view put forth by scholars such as John W. O'Malley, SJ, who see Vatican II as "making a significant break with the past."[19]

attained, and regardless of what Martin Luther had said in the sixteenth century about the importance of "sola scriptura," Catholic leaders insisted that Scripture and human reason, on their own, were not enough to understand the will of God. People needed the guidance of bishops and theologians who had pondered the mysteries of Christianity for decades and consulted the writings of those who had pondered these same mysteries before them.

Freedom, for a Catholic, was not something a person was born with, as people such as William Blackstone insisted; it was, rather, something a person *achieved*. The reason "many [people] imagine that the Church is hostile to human liberty," Pope Leo XIII explained, was that human beings tended to "pervert the very idea of freedom, or they extend it at their pleasure to many things in respect of which man cannot rightly be regarded as free."[20]

The ability to act "as one thinks fit" did not, in and of itself, constitute freedom, according to Leo. "Man is, indeed, free to obey his reason [and] to seek moral good," the pope observed. "Yet he is free also to turn aside to all other things; and in pursuing the empty semblance of good, to disturb the rightful order and to fall headlong into the destruction which he has voluntarily chosen." Human beings had the power to think it "fit" to act in ways that were sinful. "The possibility of sinning," Leo insisted, "is not freedom, but slavery." When a man sinned, he became a slave to the passions that fueled that sin – and people chose to sin because they were incapable, on their own, of understanding the will of God. "The condition of human liberty," therefore, "necessarily stands in need of light and strength to direct its actions to good and to restrain them from evil. Without this, the freedom of our will would be our ruin."[21]

Proper societies, the Catholic Church taught, were not societies that placed the fewest and least confining restraints on human behavior; they were, rather, societies where leaders and citizens alike were guided by the light and strength of the Catholic Church.[22] This pre-Vatican II understanding of church–state relations brought an unavoidable sense of urgency to beliefs like the one Sam Adams expressed in 1772, when he asserted that Catholics, by "recognizing the pope in so absolute a manner ... introduce as far as possible into the states, under whose protection they enjoy life, liberty, and property, that solecism in politicks, Imperium in imperio, leading directly to the worst anarchy and confusion, civil discord, war and bloodshed."[23]

Imperium in imperio – a state within a state. Would American Catholics accept that the new states in America would not be guided by the "wisdom" of the Catholic Church, since those states' residents, overwhelmingly, subscribed to a Protestant understanding of freedom? Could Catholics be trusted not to allow their clerical leaders to become a state within a state – one that would stand in opposition to the foundation of individual freedom upon which America was to be built?

Colonial leaders' answers to these very real questions were more complicated than the rhetoric from the period might suggest – as Congress' solicitations to the French Catholic Canadians make clear. The rhetoric was not just for show. When they created new constitutions for themselves in the 1770s, six states barred Catholics from holding office at the time of the Founding, and two of them, New Jersey and New Hampshire, held onto their religious tests on office-holding until well into the 1870s.[24] Protestant lawmakers worried not just that the Catholic clergy would form a tyrannical state within a state, but also that Catholics were incapable of handling the responsibilities that came with republican government. Men who had grown up deferring to a priestly hierarchy, these lawmakers believed, simply could not develop the sense of virtue and individual judgment essential to the success of any experiment in republican government.

But seven states – including the fiercely Protestant state of Massachusetts – did not constitutionally bar Catholics from holding office.[†] In one state, Maryland, voters actually elected a Catholic convert, Thomas Sim Lee, as their governor before the Revolutionary War was even over. Those same voters sent a Catholic, Charles Carroll of Carrollton, to the Second Continental Congress; he was there when Congress signed off on the letter to the people of Great Britain that was so insulting to Canada's Catholics. Charley Carroll's Catholic cousin, Daniel, represented Maryland at the Constitutional Convention in 1787. Pennsylvania's voters, too, sent a Catholic to that gathering. Thomas Fitzsimons was descended from people in County Wexford who had survived Oliver Cromwell's genocidal incursions into Ireland in the 1640s; he and his parents immigrated to Philadelphia in the mid-1750s, and they helped to build the first free-standing Catholic chapel in that city.[25]

[†] Although Massachusetts' constitution did not stipulate that the state's officeholders had to be Protestant, the people of Massachusetts did not completely forget their fears of popery. Their constitution still required officeholders to swear that "no foreign prince, person, prelate, state, or potentate" had jurisdiction in the state.

Although people such as Sam Adams worried that Catholics would constitute an "imperium in imperio" within the new United States, the reality is that the vast majority of non-Canadian Catholics living in the British colonies at the time of the American Revolution did not subscribe to the understanding of church–state relations that was advocated by the Vatican. They do seem to have subscribed to the Catholic belief that Scripture and human reason, on their own, were not enough to know the will of God, as evidenced by the numerous theological books and pamphlets, written by priests, that they owned and lent out to their co-religionists throughout the eighteenth century. But America's Catholics had a deep appreciation for the Protestant understanding of "freedom." When, after fleeing religious oppression in Ireland, Charley Carroll's grandfather, Charles, changed his family's motto from *In Fide et in Bello Forte* ("Strong in Faith and in War") to *Ubicumque cum Libertate* ("Anywhere so long as there is Freedom"), achieving the will of God was not the "freedom" he had in mind. Charles Carroll the Settler left Ireland in 1688 and traveled to colonial Maryland so that he could have the power to act as he thought fit.[26]

Strikingly, the force that played the strongest role in preparing America's first Catholics to embrace an individualistic, rights-oriented, Protestant understanding of freedom was anti-Catholicism. One of the many ironies of the American Revolution is that the same religious fears that convinced America's Protestants to rise up against their king also convinced America's Catholics to join them in this endeavor. Protestants, it must be said, were more than happy to have these Catholics in the fight – even as they burned the pope and King George in effigy and carried signs that read "GEORGE III REX. AND THE LIBERTIES OF AMERICA. NO POPERY."[27]

Fears of Catholicism at the time of the Founding were very real; fears of actual Catholics, however, tended not to materialize, especially among Protestants in Maryland and, to a lesser extent, Pennsylvania and New York, which was where nearly all of British North America's non-Canadian Catholics lived. Protestants in these colonies lived near, worked with, and were sometimes even married to and descended from people who subscribed to the Roman Catholic faith. They trusted Catholics, even as they feared Catholicism and took steps throughout the eighteenth century to ensure that "popery" would never get the upper hand in their colonies and trump liberty. The experiences that America's first Catholics had in these colonies – right before, during, and then after the war for independence – reveal the complex nature of anti-Catholicism at the time of the Founding.

THE RHETORICAL POWER OF POPERY

By the time Thomas Secker, the Archbishop of Canterbury, put forward a plan in 1763 to assign an Anglican bishop to the American colonies, New England's Puritans were well-poised to see the move as tyrannical. Secker had been insulting New Englanders for more than 20 years by that point. He didn't seem to recognize any shared "Protestant Interest" between himself and the New World's Calvinists. Even before he became the Archbishop of Canterbury in 1758, Secker often implied that Congregationalists were little better than Native Americans in terms of their understanding of the Christian faith. It didn't help that two years before Secker announced his plans for an American bishop, an Anglican minister in Boston finished building a large and grandiose house just outside the gates of Harvard. Massachusetts' Puritans were convinced this house was meant to be the "palace" of Secker's American bishop – and that they would soon be forced to pay for its maintenance.[28]

The shared "Protestant Interest" that New England's Calvinists had been carefully cultivating with their Anglican countrymen for the last 70 years was under attack; that interest was being threatened by a powerful man in London who had no respect for Calvinism. The Puritans believed they were able to recognize Thomas Secker's tyrannical intentions because they'd seen them before – or at least their grandparents and great-grandparents had seen them, in the age before the Glorious Revolution. The language the Puritans used to express their anxieties, therefore, was the same language their ancestors had used to express theirs; it was familiar language of "anti-popery."

Thomas Secker's proposed bishop was one of the "popish schemes of men who would gladly ... look on popery as a religion most favorable to arbitrary power," according to Samuel Langdon, the Congregational president of Harvard College. Supporters of the bishop's plan wanted to subject the American people to the "horrid rites of idolatry and the solemn fooleries of popery," according to William Livingston, an attorney who would soon become the first governor of the free state of New Jersey. In Boston, Jonathan Mayhew, who preached to Congregationalists in the city's Old West Church, saw Secker's proposal as a sign that "popery was fast gaining ground" in England. "I myself hear some episcopalians among us," the preacher claimed, using a new term for Anglicans that was starting to become common in America, "who ... say they should prefer the communion of the Church of Rome to Ours."[29]

In reality, Thomas Secker's "scheme" had almost no support in Parliament and little chance of ever being executed. Understanding that

New England's fiercely individualistic Calvinists chafed against clerical hierarchies, many leaders in Great Britain worried that such an appointment would "stir up dangerous *uneasiness* abroad." This concern became more acute after 1764, when the colonists started resisting the taxes that Parliament had imposed upon them to pay for the French and Indian War. Writing in 1768, less than a year after Parliament had placed a duty on all lead, paper, paint, glass, and tea sold in the colonies, Francis Blackburne, the Archdeacon of Cleveland, insisted that "nothing could be more unseasonable" than to appoint a bishop to the colonies "at a time when every wise and good man, and every well-wisher to the peace and prosperity of his Majesty's government, saw how necessary it was to avoid all occasions of irritating the *British* colonists of *America*."[30]

But no matter how little interest Parliament showed in the idea of an American bishop – and no matter how many Church leaders in England stood up and publicly criticized Thomas Secker's idea – England's North American colonists were convinced by the late 1760s that the Parent Country wanted to force an Anglican bishop upon them. The idea was so distasteful that even some Anglicans expressed opposition to it. In 1771, four Anglican ministers in Virginia publicly chastised Secker, insisting that if he appointed a bishop to America, it would undermine their efforts to bring people into the Anglican Church. The members of Virginia's House of Burgesses quickly passed a resolution, thanking these clergymen for the "wise and well-timed opposition they have made to the pernicious project of a few mistaken clergymen for introducing an American bishop." Explaining his support for the resolution, Colonel Richard Bland insisted "I profess myself a sincere son of the established church, but I can embrace her doctrines without approving of her hierarchy, which I know to be a Relick of the Papal Incroachments upon the Common Law."[31]

Part of the reason the colonists refused to believe that London wouldn't send a bishop to North America was that in 1766, King George III agreed to allow Rome to appoint a Catholic bishop to the newly English colony of Quebec. Bishop Jean-Olivier Briand arrived in Montreal in September of that year, and, according to a correspondent for the *London Magazine*, the Quebecois were delighted by his arrival. "It was generally affecting to see them congratulate one another wherever they met," the correspondent reported after Briand had assumed his post. "It is likely that this favor conferred on the Canadians will effectually attach them to the British government."[32]

In fact, George's decision to allow Rome to appoint Briand to Quebec proved to be a good one. The bishop turned out to be a reliable and effective ally when war finally broke out with the lower thirteen colonies. In December of 1776, one year after Benedict Arnold and Richard Montgomery were defeated on the Plains of Abraham, just outside Quebec City, Briand hosted a "solemn mass in Thanksgiving" to celebrate the anniversary of the defeat. Calling the Americans' failure to take Quebec a "singular dispensation of Providence," Bishop Briand explained that the Mass would honor God for protecting and assisting the British soldiers who "restored to us, and not only us but the whole colony, the blessing of liberty."[33]

In addition to the Mass, Briand censured three priests from Quebec who were sympathetic to the American cause. All three clergymen had offered absolution to Catholic Canadians who assisted the American army, and one of them, Pierre Flouquet, had even had Father John Carroll of Maryland over to his house for dinner when Carroll was in Montreal on behalf of the Continental Congress.[34]

As galling as this censure was, however, it was Briand's instructions to his clergy to deny the Sacraments to any laypeople who assisted the Americans in their bid for independence that really convinced Protestants in the lower thirteen colonies that the Catholic bishop was a tyrant. If a Catholic bishop could be a tyrant, an Anglican bishop could be one, too. It was a rhetorical leap that may not seem obvious or even logical to readers today, but in the minds of most Americans in the 1770s there was no difference between an Anglican and a Catholic bishop. Both kinds of bishops had become tools used by the "tyrant hand of popish power."[35]

"Popery" was not exactly the same thing as "Catholicism." The two terms were intimately related to one another – and certainly many Protestants at the time of the Revolution believed that it was not possible to worship within the Catholic Church without developing the habits of popery (hence the term's allusion to the pope in Rome). But as the rhetoric about Thomas Secker's bishop plan made clear, people in the eighteenth century who were not Catholic could be accused of exhibiting popish impulses, too. They merely had to adopt what was frequently referred to as a "slavish" mentality – that is, one that admired and utilized the tactics of tyrants and/or willingly succumbed to those tactics.

"I did verily believe, and do so still," Sam Adams wrote anonymously in the *Boston Gazette* in 1768, "that much more is to be dreaded from the growth of popery in America than from Stamp-Acts or *any other* acts destructive of men's *civil* rights." It was a powerful statement, coming as it did from the man who had hated the Stamp Act so much that he'd organized a series of street protests against it that (among other things) led to the destruction of Governor Thomas Hutchinson's house in Boston in August of 1765.[36]

Yet, right after declaring that popery was a greater threat to America than the Stamp Act, Adams told his readers that he thought "the Stamp-Act was contrived with a design only to inure people to the habit of contemplating themselves the slaves of men, and the transition from thence to a subjection to [the pope], is mighty easy." Why – if the Stamp Act was the force that habituated men to slavery and, in so doing, made it possible for the pope to enslave them – was *popery*, and not the Stamp Act, the phenomenon that Samuel Adams was most concerned about? If the Stamp Act prepared people to accept the pope's enslavement, after all, subjection to the pope was the *result*, rather than the cause of unjust taxes like the one Parliament had placed on newspapers and legal documents three years earlier. Why, then, did Sam Adams insist that popery was "more dreaded" than the Stamp Act? If the Stamp Act inured people to the pope's enslavement, shouldn't *it* have been the "more dreaded" phenomenon?

The answer to this puzzle lies with Sam Adams' understanding of the term "popery." When he used the word, Adams meant both a *cause* and an *effect* of tyranny. Popery was the result of injustices like the Stamp Act, but it was also the fertile soil in which such injustices could be planted. More than one force, in other words, was capable of cultivating popery among the people, and these multiple forces fed upon one another, each one making it easier for the next one to succeed in rendering the people incapable of recognizing and challenging tyranny. The oldest force, of course – the force that was so good at creating the habits of popery that lovers of liberty used the word "popery" as a synonym for it – was Catholicism.

Thus, people in eighteenth-century America could speak of "Popery and Mahometanism," meaning Catholicism and Islam, and also speak of "popery and arbitrary power," meaning despotism and laws that were derived not from the will of the people, but from the whims of a single individual, be he a king or a pope. They could accuse Jesuit missionaries of perpetuating "the fatal errors of atheism, infidelity, and popery" among the Indians they converted in Canada, and at the same time accuse the Protestant residents of Charlestown, Massachusetts, of being "not so much on [their] guard against popery" because voters there had sent a Tory, i.e., a supporter of the king's prerogative, to represent them in Massachusetts' colonial assembly. They could accuse the spiritual leader of the Church of England of doing the work of "that foulest Hydra Popery" because he had proposed an American bishop, and they could recall, after the Revolutionary War was over, that "real fears of popery" had "stimulated many timorous people to send their sons to join the military ranks." "The common word then," according to one veteran of the Revolution, "was 'No King, No Popery.'"[37]

Fears of popery were a standard part of the rhetoric that fueled the cause of independence. Typically, Patriot leaders used popery to undermine the authority of the king and to explain why England – which had once been such a great defender of humanity's God-given rights that people on both sides of the Atlantic called these rights "the rights of Englishmen" – should now be viewed as a tyrannical usurper of liberty.[38] Following the passage of the Quebec Act, Sam Adams declared that George III wanted Americans up and down the eastern seaboard to "submit to Popery and Slavery." His distant cousin, John Adams, worried that "the barriers against popery, erected by our ancestors" would be "suffered and destroyed" by the act, "to the hazard even of the Protestant religion."[39]

Outside New England, where the proximity to Canada (not to mention the prevalence of Calvinists) might have explained the fear, the reaction to the Quebec Act was equally overblown. "Does not your blood run cold, to think an English Parliament should pass an Act for the establishment of Popery and arbitrary power?" Alexander Hamilton asked his colleagues in New York City. In South Carolina, Judge William Henry Drayton predicted that a "tyranny under which all Europe groaned for many ages" would sweep the colonies now that the king had approved the Quebec Act. A "most cruel tyranny in Church and State," Drayton predicted, would be "fed with blood by the Roman Catholic doctrines."[40]

In Maryland, several newspaper editors also decried the passage of the Quebec Act. On the pages of the *Maryland Journal*, the Quebec Act became a sign that George III wished to extend "the medium of French law and popery" across North America, "the one enslaving the body, the other the mind." In Annapolis, the editors of the *Maryland Gazette* declared that the Quebec Act was "worse in tendency ... than the Stamp Act" because it "immovably fixed" the "standard of despotism" throughout England's colonies. One contributor to that paper insisted that the king had empowered "a body of popish slaves" to "serve as a curb upon [Protestants]" in the colonies. It was "high time," another contributor wrote, "for the protestants of all denominations in these kingdoms to take some effectual measures for the safety and security of their civil and religious liberties."[41]

Yet, the rhetoric in Maryland's newspapers did not always reflect the reality on the ground. When that colony's leaders convened in Annapolis in the fall of 1774 and the spring of 1775 to discuss their grievances with England, George III's decision to allow the free practice of Catholicism in Canada never came up – in spite of what people were reading in the papers. Maryland's leaders were disturbed by the British government's decision to shut down the port of Boston following the Boston Tea Party; they also found England's decision to disband Massachusetts' colonial assembly to be a point of great concern. But not a single person in attendance at either of the two gatherings even mentioned the Quebec Act, let alone pointed to it as evidence of the king's "popery."[42]

The silence may have been a consequence of the fact that Catholics were actually present at both meetings. Ignatius Fenwick represented St. Mary's County; Thomas Semmes represented Charles County; and Charles Carroll of Carrollton represented Frederick County. Indeed, Charley Carroll was one of seven men selected from within the ranks of the Maryland Convention to serve on the committee of correspondence that would communicate Maryland's ideas and experiences to Patriot leaders in other colonies. He joined Maryland's delegation to the First Continental Congress as an advising, but non-voting member in 1774, and then from 1775 until the end of the war he fully represented the colony at the Second Continental Congress, even putting his life and sizable fortune on the line to sign the Declaration of Independence.[43]

When Fenwick, Semmes, and Carroll represented their counties at the Maryland Convention, Catholics were still barred by law from serving in Maryland's colonial assembly or voting for anyone who served in that body. Following their take-over of the Catholic proprietor's government in 1689, the Protestant Associators had stripped Catholic men of the franchise and denied them the right to practice law. Those mandates had remained in effect in the colony for more than eighty years, in spite of numerous efforts by prominent Catholic landowners to get the laws changed.[44] When Protestants in Maryland sent Fenwick, Semmes, and Carroll to the Maryland Convention to represent them, in other words, the laws that barred Catholics from voting and holding office were still technically in effect; Maryland's Protestants simply ignored them.

The laws were colonial laws, after all, and Maryland's people were no longer interested in being colonists. The reason Marylanders didn't want to be colonists anymore was that Charles Carroll of Carrollton had actually convinced them of the wisdom of one of the primary political arguments in favor of independence – namely, the idea that each of

England's colonies had its own separate and distinct "constitution," and that Parliament was violating those constitutions when it passed laws meant to govern the lives of people living in America.

When he convinced his neighbors of the wisdom of this argument, Charley Carroll was not actually addressing the issue of whether Parliament had a right to tax the colonists; he was addressing a local matter that had nothing to do with Parliament. Carroll also wasn't speaking about his experiences as a Catholic man in a colony that had taken rights away from people of that faith. Yet, when he published essays in the *Maryland Gazette* in 1773 that were critical of the fee schedule for judges and probate officers that Governor Robert Eden had enacted, Charles Carroll of Carrollton was very much drawing upon his experiences as a politically marginalized religious minority to make his argument. He was also making an argument that he knew had direct consequences for the Patriots' cause – a cause that he fully supported, even as leaders of that cause railed against the "tyranny of popery."

MARYLAND'S REVOLUTIONARY RELUCTANCE

It's not something that's generally emphasized at Fourth of July gatherings nowadays, but the fact of the matter is that most of the people living in British colonial America at the time of the Revolution were not ardent Patriots. To be sure, Massachusetts, Virginia, and Pennsylvania were all hotbeds of revolutionary sentiment by the early 1770s; as many as 60 percent of the white residents in those colonies contributed supplies, labor, and rhetoric to the war effort. But in general, the flames of rebellion burned surprisingly low along the eastern seaboard, even at the height of the war, with roughly a third of the residents actively in favor of independence, a fifth actively opposed, and the remaining half far too distracted by the challenges of daily life to formulate a strong opinion on the subject, one way or the other.[45]

Among those colonies where support for independence in the years leading up to the war was lukewarm, Maryland may have been the most tepid. The Currency Act of 1764, which angered so many colonial leaders when it prohibited the colonies from issuing paper money, did not create the stir in Maryland that it did in Massachusetts and New York. Maryland's assembly had £25,000 sterling in the Bank of England, which allowed it to get around the prohibition and issue nearly £40,000 in paper bills in 1766 – something no other colony could do. As a consequence, Maryland's governor, Horatio Sharpe, was able to report to officials in England in 1767 that "whatever occasion might have been taken from the Proceedings of the Boston people & the Assembly of New York to represent all the Colonies as ready to set up for Independency, I am persuaded few people here entertain such a thought."[46]

The Townshend Duties also failed to provoke the ire of lawmakers in Annapolis. Baltimore's merchants did eventually agree to protest the duties in 1769, nearly two years after the passage of these infamous taxes on lead, paper, paint, glass, and tea. The merchants agreed to participate in a multi-colony boycott of all British imports. But the merchants' commitment to the boycott was sporadic, and their reasons for agreeing to it do not seem to have been rooted in any genuine anger about parliamentary taxation. Rather, Maryland's merchants were responding to the demands of their colleagues in Philadelphia, who were adamant about the need for a boycott. In an age before dredging, when Baltimore's harbor could not handle ships that had a draft of more than eight feet, the merchants in Baltimore relied heavily upon the port of Philadelphia to conduct their business. They were in no position, therefore, to offend the merchants who dominated that port.[47]

Historians have traditionally concluded that the reason Maryland's residents were so slow to react to the growing imperial crisis was that they were distracted by the disagreements they frequently had with their proprietor. Frederick Calvert, the sixth Lord Baltimore, was a Protestant, but that didn't mean that people in Maryland automatically agreed with everything he said or did. Throughout the 1750s and 1760s, members of the so-called "Country Party" in Maryland's politics chafed under the collar of proprietary rule and clashed with Lord Baltimore over tobacco inspections, ministerial salaries, officer's fees, and poll taxes. These Country Party lawmakers were unable, at first, to see Parliament's actions as inappropriate or oppressive because they were too busy interpreting Lord Baltimore's actions in a tyrannical light.[48]

But a narrative that stresses the Country Party's animosity toward Maryland's proprietor does not explain why the people of Maryland did finally direct their anger against Parliament instead of Lord Baltimore, nor is it an adequate explanation for why they were slower than the people in other colonies to do so. William Penn's sons, after all, were also labeled "tyrants" as they clashed with the people who lived within the boundaries of their proprietary inheritance, and yet Pennsylvanians were still highly critical of Parliament in the 1760s.[49]

The reason Maryland's freemen were hesitant to direct their anger against Parliament is that most of the arguments that were articulated in the 1760s against that body's actions in the colonies were predicated on an idea that the people of Maryland rejected. That idea was that parliamentary laws like the Stamp Act and the Townshend Act were unjust because the colonies had their own "constitutions" – that is to say, long-standing governing traditions, grounded in laws, customs, history, and experiences that were unique to each colony.[‡] Those constitutions were separate from that of the Parent Country, and because of that, Parliament's authority in the colonies was extremely limited. Indeed, people like Benjamin Franklin insisted that the separate nature of the colonies' constitutions meant that Parliament "has a power to make no laws for us."[50]

But the "separate constitutions" argument didn't resonate with a majority of the people in Maryland because that colony's assembly had spent the bulk of the eighteenth century actually *denying* that there was any constitutional separation between Maryland and England. The reason lawmakers in Maryland tied themselves so tightly – legally and rhetorically – to England's constitution was that they saw that constitution as the best way to control an element that existed almost exclusively within their borders and staked a solid, if unfortunate claim to their colony's history. That element was Roman Catholicism.

CURBING THE GROWTH OF POPERY

In the decades that followed the Glorious Revolution, Protestants in Maryland came to believe that to defend their liberty, they needed to preserve their English identity; to preserve their English identity, they needed to "curb the growth of popery in this province"; and to curb the growth of popery, they needed to solicit the help of Parliament.[51] Unlike England's other colonies, Maryland had to prove its English bona fides in the years that followed James' ouster from the throne. The colony's proprietor, after all, had been Catholic, just like James. He had also tolerated Catholics, just as James had – and the fruits of that toleration still lived, worked, and loved within the colony, in numbers that were far greater than anything found in England or elsewhere in the English-speaking world.

[‡] Unlike the constitution that America's Founders adopted in 1787, England's constitution was not – and still is not – a written document. When the colonists insisted each colony had its own "constitution," therefore, they were not referring to the kind of written document that each of the states ultimately adopted. Rather, they were referring to a governing ethos that was a product and a reflection of how things had always been done in each colony.

To be sure, the eighteenth century was not an endless stream of popery-curbing in Maryland. For many years, in fact, relations between Protestants and Catholics in the colony were quite good. Catholics were a known and (for the most part) trusted quantity in Maryland, and, because of that, the fight against popery there remained largely a rhetorical one – a perpetually popular ingredient in the speeches that lawmakers delivered in the assembly, but a fight that only occasionally resulted in the proposal or passage of actual legislation.

It was when Maryland's settlers felt that their colony's claim to "English" identity was being threatened that anti-Catholic rhetoric transmogrified into laws that restricted Catholics' rights. The developments that made Maryland's Protestants most uneasy tended to involve an influx of new Catholics into the colony. In the 1710s and 1720s, for instance – and then again in the 1740s – the British government sent hundreds of Jacobite prisoners to North America to work as convict-laborers. "Jacobites" were supporters of King James II; in the first half of the eighteenth century, they launched several failed efforts to get the deposed king's son and then grandson onto the throne, including two violent rebellions in 1715 and 1745. When Jacobite prisoners arrived in colonies such as Virginia and North Carolina, they provoked little anxiety among the residents there. But in Maryland, where a third of the residents in some counties were already Catholic, lawmakers responded by passing laws that they hoped would retard the growth of the Catholic population, such as one that placed a special tax on all "Irish Papist servants" brought into the colony.[52]

Maryland's Protestants were also spooked in the 1750s when hundreds of refugees from Acadia – or what the English called "Nova Scotia" – began arriving in the colony. These French-speaking Catholics had been living in what was, technically, an English colony for more than forty years by the time the French and Indian War broke out in 1754; France had been forced to give Acadia up to the English in 1713, as a provision of the Treaty of Utrecht. Even though two generations of Acadians had grown up under British rule – and the Acadians had themselves pledged to remain neutral during any conflict between England and France – England's military commanders were uncomfortable with the high concentration of French-speaking Catholics who lived in Nova Scotia. Between 1755 and 1763, therefore, they forced more than 14,000 Acadians to leave their homes, parceling the refugees out in dribs and drabs to England's other colonies.

Many of the refugees eventually made their way to the French settlement of New Orleans, where they became known as "Cajuns" (a bastardization of the word "Acadians"). More than 900 of them, however, arrived in Maryland first. Catholics there tried to put them up in their homes and provide them with resources that would allow them to recover from their journey; most of the Acadians had been forcibly marched from Nova Scotia to the Chesapeake with only those possessions they were able to carry. Maryland's lawmakers, however, barred Catholics from hosting the Acadians, worrying that such hospitality – when extended by Catholics to Catholics – would constitute a security risk. "A real or pretended Jealousy inclined this government not to suffer [the Acadians] to live with the Roman Catholics," Charles Carroll of Annapolis wrote to his son, Charley, in 1756, when Charley was away at school in Europe. The policy was particularly frustrating to Carroll, since Protestant lawmakers had also refused to allocate public money toward the refugee crisis, insisting instead that the Acadians needed to be "entirely supported by private charity."[53]

Some of Maryland's lawmakers doubted their ability to control the growth of popery in the colony. The problem, they believed, was that several members of the Upper House of the Assembly, though Protestant, were related to prominent Catholics in the colony and were reluctant, therefore, to vote for anything that was too oppressive or restrictive. Local legislation was an insufficient check on the Catholic population. Members of the Lower House of the Assembly, therefore, looked to England for help whenever they felt that their colleagues in the Upper House were blocking them, rightly recognizing that England's anti-Catholic laws were more restrictive than the ones they were able to pass in Maryland.

Maryland's lawmakers tried on several occasions in the eighteenth century to apply Parliament's anti-Catholic laws directly to the colony. When they did this, they essentially denied the premise of what became the independence movement – namely, the idea that the colonies were constitutionally different from England. Until Maryland's lawmakers broke out of this mentality and stopped looking to England for help with their legislative dilemmas, arguments about parliamentary "usurpations" and the need for complete independence from England were not going to gain any traction in Maryland.

And yet, when they attempted to defer to England's laws, Maryland's Protestants provided their Catholic neighbors with an opportunity to articulate an understanding of the colony's relationship with England that was surprisingly similar to the understanding the Patriots put forth in the 1760s. Indeed, Catholics came to the conclusion that Maryland had a constitution that was separate from – and even better than – the constitution of England nearly fifty years before the Patriots did, and Protestant deference to England was the reason why.

CATHOLIC CONSTITUTIONALISM IN EIGHTEENTH-CENTURY MARYLAND

The bill that inspired Catholics to argue that Maryland and England were different from one another was introduced into the Lower House of the Assembly in 1718, about a year and a half after 150 Jacobite prisoners had arrived in Maryland as involuntary indentured servants. This new addition to the colony's Catholic population was seen by many Protestants as a challenge to Maryland's security and – more broadly – its identity as a loyal English colony.[54]

In May of 1718, several members of the Lower House initiated a measure that they hoped would discourage Catholics from coming to the colony – and maybe even encourage some of the ones who were already there to leave. Their strategy was tricky. What the lawmakers proposed was an all-out repeal of a statute that Maryland's Assembly had enacted in 1704, entitled "An Act to Prevent the Growth of Popery in this Province." That law denied Catholics the right to vote or hold office in Maryland.

The purpose of the proposed repeal was not to give voting rights back to Catholics, however; rather, the assemblymen wanted to throw out Maryland's law so that they could defer to an anti-Catholic law in England instead. That law was stricter than Maryland's. Not only did it deny voting rights to Catholics, it also required Catholics to pay extra taxes on their land, and it denied priests the right to inherit property.

When the lawmakers introduced their proposal, they noted that the law passed by Maryland's assembly in 1704 had not worked. The "growth of popery" had not been prevented; indeed, "professed Papists still multiply and increase in Number," as the latest injection of Jacobite servants made clear. The situation was not a fait accompli, however. "By one Act of Parliament made in ... the Reign of His late Majesty, King William the Third," the assemblymen observed, "there is good Provision made to Prevent the Growth of Popery, as well in this Province, as throughout all others his Majesty's Dominions." Maryland's Protestants need not resign themselves to being outnumbered by propagating papists, in other words; they simply had to stop trying to solve the problem on their own.[55]

The proposal was a flagrant violation of Maryland's separate constitution – at least according to Peter Atwood, an English-born Jesuit who had begun serving in Maryland six years earlier, in 1712. Atwood was, of course, very concerned about the lawmakers' anti-Catholic goals. Knowing that he could not rely upon the religious sympathies of Maryland's lower assemblymen,

however, the priest chose to protest the proposal by emphasizing the autonomy that Maryland's lawmakers would be giving up if they implemented their
plan.

"That the Penal Laws of England extend not hither was for seventy
years and more the opinion of all in Maryland," Atwood reminded the
Assembly, drawing their attention to the distinctive nature of the principles and practices that animated society in colonial Maryland. Criminal
laws in the colony had always been drafted by Maryland's assembly, not
by Parliament. Any attempt to extend anything to the colony other than
those English laws "deemed an Englishman's birthright," therefore, was
"highly prejudicial to, if not destructive of our constitution."[56]

The word "constitution" cropped up time and again in an essay that
Atwood wrote to defend Maryland's Catholics against the effort to subject them to the laws of Parliament. "Altho our Government is framed ...
according to the model of that of England," the priest told his readers,
Maryland had its own assembly, and the separate and unique nature of the
constitution that guided that assembly had made it such that religious
toleration was "far from ... inconsistent" with the colony's identity.
Respect for the collective Catholic right to worship freely may not have
been a characteristic of life in England, but in Maryland it was a "fundamental part of our constitution," according to Peter Atwood. Indeed,
"Liberty of Conscience" was the "reason behind the peopling of this
province" and the "perpetual and inherent birthright of each
Marylandian."[57]

It's noteworthy that Peter Atwood spoke of both "an Englishman's birthright" and the "birthright of each Marylandian." The distinction was
essential to his argument in 1718, and it was one that would ultimately
have revolutionary ramifications when it was articulated in a different
context by Protestant leaders in New England and Virginia fifty years
later. Even as they insisted that they were good Englishmen, deserving of
English rights, Maryland's Catholics did not – and *could* not – make their
argument without appealing to a related, but different birthright: the one
that they had as residents of a colony that, unlike England itself, had been
founded with their best interests in mind.

The assemblymen in the Lower House failed in 1718 to repeal
Maryland's law. Over the course of the next four decades, however,
Protestants in the colony tried several more times to apply England's
anti-Catholic laws to life in Maryland; each time the colony's Catholics
responded by resurrecting Peter Atwood's argument.[58]

To be sure, Atwood was no revolutionary. He and the lay Catholics who utilized his argument in the 1730s and 1740s were not bold enough to insist, as the Patriots later would, that they were no longer English subjects. In many respects, Maryland's Catholics did not have the freedom in the first half of the eighteenth century to make such an audacious claim. Many people in North America and England, after all, were arguing that Catholics could not be good Englishmen, by virtue of their enslavement to the pope in Rome. There was much about what it meant to be an Englishman that Maryland's Catholics wanted to claim for themselves, however – the right to be represented in the legislative deliberations that governed their lives, for starters. Catholics were therefore uninterested (in the early decades of the eighteenth century, at least) in throwing off the mantle of English identity.

But the fact is that long before Protestant colonists recognized that they had evolved into something different from their supposed countrymen in England, Catholic colonists understood that to be English in Maryland meant something different from what it meant to be English in England. When, in the wake of the Stamp Act of 1765, colonial leaders in Anglican Virginia, Congregationalist Massachusetts, and Quaker Pennsylvania started to insist that their rights as Englishmen were being violated by an English government that refused to recognize the separate nature of their colonies' constitutions, Catholics in Maryland heard an argument that was quite familiar to them.

CATHOLIC DISCOURSE IN A SECULAR CONTEXT

The development that prompted Charles Carroll of Carrollton to publish a series of essays in the *Maryland Gazette* – and, in so doing, bring Maryland's political leaders to the brink of independence – had nothing to do with parliamentary taxation. It had to do with the fees that public officials received in Maryland for their services – and, more specifically, the manner in which those fees were determined.

The fee schedule that dictated what agricultural inspectors, land commissioners, and probate judges were paid had been approved by the General Assembly in 1763. When the schedule came up for renewal in 1769, however, lawmakers in the Lower House wanted to lower the fees because they believed that some officers – including a prominent land commissioner named Daniel Dulany – were being paid too much.

The Lower House could not get the Upper House to approve the new fee schedule. Many of the men who had been appointed to the Upper House by the proprietor were also officers whose incomes would have been adversely affected by the lower schedule. Because the two houses could not reach an agreement, the fee schedule expired in October of 1770. It became illegal for any officer in Maryland to perform his job, and that included the officers who inspected the colony's tobacco. The situation had the potential to wreak havoc on Maryland's economy, and so in November of 1770, Governor Robert Eden issued a proclamation, re-instating the original fee schedule and completely ignoring the wishes of the Lower House.

The delegates in the Lower House were furious. Because Maryland's economy was running strong, however, the anger at Eden's proclamation eventually dissipated and lay dormant until the fall of 1772, when the international price of tobacco began to drop. By January of 1773, Maryland was in a recession, and the colony's residents were once again grumbling about the high fees they were paying to officers in the colony. Many pointed specifically to the governor's proclamation as illegitimate and illegal because he had circumvented the General Assembly when he made it.[59]

Daniel Dulany miscalculated the anger. On January 7, 1773, he anonymously published a fictitious dialogue in the *Maryland Gazette* that he fully expected would convince the colony's residents that Governor Eden's proclamation had been valid. The dialogue was between two "citizens": an ignorant and bumbling "First Citizen," who represented those who questioned the proclamation's legitimacy, and a "Second Citizen," whose defense of the fee proclamation was sophisticated and drew upon an extensive understanding of England's history and political landscape.

Three weeks after the fictitious dialogue appeared, however, the doltish "First Citizen" whom Dulany had created mysteriously published an answer to the Second Citizen's arguments – only this time the First Citizen wasn't such a fool. He came armed with Charles Carroll of Carrollton's impressive knowledge of not just England's constitutional history, but Maryland's constitutional history, as well.

Everyone in the colony knew who the authors were. Throughout the public exchange that followed – now known as the "Antilon-First Citizen Letters" – Carroll was careful not to rise to the bigoted challenge that Daniel Dulany issued when he reminded the *Gazette*'s readers that Carroll had been "disabled" from "interfering" in Maryland's politics because he was a "papist by profession" whose "religious principles" were "inconsistent with the security of British liberty." "Attempts to rouse popular prejudices, and to turn the laugh against an adversary, discover the weakness of a cause," was Carroll's only response.[60] But when he argued that Governor Eden's fee proclamation was unconstitutional because it reversed a fee-setting custom that had been established and followed in Maryland since the time of the colony's founding, Charles Carroll of Carrollton made an argument about the fee proclamation that reflected his religious identity and mirrored the arguments that Catholics had been making about religious intolerance since at least 1718.

Daniel Dulany's defense of the governor's proclamation rested on the idea that there was a precedent for it in England. The fees paid to officers in the colony were not taxes, he reminded the *Gazette*'s readers. Their amount, therefore, did not have to be established by men who'd been elected to the legislative assembly by the people. "No tax," Dulany acknowledged, "can be imposed except by the legislature." It was fine, however, for the governor, who'd been appointed by the proprietor, to determine fees. People who were "not vested with a legislative authority," after all, had "settled and ascertained the fees of officers" in England for decades. Dulany pointed specifically to a case from 1743 in which an unelected official had issued an order that determined the fees paid to officers in England's Court of Chancery.[61]

But when non-elected ministers in England settled officers' fees, Charles Carroll pointed out, they were still obliged to respect England's constitution – and therein lay the flaw in Dulany's argument. The constitution that Governor Eden was obliged to respect was not the constitution of England, but the constitution of Maryland. "Fees in this province have been generally settled by the legislature," Charley Carroll observed. "So far back as 1638, we find a law for the limitation of officers fees; in 1692, the governor's authority to settle fees was expressly denied by the lower house."

It did not matter, in other words, that custom in England had evolved in such a way as to allow non-elected officials to set certain officers' fees. In Maryland, the colony's duly elected assemblymen had always been the ones who'd set the fees. Quoting the Lower House's 1692 decision to deny the governor the right to set officers' fees, Carroll noted that it was "'*the undoubted right of the freemen of this province not to have ANY FEES imposed upon them but by the consent of the freemen in the general assembly*.'" Any action that did not respect that right was, in Carroll's words, "a deviation from the principles of the constitution" and "contrary to the spirit of *our constitution* in particular."[62]

Throughout their entire exchange, the "constitution" Daniel Dulany referred to was always the "the constitution of England" or "England's constitution." In contrast, Charles Carroll spoke of two constitutions – England's and Maryland's – and insisted that both were equally relevant, as far as the debate over Governor Eden's fee proclamation was concerned. England's constitution was important because Maryland's constitution was indebted to it. Maryland's constitution had evolved from the customs and usages that were possible under the charter, and that charter had been issued so that the constitutional rights that Maryland's first settlers had as Englishmen would be protected, even as they lived far away from England. But the constitution that Governor Eden was bound to respect in 1770 was *"our constitution* in particular," according to Charley Carroll – a collection of precedents and practices that had developed in Maryland over the course of 140 years. Regardless of what England's constitution demanded, Maryland's constitution demanded that all officers' fees be subject to legislative oversight.

It was an argument that said nothing about religion; and yet, Charles Carroll of Carrollton's identity as a Catholic was deeply embedded within it. He was telling his neighbors that Maryland was different from England – that it had always been different from England – and in the context of the fee proclamation controversy, even those neighbors who served in the Lower House of the Assembly and wanted to "curb the growth of popery" were eager to embrace this argument.

CHAPTER CONCLUSION

The anti-Catholic tone of the Patriots' rhetoric subsided after the colonies formally declared their independence in July of 1776. The Continental Congress knew from the get-go that the Americans weren't going to be able to win the war on their own; they quickly initiated negotiations with England's greatest enemy, therefore, and in May of 1778, thousands of French Catholic soldiers and sailors began arriving in Boston, Newport, White Plains, Yorktown, and Savannah, having been sent there by their king to help the Patriots win the fight.[63]

Part of the reason the Americans toned down their rhetoric was that they'd learned from their experiences with the Canadians; it just didn't make sense to be insulting the faith of the very people you were trying to charm. But one other relevant factor may have been that the alliance with France afforded Protestants who had never met a Catholic the chance to see Catholics – and French Catholics, at that – engaged in activities that were designed to promote freedom as Protestants understood the term.

"Before the Revolution," the Boston native Samuel Breck recalled, "the colonists had little or no communication with France, so that Frenchmen were known to them only through the prejudiced medium of England." That medium had made Boston's residents suspicious of the French alliance when Congress first announced it, and they were convinced the king of France would be sending only his weakest, most incompetent men to defend the cause of liberty in America. "How much were my good townsmen astonished," Breck wrote, when they ran to the wharves in 1778 to "catch a peep" of the Chevalier de Sainneville's fleet, only to discover that the king has sent "plump, portly officers and strong, vigorous sailors" to Boston Harbor, instead of the "gaunt, half-starved, *soup-maigre* [i.e. "meatless"] crews" the Bostonians expected.[64]

Certainly, American Catholics themselves were partially responsible for the less religiously inflammatory tone of the Patriots' rhetoric. Charles Carroll of Carrollton wasn't the only Catholic to support the independence movement; indeed, the muster rolls from St. Mary's County – where the bulk of Maryland's Catholics lived – indicate that Catholic support for the war effort may have been proportionately greater than Protestant support. An astounding 79 percent of the Catholic men who married in St. Mary's County between 1767 and 1784 swore their allegiance to the free state of Maryland, donated money and supplies to the American war effort, and served in the Continental Army or the St. Mary's County Militia; 58 percent of the men who belonged to the Jesuits' congregation at St. Inigoes Manor in 1768 did the same.[65]

The decades that followed the revolution also proved to be more religiously tolerant times in America, as Protestants across the spectrum worked to minimize their differences and focus on the core, theological beliefs that they all shared.[66] Catholicism was still a hard pill for these Protestants to swallow, and the hand of post-revolutionary ecumenism was never fully extended to Catholics. Nevertheless, the first thirty years or so of America's identity as an independent nation were a time of new freedom for American Catholics, an era when they didn't have to struggle against laws that restricted their rights, and they didn't have to prove their loyalties – or even their legitimacy as Christians – to their countrymen.

Instead, Catholics were able to focus on building an episcopal infrastructure for their faith, something that had been completely absent from the Catholic experience in British colonial America. Unlike Quebec, Maryland had had no resident bishop during its time as an English colony; in 1789, however, John Carroll became the first Catholic bishop in the United States, his religious jurisdiction extending to all Catholics in the country, wherever they were.

Carroll's effort to impose some degree of institutional discipline onto America's Catholics revealed just how "American" these Catholics had become. America's Catholics resisted his efforts because they resisted the Vatican's understanding of freedom and lay-clerical relations. They pushed to retain the control they'd had over their Church during the years when there were few priests serving in the colonies and no residential bishops. As an American himself, Carroll understood this resistance and worked to accommodate it to some degree. At the end of the day, however, he was the pope's representative in America – and it was his job to make the Church in America truly "Catholic."

NOTES

1. Brendan Morrissey, *Quebec, 1775: The American Invasion of Canada* (Oxford, UK, 2003), 7–72; Roger Riendeau, *A Brief History of Canada* (New York, 2007), 98–99.
2. Bernard Bailyn, *The Ideological Origins of the American Revolution* (Cambridge, MA, 1967, 94–143; Samuel Seabury, *A View of the Controversy between Great Britain and Her Colonies* (New York, 1774), 19. Seabury actually believed that these assertions were exaggerations.
3. Bailyn, *The Ideological Origins of the American Revolution*, 119.
4. Ruth H. Bloch, *Visionary Republic: Millennial Themes in American Thought, 1756–1800* (New York, 1988), 58–60.
5. Ezra Stiles, *The Literary Diary of Ezra Stiles*, Franklin Bowditch Dexter, ed. (New York, 1901), 1:455.
6. "To the Inhabitants of the Province of Quebec," October 26, 1774, in *Journals of the Continental Congress, 1774–1789*, Worthington Chauncey Ford, et al., ed. (Washington, DC, 1904), 1:105; Francis D. Cogliano, *No King, No Popery: Anti-Catholicism in Revolutionary New England* (Westport, CT, 1995), 63; Edward J. Davies, *The United States in World History* (New York, 2006), 26.
7. Quoted in Cogliano, *No King, No Popery*, 64; "Extract of a Letter from Canada, dated Montreal, March 24, 1775," *American Archives*, 4th Series (Washington, DC, 1846), 2:229.
8. "Extract," ibid.
9. Ibid.
10. "To the People of Great Britain," October 21, 1774, in *Journals of the Continental Congress*, 1:88, 99–101.
11. Ibid.; Bailyn, *The Ideological Origins of the American Revolution*, 19; Brendan McConville, *The King's Three Faces: The Rise and Fall of Royal America, 1688–1776* (Chapel Hill, NC, 2006), 282, 288–290; Alfred P. James, *The Ohio Company: Its Inner History* (Pittsburgh, 1959), 45;

Archibald Henderson, *Dr. Thomas Walker and the Loyal Company of Virginia* (Worcester, MA, 1931), 80.

12. "To the People of Great Britain" and "To the Inhabitants of the Colonies," *Journals of the Continental Congress*, 1:88–99, 101.

13. "Massachusettensis" (Daniel Leonard), "To The Inhabitants of Massachusetts Bay," Boston Gazette, March 27, 1775, rpt. in John Adams and Jonathan Sewall, *Novanglus and Massachusettensis: Political Essays Published in the Years 1774 and 1775* (Boston, 1819), 221; John Lind, *An Englishman's answer, to the address, from the delegates, to the people of Great Britain, in a letter to the several colonies which were represented in the late Continental Congress* (New York, 1775), 24; Samuel Johnson, *Hypocrisy Unmasked; or, A Short Inquiry into the Religious Complaints of Our American Colonies* (London, 1776), 17. Adams mistakenly thought that Massachusettensis was Jonathan Sewall, the colony's attorney general, and so when he published the exchanges, he put Sewall's name on the collection. See Lorenzo Sabine, *Biographical Sketches of Loyalists of the American Revolution* (Boston, 1864), 11.

14. Brantz Mayer, "Introductory Memoir Upon the Expedition to Canada," in Charles Carroll, *Journal of Charles Carroll of Carrollton during His Visit to Canada*, Brantz Mayer, ed. (Baltimore, 1876), 30; "Commission of Dr. Franklin, Samuel Chase, and Charles Carroll, as Commissioners to Canada," in *American Archives, Fourth Series*, Peter Force, ed. (Washington, DC, 1853), 5:411.

15. William Blackstone, "Of the Rights of Persons," *Commentaries on the Laws of England, in Four Volumes* (Oxford, 1765–1769), rpt. (New York, 1853), 1:89, 125, 140.

16. Blackstone, "On Private Wrongs," in ibid., 3: 337.

17. John Leland, "The Rights of Conscience Inalienable" (1791), in *The Writings of the Late Elder John Leland*, L.F. Greene, ed. (New York, 1845), 181.

18. Ibid., 185.

19. Benedict XVI, "A Proper Hermeneutic for the Second Vatican Council," and Avery Cardinal Dulles, "Nature, Mission, and Structure of the Church," in *Vatican II: Renewal Within Tradition*, Matthew L. Lamb and Matthew Levering, eds. (New York, 2008), ix–xvi, 25–36; John W. O'Malley, "The Style of Vatican II," *America*, February 24, 2003, accessed on July 19, 2017: www.americamagazine.org/issue/423/article/style-vatican-ii.

20. Leo XIII, "Libertas: On the Nature of Human Liberty," June 20, 1888, *Papal Documents Online*, accessed January 14, 2016: http://w2.vatican.va/content /leo-xiii/en/encyclicals/documents/hf_l-xiii_enc_20061888_libertas.html.

21. Ibid. Leo did not become pope and issue his encyclical until many decades after the Revolutionary War. His letter, however, is considered to be the definitive Catholic statement on liberty prior to the reforms of the Second Vatican Council; as such, it is a distillation and embodiment of centuries of Catholic thought on the issue of liberty and accurately reflects the Church's understanding of freedom at the time of the American founding.

22. Samuel Moyn, "Religious Freedom between Truth and Tactic," in *Politics of Religious Freedom*, Winnifred Fallers Sullivan, Elizabeth Shakman Hurd, Saba Mahmood, and Peter G. Danchin, eds. (Chicago, 2015), 135–141;

Avery Dulles, "Dignitatis Humanae and the Development of Catholic Doctrine," in *Catholicism and Religious Freedom* (New York, 2006), 43–66.

23. Samuel Adams, "The Rights of the Colonists," November 20, 1772, *The Writings of Samuel Adams*, Harry Alonzo Cushing, ed. (New York, 1904), 8:359.

24. Patrick T. Conley and Robert G. Flanders Jr., *The Oxford Commentaries on State Constitutions: Rhode Island* (New York, 2011), 65; Paul Finkelman, ed. *The Encyclopedia of American Civil Liberties*, Volume I (New York, 2006), 136.

25. Maura Jane Farrelly, *Papist Patriots: The Making of an American Catholic Identity* (New York, 2012), 256, 253; "America's Founding Fathers: Delegates to the Constitutional Convention," *The Charters of Freedom: The National Archives and Records Administration*, accessed on December 6, 2015: www .archives.gov/exhibits/charters/constitution_founding_fathers.html.

26. Farrelly, *Papist Patriots*, 159–160; Scott McDermott, *Charles Carroll of Carrollton: Faithful Revolutionary* (New York, 2001), 25.

27. Massachusetts *Spy*, March 17, 1775.

28. John McWilliams, *New England's Crises and Cultural Memory: Literature, Politics, History, Religion, 1620–1860* (New York, 2004), 196–197; Thomas Secker, Bishop of Oxford, *A Sermon Preached before the Incorporated Society for the Propagation of the Gospel in Foreign Parts* (London, 1741).

29. Samuel Langdon, "Election Sermon," May 31, 1775, quoted in Martin I.J. Griffin, "Catholics and the American Revolution," *American Catholic Historical Researches* 1(1906), 31; "American Whig," aka William Livington, *The New York Gazette*, May 1, 1769; Jonathan Mayhew, *Remarks on an Anonymous Tract, Entitled An Answer to Dr. Mayhew's Observations on the Charter and Conduct of the Society for the Propagation of the Gospel in Foreign Parts* (Boston, 1764), 75, 79.

30. Patricia Bonomi, *Under the Cope of Heaven: Religion, Society and Politics in Colonial America* (New York, 1986), 199–209; Francis Blackburne, *A critical commentary on Archbishop Secker's letter to the Right Honorable Horatio Walpole, concerning bishops in America* (Philadelphia, 1771), 5–6.

31. Richard Bland to Thomas Adams, August 1, 1771, rpt. in *William and Mary Quarterly* 5(1897), 153–154. See also James E. Pate, "Richard Bland's Inquiry into the Rights of the British Colonies," *William and Mary Quarterly* 11 (1931), 24; and Nancy L. Rhoden, "Anglicanism, Dissent, and Toleration in Eighteenth Century British Colonies," in *Anglicizing America: Empire, Revolution, Republic*, Ignacio Gallup-Diaz, Andrew Shankman, and David J. Silverman, eds. (Philadelphia, 2015), 136.

32. Quoted in Philip Lawson, *The Imperial Challenge: Quebec and Britain in the Age of the American Revolution* (Montreal, 1989), 76.

33. Jean-Oliver Briand, "Pastoral Letter, December 29, 1776," in *Catholics and the American Revolution*, Martin Ignatius Joseph Griffin, ed. (Ridley Park, PA, 1907), 1:97–99.

34. James Hennesey, *American Catholics: A History of the Roman Catholic Community in the United States* (New York, 1981), 65; Steve O'Brien, *Blackrobe in Blue: The Naval Chaplaincy of John P. Foley, S.J.* (New York, 2002), 8–9; McDermott, *Charles Carroll of Carrollton*, 127.

35. Hennesey, American Catholics; anonymous colonist, quoted in Bloch, *Visionary Republic*, 59.

36. Samuel Adams, aka "A Puritan," Boston *Gazette*, April 11, 1768, in *The Writings of Samuel Adams*, 1:204; Gary B. Nash, *The Unknown American Revolution: The Unruly Birth of Democracy and the Struggle to Create America* (New York, 2006), 45–58.

37. Jonathan Mayhew, *Observations on the Charter and Conduct of the Society for the Propagation of the Gospel in Foreign Parts* (Boston, 1763), 75, 78, 20; James Otis, *The Rights of the British Colonies Asserted and Proved* (Boston, 1766), 27; Samuel Adams, *Boston Gazette*, April 11, 1768.; John C. Miller, *Sam Adams: Pioneer in Propaganda* (Stanford, CA, 1936), 127; Thomas Hollis to Jonathan Mayhew, December 18, 1864, in *Memoirs of Thomas Hollis, Esq.*, Francis Blackburne, ed. (London, 1780), 214; Daniel Barber, *The History of My Own Time* (Washington, DC, 1827), 17.

38. McConville, The King's Three Faces, 281–282.

39. Samuel Adams, "Address of Massachusetts to Mohawk Indians," 1775, in *The Writings of Samuel Adams*, 3:213; John Adams, *The Works of John Adams, Second President of the United States*, Charles Francis Adams, ed. *(Boston, 1850)*, 2:252; Stiles, *The Literary Diary of Ezra Stiles*, 1:455.

40. Alexander Hamilton, *A Full Vindication of Matters of Congress from Calumnies of Their Enemies* (1774), rpt. in *The American Catholics Historical Researches* 6 (1889), 160; William Henry Drayton, "Charge of William Henry Drayton" in *American Archives*, 4th Series, 6:959; C.H. Van Tyne, "The Influence of the Clergy, and of Religious and Sectarian Forces on the American Revolution," *American Historical Review* 19 (1914), 59–62.

41. *Maryland Journal*, September 7, 1774; *Maryland Gazette*, October 13, December 22, and November 10, 1774.

42. *Proceedings of the Conventions of the Province of Maryland Held at Annapolis, 1774, 1775, 1776* (Baltimore, 1836), 210–215.

43. *Archives of Maryland*, William Hand Brown et al., ed. (Baltimore, 1883–present), *Archives of Maryland Online*, 78:209, accessed on May 30, 2016: http://aomol.msa.maryland.gov/html/index.html.

44. Ibid., 8:107, 448; 20:144; 22:487; 26:289, 349; 27:371: 33:109.

45. Robert Middlekauff, *The Glorious Cause: The American Revolution, 1763–1789* (New York, 2005), 563–564.

46. Jack P. Greene and Richard M. Jellison, "The Currency Act of 1764 in Imperial-Colonial Relations, 1764–1776," *William and Mary Quarterly* 18 (1961), 493–494; Katherine L. Behrens, *Paper Money in Maryland* (Baltimore, 1923), 51–52; Horatio Sharpe to Hugh Hammersley, June 9, 1767, in *Archives of Maryland Online*, 14:392.

47. Charles Albro Barker, *The Background of the Revolution in Maryland* (New Haven, 1940), 291–293; 315–316; Ronald Hoffman, *A Spirit of Dissension: Economics, Politics, and the Revolution in Maryland* (Baltimore, 1973), 37–43; 60–88.

48. David Curtis Skaggs, "Maryland's Impulse Toward Social Revolution, 1750–1776," *The Journal of American History* (1968), 771–786, and *Roots of Maryland Democracy, 1753–1776* (Westport, CT, 1973);

Hoffman, *Spirit of Dissension*; Barker, The Background of the Revolution in
Maryland; and Aubrey C. Land, *Colonial Maryland: A History* (Millwood,
NY, 1981).

49. Carl and Jessica Bridenbaugh, *Rebels and Gentlemen: Philadelphia in the Age
of Franklin* (New York, 1942); Stephen Brobeck, "Revolutionary Change in
Colonial Philadelphia: The Brief Life of the Proprietary Gentry," *William and
Mary Quarterly* (1976), 410–434; Lorett Treese, *The Storm Gathering: The
Penn Family and the American Revolution* (State College, PA, 1992); Rhys
Isaac, *Landon Carter's Uneasy Kingdom: Revolution and Rebellion on a
Virginia Plantation* (New York, 2004); Jack P. Greene, "Society, Ideology,
and Politics: An Analysis of the Political Culture of Mid-Eighteenth-Century
Virginia," in *Society, Freedom and Conscience: The American Revolution in
Virginia, Massachusetts, and New York*, Richard M. Jellison, ed. (New York,
1976), 14–76; Jack P. Greene, "'Virtus et Libertas': Political Culture, Social
Change, and the Origins of the American Revolution in Virginia, 1763–
1766," in *The Southern Experience in the American Revolution*, Jeffrey J.
Crow and Larry E. Tise, eds. (Chapel Hill, 1978), 55–108.

50. Jack P. Greene, *Peripheries and Center: Constitutional Development in the
Extended Polities of the British Empire and the United States, 1607–1788*
(Athens, GA, 1986), 12, 95–97, 103–104; 110–124. The Franklin quote is on
p. 12.

51. *Archives of Maryland Online*, 26:46, 340.

52. *Archives of Maryland Online*, 33:109; 46: 349–550, 52:558.

53. Glenn R. Conrad, ed. *The Cajuns: Essays on Their History and Culture*
(Lafayette, LA, 1983); Charles Carroll of Annapolis to Charles Carroll of
Carrollton, July 26, 1756, in *Dear Papa, Dear Charley: The Peregrinations of
a Revolutionary Aristocrat*, Ronald Hoffman, Sally D. Mason, and Eleanor S.
Darcy, eds. (Chapel Hill, NC, 2001), 1:30.

54. Ronald Hoffman, *Princes of Ireland, Planters of Maryland: A Carroll Saga,
1500–1782* (Chapel Hill, NC, 2000), 82–90; *Archives of Maryland Online*,
30: 334; Margaret Sankey, *Jacobite Prisoners of the 1715 Rebellion:
Preventing and Punishing Insurrection in Hanoverian England* (Burlington,
VT, 2005), 67–69.

55. *Archives of Maryland Online*, 33:288–289; "William III, 1998–99: An Act
for the Further Preventing the Growth of Popery" (11 and 12 William III, c.
4), in *Statutes of the Realm, 1695–1701*, John Raithby, ed. (London, 1820),
7:586–587.

56. Peter Atwood, "Liberty and Property, or the Beauty of Maryland Displayed,"
rpt., *United States Catholic Historican Magazine* (1889–90), 248–249.

57. Ibid., 252, 242.

58. Farrelly, Papist Patriots, 201–203.

59. Hoffman, *Spirit of Dissension*, 92–103; Peter S. Onuf, *Maryland and Empire,
1773: The Antilon-First Citizen Letters* (Baltimore, 1974), 13–16.

60. Antilon's *Third Letter* (April 8, 1773) and *Fourth Letter* (June 3, 1773); First
Citizen's *Third Letter*, (May 6, 1773), in Onuf, *Maryland and Empire*, 122,
186, 188, 125.

61. Antilon's *Fourth Letter, Second Letter*, February 18, 1773, and *Third Letter*, in ibid., 157, 71, 101; Nicholas B. Wainwright, "Tale of a Runaway Cape: The Penn-Baltimore Agreement of 1732," *The Pennsylvania Magazine of History and Biography* (1963), 251–293.

62. First Citizen's *Third Letter*, in Onuf, *Maryland and Empire*, 134–135, 78.

63. Cogliano, *No King, No Popery*, 89–106; Henry Lumpkin, *From Savannah to Yorktown: The American Revolution in the South* (Lincoln, NE, 1987), 234–253.

64. Samuel Beck, *Recollections of Samuel Beck, with Passages from His Note-Books (1771–1862)*, H.E. Scudder, ed. (Philadelphia, 1877), 24–25.

65. Maura Jane Farrelly, "American Slavery, American Freedom, American Catholicism," *Early American Studies* 10 (2012), 82, n. 24.

66. Chris Beneke, *Beyond Toleration: The Religious Origins of American Pluralism* (New York, 2008), 3–48.

4

"The Catholic Religion is Modified by the Spirit of the Time in America"

Anti-Catholicism and the New Republic

John Carroll's first visit to Boston as America's new Roman Catholic bishop was surprisingly enjoyable. The city was home to around 18,000 people by the summer of 1791, and although "scarcely a hundred souls" of them were Catholic, this number was still far greater than it had been just twenty-five years earlier, when John Adams noted (with some relief) that Catholics in New England were as rare as comets and earthquakes.[1] The growth of Catholicism in a city that had been founded by anti-Catholic Puritans was a development that America's first Catholic bishop welcomed heartily; nevertheless, Carroll had some reservations as he headed north from his home in Maryland to visit Boston's Catholics. New England, after all, had a long history of opposition not just to Catholics, but to bishops, as well.

Carroll was delighted, therefore, when several prominent Protestants – including even Massachusetts' Congregationalist governor, John Hancock – attended a Mass he delivered in a Huguenot church that Catholics had been renting on School Street. The bishop was also invited to deliver the benediction at the annual banquet for the Ancient and Honorable Artillery Company of Massachusetts. This militia group, which still exists today as an honor society, was founded in 1638 by John Winthrop to provide for the colony's defense.[2]

When he returned to Baltimore, Carroll wrote to Governor Hancock that he was "astounded and confounded" by the "innumerable favors & civilities" he had received during his time in Boston. "I had always heard that the town of Boston was distinguished for its hospitality," the Catholic bishop wrote. "But everything was beyond my highest expectations."[3]

In a letter he wrote to an old friend in England, John Carroll was a bit more honest about Boston, admitting to Charles Plowden that the city was not at all "distinguished for its hospitality," at least not when it came to Catholics. New England's largest city was, in fact, a place "where a few years ago, a popish priest was thought to be the greatest monster in creation. Many here, even of their principal people, have acknowledged to me that they would have crossed to the opposite side of the street rather than meet a Roman Catholic some time ago."[4]

But things had changed in America, Carroll told his English friend. The American people were citizens of a new nation now – one where the Constitution included a clause that eliminated religious tests on national office-holding, and one where an amendment to that constitution would soon be ratified, prohibiting the federal government from ever establishing a national church or impeding the expression of any religious belief. "In these United States," John Carroll proudly told not just Charles Plowden, but many of his fellow Catholic clergy in Europe, "our religious system has undergone a revolution, if possible, more extraordinary than our political one."[5]

CHAPTER OVERVIEW

The first few decades that followed the American Revolution were a time of unusual freedom for Catholics in the United States. Cultural and legal discrimination against them did not fully disappear, but Protestants in the new country did prove to be remarkably civil toward them in the years that followed the war. Every state allowed Catholics to vote, and a few of them even allowed Catholics to hold office. The first generation of citizens in the United States seemed to take the premise of their revolution pretty seriously (at least when it came to religion); they understood that the "unalienable rights" they'd fought for belonged to Catholics, as well.

This more tolerant landscape had an unexpected side-effect: It made America's Catholics rather contentious. New England's history of animosity toward Catholicism wasn't the only reason John Carroll was a little apprehensive about his trip to Boston. He was also worried that he might be walking into a hornet's nest his own people had built. The bishop traveled to New England in the summer of 1791 for two reasons: 1) a prominent Catholic priest in the city was openly antagonizing Protestants, and Carroll hoped to rein him in; and 2) Boston's Catholics were fighting with one another about who their priests should be and where their Masses should be said, and the bishop hoped to resolve those disagreements. Carroll probably didn't realize it, but the religious "revolution" that he praised was the reason Catholics in Boston were irritating

Protestants and clashing with one another. That radical change in the way America's Protestants treated Catholics had given his co-religionists the freedom to be openly disagreeable.

At the dawn of the nineteenth century, most of Boston's Catholics were French – soldiers and sailors who'd stayed in Massachusetts following the Revolutionary War. These Catholics wanted to be ministered by the priest John Carroll had sent to Boston in 1789, Father Louis de Rousselet. Rousselet was one of nearly 30,000 priests who fled France between 1789 and 1800 in order to avoid being killed. France's revolutionary leadership believed the Catholic Church had been complicit in the abuses committed by the French monarchy; they therefore executed thousands of priests and nuns during a period of heightened "de-Christianization" in France in the 1790s.[6]

Carroll sent Rousselet to Boston after the city's first priest, Claude Bouchard de la Poterie, proved to be a bad match for the region. Poterie had arrived in New England in 1778, along with the French Navy, and he liked to emphasize his fancy, old-world titles to Boston's fiercely republican Protestants – titles such as "Knight of the Order of the Holy Sepulchre at Jerusalem" and "Doctor Protonotary of the Holy See of Rome." These titles, Carroll believed, were at odds with "the temper & habits of thinking in America; where more caution is required in the Ministers of our Religion, than perhaps in any other Country."[7]

Boston's few dozen Irish immigrants, who were not yet the demographic force they would one day become, wanted to be ministered by Father John Thayer, a Boston native who'd begun his adult life as a Yale-trained Congregational minister. Thayer had served as a chaplain in the Continental Army during the Revolutionary War. He converted to Catholicism in 1783 after spending several months in Rome, where he studied the theology of the Catholic Church "for the same reason that I should have wished to know the Religion of Mahomet, had I been at Constantinople."[8]

John Carroll had sent Thayer to Boston in 1790 to assist Rousselet with New England's growing Catholic population. It was a decision the bishop soon came to regret. Almost immediately, John Thayer started sowing discord among Boston's Catholics, insisting that an American was more qualified than a foreigner to serve as the parish's head priest. Thayer also seemed determined to annoy the Protestants he encountered in his hometown. He told Benjamin Franklin that he intended to convert the entire country to Catholicism – an "unwise" announcement that Franklin saw fit to warn John Carroll about. Thayer also "rail[ed] at Calvin and Luther" during a visit to

John and Abigail Adams' house, asking John "if he believed the Bible" and confiding to the future president that he wanted to turn all of his friends into Catholics. "Mr. Adams took him up pretty short," Abigail reported to her brother-in-law, "and told him ... that his religion was a matter that he did not look upon himself accountable to anyone but his Maker."[9]

In the summer of 1790, John Thayer published an essay in one of Boston's newspapers in which he argued that Catholicism was the only true form of Christianity. He then got into a very public debate with a Protestant minister from New Hampshire who didn't like what the priest had written. At one point during that exchange, which took place on the pages of the *Columbian Centinel*, Thayer ominously warned the Reverend George Lesslie and all of New England's Protestants that "there is no salvation out of this [Roman Catholic] Church." He advised them that such a reality was one that "merits the most serious reflections, since they who despise God are not in the way of salvation."[10]

"Nothing can contribute more to vilify us in the eyes of our Protestant Brethren," Carroll chastised Thayer, "or give more pleasure to the enemies of our religion" than the clerical in-fighting and public threats of damnation that the convert priest had brought to the religious landscape in Boston. If he could have, Carroll probably would have removed John Thayer from the city. Shortly before he arrived in New England, however, America's bishop learned that Louis de Rousselet was not actually allowed to say Mass anymore; he'd been stripped of that authority by bishops in France shortly before he moved to the United States, for reasons that are no longer known. John Carroll's hands were tied, at least for the time being; he needed John Thayer to stay in Boston. He did warn the convert priest to curb his argumentative behavior, however. He also required Thayer to sign a pledge, in which the priest agreed to submit to any decision that Carroll made as Bishop of the United States.[11]

Relations between Catholics and Protestants in Boston were smooth for a few years after Carroll's visit, but in the fall of 1793, John Thayer started debating Protestants again. In September of that year, a Congregational minister named John Lathrop delivered a lecture at Harvard College as a part of that school's annual "Dudleian" series. The Dudleian Lectures were endowed in 1755 by Massachusetts' former Chief Justice, Paul Dudley; in his will, Dudley had stipulated that every fourth lecture had to address "the idolatry of the Romish church, their tyranny, usurpations, damnable heresies, fatal errors, abominable superstitions, and other crying wickedness." To that end, Lathrop had delivered a lecture that focused on the ways in which the Church of Rome tried to usurp the authority of Christ.[12]

As Dudeleian lectures went, Lathrop's was actually remarkably tame, reflecting some of the spirit of that religious "revolution" that made John Carroll so proud. In a nod to the Christian heritage that Catholics and Protestants shared, Lathrop was careful throughout his speech to refer to Roman Catholics as "our Catholic brethren." Before launching into a criticism of Catholicism's "errors," Lathrop also informed his audience that many educated people "highly esteem [Catholics] for their learning and piety," and he insisted that "the usurpations of the Romish church are by no means so threatening to the liberties and happiness of mankind, as they were at the time when our fathers separated from her."[13]

But John Thayer was unimpressed by these ecumenical overtures. "Your pamphlet is called *A Lecture on the Errors of Popery*," he wrote to the Congregational minister, utilizing a degree of sarcasm that was unusual, even for him. "A more proper title would have been *The Errors of Dr. Lathrop*." Thayer went on to enlighten John Lathrop about the history of the Roman Catholic Church, seemingly oblivious to the fact that Lathrop was a fellow in the American Academy of Arts and Sciences, a group that still stands today as one of the most prestigious honor societies in the United States. "We should not have seen you undertake, in these days of liberal sentiment," Thayer remarked, "to rake together a few, scattered transactions, performed in different ages by *individual* Catholics, and charge them to the *whole church*, of which they were members."[14]

Carroll probably agreed with Thayer's evaluation of Lathrop's lecture. Nevertheless, the bishop worried that Thayer's vicious and arrogant reaction to the musings of a well-respected minister might undo the interdenominational progress that, paradoxically, the anti-Catholic lecture had represented. Concluding that John Thayer lacked the necessary diplomatic skills to work in an urban setting, Carroll shipped the New Englander off to the sparsely populated new state of Kentucky, where Thayer's charismatic preaching style proved pleasing enough to draw some Protestants to his services. Indeed, Thayer's charisma caused several Protestant ministers in Kentucky to "look upon him with an envious eye, seeing their meeting deserted by numbers of their hearers."

Soon, though, Thayer was picking fights again. He referred to Kentucky's Methodists as "fools" and openly condemned slavery, even as he owned – and by some accounts abused – a slave woman named Henny. After Thayer was accused by a female parishioner of asking her to "draw up her cloathes & shew him her private parts" during the Sacrament of Confession, John Carroll decided that he had had enough.

He removed the priest from the frontier and arranged for him to be transferred to Ireland, where Thayer died in 1815 – the same year John Carroll did.[15]

John Thayer was an anomaly – an unusually cantankerous fellow who, as a convert, exhibited an obnoxious zeal for his faith that few of his clerical colleagues shared. The discord that he brought to – or more accurately, capitalized on – in the parishes he served, however, was far from unusual among the Catholic congregations that began to spring up in America following the Revolution. In Louisiana, Georgia, South Carolina, Virginia, Kentucky, Maryland, Pennsylvania, New York, and Massachusetts, native-born Catholics feuded with immigrants; French Catholics feuded with Irish Catholics, who feuded with German Catholics; wealthy Catholics feuded with their poorer religious brethren; and lay Catholics of all classes and nationalities feuded extensively with their priests.

Part of the reason early American Catholics had the freedom to argue with one another over who their priests would be and where their churches would be built was that John Carroll had been right when he said that America had undergone a religious revolution "more extraordinary than our political one." It would be wrong to say that Protestants in the United States forgot all of their animosity toward Catholics and welcomed Papists into their religious and political conversations with open arms – as John Lathrop's Dudleian lecture clearly showed. But as Lathrop's lecture also showed, America's Protestants had come a long way since the age of Roger Williams, when even the most tolerant of Calvinists considered Catholics to be the "Anti-Christ."

In the words of Benjamin Rush, a Presbyterian doctor from Philadelphia who signed the Declaration of Independence and served as a surgeon in the Continental Army, "pains were taken" in the decades immediately following the war, "to connect Ministers of the most dissimilar religious principles together, thereby to show the influence of a free government in promoting christian charity."[16] America's Protestants, in other words, took the religious commitments articulated in their national constitution seriously. They would never consider voting for a Catholic candidate, to be sure – but they'd never deny the franchise to Catholics, either, as Protestants in every colony except Pennsylvania and Rhode Island had done in the eighteenth century. They'd also never lock a Catholic church, tear it down, and then use its bricks for salvage, as Protestants in colonial Maryland had done; nor would they ever put a man on trial for having delivered the Catholic Sacrament of Penance to a slave, as Protestants in New York did in 1741.[17]

Because Catholics in the new republic weren't facing the kind of Protestant animosity that their colonial ancestors had faced, they had the freedom to focus on doing what they needed to do to make their denomination a vibrant, vocal, and powerful participant in America's experiment with religious pluralism. And because they were building up their faith in a country that had just successfully challenged several long-standing, traditional hierarchies and replaced them with the "truth" that "all men are created equal," lay Catholics in the United States felt entitled to be full participants in the process that would determine what their Church was to become in the new nation. This was the reason the laity frequently clashed with each other, their Protestant neighbors, and – more particularly – their *priests* in early America, a habit that many bishops considered to be "scandalous" and one that they worked hard in the early nineteenth century to curtail.[18]

LIBERTY, NOT TOLERATION

When he proposed what became Article VI, Clause Three of the US Constitution, Charles Pinkney of South Carolina told his colleagues at the Constitutional Convention that the provision was one "the world will expect ... in the establishment of a System founded on Republican Principles, in an age so liberal and enlightened as the present." The promise that "no religious Test shall ever be required as a Qualification of any Office or public Trust under the United States" was one that the Founders had more or less committed themselves to, Pinkney insisted. They'd made that commitment eleven years earlier, in July of 1776, when they told the world that theirs was a revolution premised on the idea of natural rights.[19]

Not everyone agreed with Pinkney that the mandates of a "liberal and enlightened" age required America's Founders to create a government that allowed anyone of any religious persuasion to serve in office. When they were presented with the text of the Constitution and asked to ratify it in February of 1788, several members of Massachusetts' state legislature suggested that Article VI was "a departure from the principles of our forefathers, who came here for the preservation of their religion." More specifically, they worried that the third clause "would admit deists, atheists, &c. into the government," and they "shuddered at the idea that Romanists and pagans might be introduced into office." In Maryland, one delegate to the Convention explained his vote against the Constitution by pointing to Article VI, Clause Three and asking his colleagues why it had become so "unfashionable" to think "that in a Christian country, it would be at least decent to hold out some distinction between the professors of Christianity and downright infidelity or paganism?"[20]

The lawmaker who asked this question, Luther Martin, held a belief that was not uncommon at the time – and one that was actually *shared* by many of the men who parted ways with him and voted to ratify the Constitution. That belief was that in order for a republican democracy to work, voters needed to be virtuous, and in order for voters to be virtuous, society needed to cultivate religion. "It is religion and morality alone which can establish the principles upon which freedom can securely stand," John Adams wrote in 1776. "The only foundation of a free constitution is virtue." His colleague in the Continental Congress, Benjamin Rush, echoed this idea ten years later, when he sought to create a system of public education in his home state of Pennsylvania. "The only foundation for a useful education in a republic is to be laid in Religion," Rush wrote. "Without this there can be no virtue, and without virtue, there can be no liberty."[21]

Adams and Rush were both Federalists, meaning they strongly supported the Constitution as it was written in 1787 – and this support included an endorsement of the provision against religious tests.[22] The fact that they didn't want a religious test on national office-holding did not mean, however, that Rush and Adams believed the government had no interest in promoting religious belief. They simply felt– unlike Luther Martin – that the best way for the government to promote religion was for the government to stay out of the business of requiring it. They also felt that the kind of religion the new republic needed ought to be generic and devoid of the pedantic theological differences that separated one denomination from another.

Certainly there were some Founders who had little patience for religion. Thomas Jefferson famously wrote in 1787 that it "does me no injury for my neighbor to say there are twenty gods or no god. It neither picks my pocket nor breaks my leg." His good friend, Tom Paine, pushed this idea to its extreme, writing in 1794 that "all national institutions of churches, whether Jewish, Christian, or Turkish, appear to me no other than human inventions, set up to terrify and enslave mankind, and monopolise power and profit."[23]

But Jefferson and Paine were in the minority in the late eighteenth century. Most of their contemporaries were scandalized by Paine's book, *The Age of Reason*. Few people realize it today, but the author of *Common Sense* – the now-famous pamphlet that made the case for independence to the American people and, in so doing, launched the Revolution – died with few friends. Not even the Quakers in his community would allow his body to be buried in their cemetery, though Quakers were known the world over for their tolerant approach to religious differences.* Paine's thirteen-line obituary in the *New York Evening Post*, unceremoniously squeezed between a marriage announcement and a list of the ships that had been cleared to enter New York Harbor the week before, perfectly conveyed the general American sentiment toward the revolutionary at the time of his death in 1809: "I am unacquainted with his age," the author wrote, "but he had lived long, done some good, and much harm."[24]

The fact is that most of the men who constructed the United States' form of government wanted the American people to be religious. But they also wanted the American people's religiosity to be a *choice*. The delicate and nuanced nature of this goal – forgotten by many people today on both sides of the debate about the place of religion in the public square – is revealed in the Northwest Ordinance, Congress' plan for how they would govern the Ohio Country (i.e., the southern part of Quebec that England had ceded to the United States) before it was populated enough to be broken up into states. "No person demeaning himself in a peaceable and orderly manner shall ever be molested on account of his mode of worship, or religious sentiments in the said territory," the Ordinance from 1787 stipulated. Yet, "religion, morality, and knowledge being necessary to the success of good government and the happiness of mankind, schools and the means of education shall ever be encouraged."[26]

The "religion" that Congress recognized as being "necessary" to good government was non-specific – and deliberately so. Most of the Founders believed that issues like whether a person should be baptized as an infant or an adult, or whether a proper baptism involved "sprinkling" water onto the head of a candidate or "dunking" him entirely into a river or lake, were inconsequential when it came to the question of what conditions best sustained good government. It was fine for beliefs about baptism to separate Congregationalists from Baptists and Baptists from Methodists (a movement within Anglicanism that started in the eighteenth century and eventually became its own denomination). It was not fine, however, for those beliefs to separate one American from another.

* Tom Paine was buried on his farm in New Rochelle, New York. His reputation was rehabilitated in the mid-nineteenth century by abolitionists who believed (probably incorrectly) that he was the first person in America to call for the complete emancipation of all slaves. One of these abolitionists dug his remains up and shipped them to Paine's native England for re-internment, but the bones were lost along the way. It's not clear what happened to them, but a family in Australia today claims to be in possession of Paine's skull.[25]

Indeed, more than a few of the framers of America's system of government weren't even convinced that accepting the divinity of Christ was something citizens needed to do in order to maintain the virtue that made it possible for republican democracy to work. They believed that citizens had to look beyond themselves and their friends and neighbors in order to find a standard of virtue that wasn't unavoidably riddled with humanity's flaws; "God," in other words – or what the Declaration of Independence called a "Creator" – was a concept that the Founders felt was probably important to the accomplishment of good, democratic government. But the question of whether Christ needed to be a part of that standard of virtue, men such as James Madison, John Adams, and Benjamin Franklin believed, was not one for society or government to answer.

"Before any man can be considered as a member of Civil Society," James Madison wrote in 1785, "he must be considered as a subject of the Governor of the Universe."[27] Madison's language reflected his keen interest in Deism, a philosophy of religion that came to prominence among educated people in Europe and America in the eighteenth century and implicitly rejected the divinity of Christ. Deists insisted that the creator of the universe did not intercede in world events beyond his original act of creation, and this divine non-involvement applied to everything that had ever happened in the history of the world – including even the events that may have transpired in a manger in Bethlehem roughly 1,800 years earlier.[28]

But his Deistic language aside, it's not clear that James Madison actually was a Deist. The author of the First Amendment was born into an Anglican family and educated by Presbyterian ministers, and at one point he even expressed an interest in becoming a Presbyterian minister himself. It's not unreasonable, in other words, to think that Madison might have considered Jesus to be the son of God, at least when he was still young and helping to design America's system of government.[29] But the man who would become America's fourth president very deliberately did not include Christ in the equation whenever he spoke of the "duty" that Americans had to render "homage" to "the Creator," or the interest that government had in the cultivation of "virtue in the people." That's because the question of Christ's divinity – much like sprinkling versus dunking – was one that Madison believed could be "directed only by reason and conviction," and the resolution of these issues was certainly not something that the "preservation of free Government requires."[30]

But if people such as Madison, Adams, and Franklin didn't think Christ's divinity was a political issue, the fact remains that many of the first Americans who were tasked with "living out" the political project they designed still did.

They believed that Christianity – and Protestantism, more specifically – was the best kind of religion for a democratic republic to embrace. This is why so many states initially had provisions in their constitutions that limited office-holding to Protestants (or, in the case of Maryland, Delaware, Massachusetts, and Rhode Island, to "Christians"). It's also the reason Connecticut and Massachusetts continued until well into the nineteenth century to collect taxes "to make suitable provision . . . for the institution of the public worship of God and for the support and maintenance of public Protestant teachers of piety, religion, and morality."[31]

But on the national level, at least, most Americans at the dawn of the nineteenth century seemed willing to accept the premise of the Founders that the theological boundaries that separated one denomination – or even one religion – from another were unimportant when it came to the administration of good government. This is why the people's representatives in the state legislatures voted to ratify the US Constitution, even with its prohibition on religious tests. It's why, once that constitution was fully ratified, "the Jew joined the Christian; the Episcopalian the Presbyterian; & the Seceder the Roman Catholic" to celebrate the new plan of government, marching "arm in arm" down Philadelphia's Market Street in a parade that was a "complete triumph over religious prejudices," according to one observer.[†] And it's why, in the summer of 1790, George Washington proclaimed that "all possess alike liberty of conscious and the immunities of citizenship" when explaining to a group of Jews in Newport, Rhode Island, that "it is no more that toleration is spoken of as if it were the indulgence of one class of people, that the other enjoyed the exercise of their inherent natural rights."[32]

In making this declaration, Washington was drawing a subtle but important distinction between "religious toleration" and "religious liberty" – and insisting, then, that *liberty* was the foundation upon which the new country's religious culture would and should be built. Strictly speaking, "toleration" was what Parliament and King George III had implemented in Canada in 1774. Although the Quebec Act allowed Catholics to practice their faith freely, it was still premised on the idea that Catholics were wrong to believe what they believed – and that they had no more "right"

[†] After the Revolution, Anglicans in the United States called themselves "Episcopalians" because they wanted to distance themselves from England, even as they continued to subscribe to the theological teachings of that country's national church. The "Seceders" were members of a tiny denomination formed in Philadelphia in 1782, when two socially conservative, break-away groups of Presbyterians came together to form the Associate Reformed Church.

to their mistaken beliefs than an engineer had to the belief that two plus two equals five.

Britain's government would tolerate Catholics' expression of their mistaken religious beliefs so long as that expression did not endanger society (the way an engineer's expression of his mistaken beliefs about math would endanger society, for instance, if he expressed those beliefs while designing a bridge). But if, at any point, the government determined that Catholics were dangerous, that toleration would end. This reality was what Congress had tried, unartfully, to warn the Canadians about in 1774, when they sent their letter to the inhabitants of Quebec before invading the colony. Toleration was no great gift, since it was dependent upon the whims and sensibilities of the giver.

Religious liberty, however, was dependent upon no one but God. It was not a philosophy of governance that gave people the freedom to be wrong; it was a bold assertion that the rightness or wrongness of a person's religious beliefs was an entirely non-political question – that it never was and never would be the obligation of government to determine how humanity relates to God. Certainly, a nation that is committed to religious liberty can still say that democratic government has an interest in encouraging people to navigate a relationship with God on their own, through the use of their reason; like John Adams and Benjamin Rush, George Washington believed "of all the dispositions and habits that lead to political prosperity, religion and morality are indispensable supports." But Washington told the Jewish residents of Newport that Americans no longer spoke of toleration as a mere "indulgence" – that they had, instead, embraced the "enlarged and liberal policy" of "liberty of conscience" – because he firmly believed that his country was changing. It was becoming a country that recognized the pointlessness of forced religion – a country that "gives bigotry no sanction, to persecution no assistance, [and] requires only that they who live under its protection demean themselves as good citizens in giving it on all occasions their effectual support."[33]

RELIGIOUS LIBERTY IN THE STATES

Of course, at the time that Washington addressed the Jews of Newport, the state of Rhode Island wasn't quite "there" yet. Americans may have adopted a posture of "liberty" when it came to their national politics, but on the state level, non-Christians still weren't allowed to vote or hold office in Rhode Island, suggesting that the legal culture there did still view Jewish beliefs as "wrong" on some level and that when Jews attended worship services openly at their synagogue in Newport, they were being "indulged" or "tolerated" by their Christian neighbors, in spite of Washington's words to the contrary.

But America's first president was not naïve to think that things were changing. The 1790s actually saw several states remove their religious restrictions on people's civil rights. South Carolina eliminated its Protestant test on office-holding in 1790, when lawmakers there adopted a second constitution that barred only the clergy from holding office. That mandate applied to all clergy, not just non-Protestant ones, and South Carolina's new constitution guaranteed that the "free exercise and enjoyment of religious profession and worship" would be enjoyed by everyone in the state.[34]

Although Pennsylvania had never formally barred non-Protestants – or even non-Christians – from holding office, requiring only that men affirm their belief in a Supreme Being before casting a vote, lawmakers in Philadelphia took steps in 1791 to modify their constitution so that it would be perfectly clear that Catholics and Jews were eligible to hold office in the state. In Georgia, lawmakers got rid of their state's Protestant test on office-holding in 1798, when they adopted a new constitution – the state's third since 1776 – that required only that lawful candidates be up-to-date on their tax payments. That same year, Rhode Island's lawmakers finally eliminated the Christian requirement on voting when they enacted a statute that declared "all men shall be free to profess, and by argument to maintain, their opinions in matters of religion, and that the same shall in no wise [sic] diminish, enlarge, or affect their civil capacities."[35]

By the turn of the nineteenth century, it was no longer acceptable in polite American society to be a rabid religious bigot. William Goddard, the co-editor of the *Maryland Journal and Baltimore Advertiser*, was an early adopter of this new set of manners. In 1785, Goddard instructed anyone who wanted to publish in his paper that essays that sought to "examine, criticize, or censure ... the Conduct and Character of Men who hold the Offices of Government" would be "received with many grateful Thanks." As the paper's editor, however, he thought it "his duty that nothing appears in his Paper which may ... ridicule and revile the religious Profession of any Set of Men."[36] It was an announcement that almost certainly would have made Cecilius Calvert smile. The religious civility that Maryland's first proprietor had hoped to achieve a century and a half earlier when he drafted the "Act Concerning Religion" in 1649 was finally becoming a reality in Maryland.

Some people believed that Americans had become more accommodating of religious differences because they were simply too busy building and expanding their new nation to care anymore about those differences. "The seasons call for their attention," the French Catholic immigrant J. Hector St. John de Crèvecoeur observed in the 1780s about his neighbors in upstate New York. They had "no time," therefore, for what he called "the foolish vanity, or rather the fury of making Proselytes." Americans' beliefs had become a "strange religious medley" that was "neither pure Catholicism nor pure Calvinism." As such, this medley did not cultivate or sustain religious bigotry.[37]

But the pressing need to plow fields and build roads aside, the fact is that many people in the United States at the time of the Founding took the spirit of freedom that had animated their revolution seriously – at least when it came to religion. (The continued existence of slavery, of course, testified to how much work Americans still had to do before their practices would truly be in line with their revolution-era principles.) "Having banished from our land that religious intolerance under which mankind so long bled and suffered," Thomas Jefferson declared in his first inaugural address in 1801, Americans recognized that "every difference of opinion is not a difference of principle." When they declared their independence from Great Britain and formed a new government, the American people had committed themselves to the principle that "the minority possess their equal rights, which equal law must protect, and to violate [those minority rights] would be oppression."[38]

In the United States, the majority could differ from the minority when it came to opinions about whether the Sabbath fell on a Saturday or a Sunday, whether the mother of Jesus was born with the stain of original sin on her soul, or whether carpets were an appropriate luxury in a house of God (an issue that started vexing Methodists not long after Jefferson became president). Such differences of opinion, however, did not require anyone in America to abandon his or her commitment to the principle of equal rights before the law. That principle, Jefferson believed, would become the source of America's strength – and its uniqueness as a nation.

AMERICANS GET A CATHOLIC BISHOP

America's Catholics took full advantage of the spirit of freedom and limited ecumenism that characterized the religious landscape in the decades immediately after the Revolutionary War. High on their list of priorities was the creation of a clerical, episcopal, and physical infrastructure to support the Catholic Church's growth in America. This goal was shared by priests and lay people alike – though it became clear very early on that the laity did not always share their priests' vision for how, exactly, their Church should grow.

John Carroll wanted his new country to have its own bishop. Technically speaking, Carroll wasn't actually the leader of the small community of Jesuits working in the United States in the 1780s; indeed, that community of priests was not even technically made up of Jesuits anymore, since Pope Clement XIV had suppressed the Society of Jesus in 1773, and the Jesuits would not have their order restored until just before Carroll's death in 1815.[‡] Carroll was probably the best-known priest in America, however, thanks to the failed diplomatic mission he'd undertaken to Quebec in 1776, along with his cousin, Charles, their fellow-Marylander, Salmon Chase, and Benjamin Franklin. Because he was well-known and well-respected by the Patriot leadership, John Carroll became the "voice" of American Catholics following the Revolution.

During the colonial period, the priests who served in British North America had been under the jurisdiction of the Bishop of London (though that bishop never actually visited the colonies). John Carroll wanted that situation changed; America, after all, was no longer a part of England. He wrote to Pope Pius VI, therefore, in 1783, explaining to the pontiff that "because of the present arrangement of government in America, we are no longer able as formerly to have recourse for our spiritual jurisdiction to bishops or vicars apostolic who live under a different and foreign government."[39] Rome responded by removing America's clergy from the Bishop of London's jurisdiction and placing them under the auspices of the Propaganda de Fide, the Vatican office that oversaw (and still oversees) the Catholic Church's global missionary efforts.

This move completely missed Carroll's point, however, as it still placed America's priests directly under the authority of a "foreign government." "I consider powers issued from the Propaganda not only improper, but dangerous here," Carroll told several of the priests he worked with in Maryland. Placing the United States under the jurisdiction of an office in Rome, "appears to be a dangerous step, and, by exciting the jealousy of the governments here may lend much to the prejudice of [Catholic] Religion, and perhaps expose it to the reproach of encouraging a dependence on a foreign power."[40]

[‡] The reasons for the pope's suppression of the Jesuits are complicated and still fraught with controversy, nearly 250 years later. One major reason, though, had to do with the pressure the pope was receiving from monarchs in Spain and Portugal, who felt that the Jesuits were stirring up the indigenous people in South America and stymieing European efforts to exploit the resources there.

Carroll's concerns were far from unreasonable, given America's long history of animosity toward Catholicism. The Maryland-born priest, however, was bothered by more than just the possibility of Protestant reproach. He hadn't been forced to join the diplomatic mission to Canada, after all; John Carroll was a Patriot, and he firmly believed that the colonies had rightfully achieved their independence and become their own nation. He also believed that that nation had undergone a religious revolution that presented great opportunities to English-speaking Catholics. The Vatican's move suggested otherwise.

In placing the United States under the jurisdiction of the Propaganda, the Vatican was implying that America was something less than a free and independent country – that there was something "temporary" about it, in other words. It was also suggesting that the culture in the United States was inherently incompatible with Catholicism – as incompatible as, say, the culture in Muslim Africa or Shinto Japan, two other places where Catholic missionaries who were under the auspices of the Propaganda de Fide labored to convert people. This suggestion was particularly troubling to John Carroll, who was proud of the religious reforms his new country had adopted. "By the constitution, our Religion has acquired equal rights and privileges with that of other Christians," he observed to his clerical colleagues. "We form not a fluctuating body of laborers in Christ's vineyard, sent hither and removable at the will of a Superior, but a permanent body of national clergy, with sufficient powers ... to choose our own superior and a very just claim to have all necessary spiritual authority communicated to him."[41]

Giving America its own bishop, Carroll believed, would be an act of diplomatic recognition on the part of the Vatican – a formal acknowledgment that a new country had been born, that that country was here to stay, and that its culture was one the Vatican respected. Carroll wanted this acknowledgment for the United States. But he also understood that framing the appointment of an American bishop as an act of diplomatic recognition was the best way to present the idea to America's Protestants, given the history of animosity toward both Catholicism and bishops in the United States.

His companion on the diplomatic trip to Montreal agreed. Benjamin Franklin was serving as the United States' ambassador to France when the Vatican placed America's Catholics under the auspices of the Propaganda de Fide. Franklin approached the Vatican's representative in Paris and encouraged him to encourage the Vatican to take John Carroll's advice and give American Catholics their own bishop instead. Franklin also suggested that that bishop should be chosen from among the group of priests who were already serving in the United States – preferably someone who was also native-born – and that America's priests, themselves, should be the ones who chose the bishop. This last idea was one that John Carroll had already presented to Rome, telling one Vatican official that "in our free and jealous government, where Catholics are admitted into all public Councils equally with the professors of any other Religion, it will never be suffered that their ecclesiastical Superior . . . receive his appointment from a foreign State."[42]

In the end, Pius VI did as both Franklin and Carroll advised. Maryland's priests voted in May of 1789, selecting not just the man they wanted to be their bishop, but also the town that they wanted to serve as the seat of the first American diocese. In November of 1789, John Carroll was consecrated as the Bishop of Baltimore, with his jurisdiction extending to Catholics living in all parts of the United States.

CATHOLIC REPUBLICANISM

Carroll's first task was to deal with the clerical shortage that had been plaguing the Catholic community in British colonial America since the early years of settlement. There'd never been enough priests in the colonies to regularly meet the needs of the Catholic population, and it was not uncommon for Catholics who lived outside Philadelphia and St. Mary's City to have to go weeks – or even months – without receiving the Sacraments of Communion or Confession. Although Philadelphia did have two free-standing Catholic chapels, Maryland had none after lawmakers there tore down the Catholic chapel in St. Mary's City in 1704. When Masses were held, they were typically held in the private chapels (or, more often, just rooms) that lay Catholics in both colonies kept in their homes. Marriages were typically arranged around the schedules of itinerate priests who traveled throughout the countryside and were frequently delayed by the weather, illness, and/or poor road conditions.[43]

At the close of the Revolutionary War, there were just twenty-one priests in the United States – serving a lay population that Carroll estimated was around 30,000. Fortunately for these priests, the Catholic population tended to be concentrated in Pennsylvania and Maryland – and even more specifically in Charles and St. Mary's Counties, on the southern tip of the Western shore of the Chesapeake. In the years that followed, however, America's lay Catholics started to spread out. Some of Maryland's Catholics moved to central Georgia, where land was cheap. Many more moved to Kentucky, since the climate there was similar to Maryland's, but the land had not been depleted of its resources by decades of tobacco farming. The federal government also handed out land-grants in Kentucky to veterans and people who had provided supplies to the Continental Army. By 1787, more than seventy Catholic families from Maryland had migrated to Nelson County, Kentucky, and more were on their way. If John Carroll wanted them to retain their Catholic identity, he was going to have to find them a priest.[44]

Carroll wanted the priests serving America's Catholics to understand and, when appropriate, reflect the republican sensibilities that animated most Americans, be they Catholic or Protestant. This is why he'd pushed to have the selection of the country's bishop put to a vote; though the vote was confined to clergy, it nevertheless gave his position a certain degree of credibility in the eyes of many Americans.

As his experience with Claude Bouchard de la Poterie in Boston showed, however, it was not easy to find priests who appreciated the spirit of the revolution that the Americans had just launched. The pool of priests that Carroll had to draw from when augmenting the clerical population in his country was European – and more specifically, it was French. Although some of the European clergy who came to the United States during the years of Carroll's episcopate did work valiantly to accommodate themselves to the needs of their fiercely republican parishioners, many of them did not – and perhaps could not – recognize the merits of republicanism. They were fleeing the rather extreme form of republicanism that had launched the French Revolution in 1789, after all – and the violent "de-Christianization" of the country that followed.[45]

These men, it must be said, were also Catholic clergy, and the hierarchical orientation of Catholicism was not a natural fit for the individualistic and self-empowering ideals of republicanism, a reality that even John Carroll was forced to confront and admit from time to time. The political culture in the United States was contractual, constitutional, and voluntary, making it far more compatible with the Protestant understanding of freedom than with the Catholic understanding of freedom. Under such circumstances, the most Carroll could hope for was that these French priests would "study our constitution, our laws, our customs" and, through that, come to respect "the American way of life."[46]

Alas, this did not always happen – and Carroll spent a good part of his episcopacy trying to broker some degree of peace between Old World priests who felt entitled to deference from their parishioners and New World laypeople who felt entitled to tell their priests what to do. These clashes were present from the very beginning in most of the new parishes that sprang up during Carroll's time as the leader of the Catholic Church in the United States: Holy Cross in Marion County, Kentucky (1785); St. Peter's in New York City (1786); Holy Trinity in Philadelphia (1789); St. Mary's in Charleston (1791); St. Patrick's in Norfolk, Virginia (1791); and Holy Cross in Boston (1803).[47]

Often, the tensions were fairly minor. Parishioners in Kentucky, for instance, wrote to John Carroll in 1806 to complain that their Flemish priest had forbidden dancing and the wearing of "finery" by women.[48] Neither prohibition was grounded in Catholic theology (indeed, the prohibitions more closely mirrored the Wesleyan theology of the Methodists who were starting to make inroads into Kentucky), and Father Charles Nerinckx's parishioners ultimately resolved the disagreement themselves by simply ignoring their priest and continuing to host parties.

Sometimes, however, the tensions became quite heated – and even public. In Norfolk's St. Patrick's parish, for instance, lay Catholics wrote to Thomas Jefferson to complain about the indecipherable French accent of the priest who'd been assigned to serve them. They asked the former president and fellow Virginian to use his influence to pass a federal law that would have required the congregational election of all pastors, regardless of denomination. Such a law, these Catholics wrote, would be "perfectly conformable to the fundamental and vital principles of the American Constitution." It was "most just and reasonable," they insisted, "that those who are most interested in the good conduct of the Pastors, and remunerate them for their labors" should be the ones to select them. Virginia's lay Catholics even went so far as to capitalize on some of the old Protestant fears of Catholicism in their effort to get rid of their priest. They told Jefferson that the pastoral elections they were calling for would force immigrant clergy to conform to the political principles of their newly adopted country, and thus the danger of "foreign influence" in the state would be mitigated.[49]

Their effort failed to move Jefferson. It testifies, however, to the strongly republican character of lay Catholics in early America. As one Protestant observer put it, "the Catholic religion is modified by the spirit of the time in America; and its professors are not a set of men who can be priest-ridden to any fatal extent." Certainly, John Carroll did not want lay Catholics in his country to be "priest-ridden"; indeed, unlike many of the clergy he brought over from Europe, he understood that such a goal was not even possible in a country where the national language was, in his words, "the language of a republican." Still, there were times when even

John Carroll wondered if the Catholic faith might have been "modified" a little too much by the "spirit of the time."[50]

Carroll promised Catholics in New York, for example, that he would "extend a proper regard" to their claim that they were entitled to a voice in "the mode of the presentation and election [of pastors]." Nevertheless, he chastised those same parishioners for acting "nearly in the same manner as the Congregational Presbyterians of your neighboring New England states" when they insisted on having certain "rights" within the community of the Church.[51] It was one thing, the Catholic leader seemed to be saying, for America's Catholics to absorb the spirit of republicanism and revel in the religious revolution that had been launched in the United States by that spirit; it was quite another for them to forget who they were and what it meant to be a Catholic.

The reason the members of St. Peter's parish felt entitled to choose their priest was that they owned and legally controlled the land on which their church was to be built; soon they would own and legally control the church building as well. During the eighteenth century, New York had no free-standing Catholic churches. At the time of the American Revolution, therefore, New York's Catholics attended Mass in the home of a wealthy Portuguese merchant, José Roiz Silva. Silva maintained the chapel and paid for the housing of the only priest in the state.

In February of 1785, twenty-one lay Catholic men joined Silva in petitioning New York's city council for a patent that would enable them to jointly purchase land as an incorporated religious association. The corporate patent would allow them to retain control of the land that they purchased and to build a church on it, but it would also provide each man with some degree of financial protection should anything go wrong with their religious 'investment.'[52]

The practice of incorporating as a religious association was common among Protestants in the United States and dated back to the founding of Plymouth and Boston. Indeed, during the colonial period, Maryland was the only colony that hadn't allowed groups of people to own church property jointly as a "corporation," and the reason for this was that lawmakers there didn't want the Society of Jesus to be able to own the farms upon which Maryland's priests lived and worked.[53] The Society of Jesus was outlawed in England, and if Maryland allowed the Jesuits to own property jointly, the colony would effectively be giving formal, legal recognition to a group considered treasonous by the parent country. In Maryland, therefore, each priest owned a certain percentage of each Jesuit farm individually – a legal requirement that complicated the Society's efforts to retain control of the property every time a priest died, since a priest could, conceivably, leave his share of the farm to someone who was not a Jesuit.[§]

In general, though, the incorporation of religious associations was quite common in colonial America, and for many decades it was the primary vehicle by which church buildings of all denominations were constructed and maintained. Each association elected a board of lay trustees, and that board made a host of decisions that affected life within the congregation, decisions ranging from whether and when a new roof should be built on a chapel to the selection of ministers and the payment of their salaries. This was how Congregationalists, Baptists, and Presbyterians had built their churches in colonial America – and it was how Catholics in Philadelphia had built St. Joseph's and St. Mary's churches in the mid-eighteenth century, as well.

John Carroll accepted the lay-trustee system as the best way to build up the Catholic Church's physical infrastructure in early America, even though it was radically different from the way the Church operated in Continental Europe, giving lay Catholics a degree of authority that was unheard of in the Old World.[**] Lay trusteeism also made it possible for disagreements that the laity had with one another to infect the governance of the Church from time to time. Nearly all of the parishes in early America were afflicted with these disagreements, to Carroll's chagrin. Philadelphia's Catholic community, however, may have been the one that was most acutely afflicted – and where the disagreements had the most obvious impact on the Catholic Church.

LAY TRUSTEEISM IN PHILADELPHIA

The disagreements that plagued Catholics in the City of Brotherly Love were a mixture of class and ethnic antagonisms. Irish Catholics resented the heavily accented English of German and French-speaking priests;

[§] The prohibition on corporate land ownership actually ended up protecting the Jesuits' property from the Vatican after Pope Clement XIV suppressed the Society in 1773. Officials in Rome tried to confiscate the Jesuits' farms and slaves following the suppression, insisting that since the Society no longer existed, everything that had once belonged to the Society now belonged to Rome. But the farms in Maryland had never legally belonged to the Society of Jesus.

[**] The closest thing in Europe to lay Catholic trusteeship was the right of *jus patronatus*, which was practiced in some German-speaking principalities. It allowed a nobleman who had donated land to the Catholic Church and paid for the construction of a church or cathedral to recommend that a certain priest be assigned to work in that church or cathedral. The nobleman could only ever make a recommendation, however – clerical assignments were still the prerogative of the bishop – and the land, the church, and everything in the church belonged to the diocese.

German and English Catholics resented the heavy drinking habits of Irish priests. Ethnic devotions to particular saints – Nicholas, Patrick, George, and Denis – became a source of competition between and among the various ethnic groups, and non-theological traditions such as congregational singing in the vernacular, which was important to Germans, and the funeral custom known as a "wake," which was important to the Irish, generated annoyance and sometimes even disgust among Catholics who were unfamiliar with these practices.[54]

The disagreements that German and Irish Catholics had with one another resulted in the founding of a whole new parish in 1788; Holy Trinity was built on land that German-speaking Catholics purchased just two blocks away from St. Mary's Church. At a time when John Carroll was facing a severe dearth of competent priests, the bishop was forced to assign a new priest to work in a new church that was just a few hundred yards away from an existing church – all because German and Irish Catholics couldn't get along.

He did so with some reluctance. When the new trustees of Holy Trinity complained to him, however, that the German-speaking priest he'd found for them was "not by any means agreeable to our wishes," that's when the bishop pulled rank on the trustees, warning them that "the authors of dissensions & sowers of discontent between Pastors & their flock have always been punished by the Church with exemplary Severity."[55] America's bishop may have accepted the American custom of lay trustee-ism as the best way to build up the Church's physical infrastructure, but that didn't mean he was willing to give the laity unlimited power.

Among the Irish, there were disagreements between those who were native-born Americans (i.e., the descendants of earlier immigrants) and those who had arrived in the country recently, after the Revolution. Those disagreements literally came to blows in the winter of 1799, when a native-born Irish-American trustee at St. Mary's Church wouldn't allow an Irish immigrant to solicit signatures from the lower-class, immigrant Irish Catholics who attended Mass at St. Mary's.

The Irishman soliciting signatures was actually Protestant; he'd reached out to his Catholic countrymen, however, because he wanted them to sign a petition opposing the Alien and Sedition Acts, a set of federal laws that made it harder for immigrants to become citizens and empowered the president to deport any immigrant he believed was "dangerous to the peace and safety of the United States."[56] The petition was a stinging rebuke of President John Adams, who had pushed for the passage of the Alien and Sedition Acts. The American-born trustees of St. Mary's Church, therefore, didn't want their fellow Catholics signing the petition because Adams enjoyed the support of many of Philadelphia's wealthier, native-born residents, Catholic and Protestant alike.

The Irish-born Catholics of St. Mary's parish wanted to sign the petition, and they made their desire perfectly clear in the kerfuffle that took place in the St. Mary's churchyard in February of 1799 – dubbed the "United Irish Riot" by one Philadelphia newspaper. The fighting was more than just fisticuffs. One native-born Catholic trustee was shot, though he did not die. Several other men – immigrant and native-born, Catholic and Protestant, all of them Irish – were severely injured.[57]

The Alien and Sedition Acts expired in 1802, and Congress chose not to renew them. The Irish in-fighting in St. Mary's parish died down for several years after that, but by the summer of 1812, old antagonisms were being revived – and stoked – by an immigrant Irish priest named William Harold. Harold's salary had been docked by the native-born trustees because his homilies were unpopular with St. Mary's wealthier parishioners. Harold made sure his fellow immigrants knew that the trustees had done this.

John Carroll was no longer the parish's bishop; Philadelphia's Catholic community had grown large enough to become its own diocese in 1808, and the bishop tasked with resolving the disagreement was an Irish-born Franciscan named Michael Egan. Even though he, too, was an immigrant, Egan did not like Harold's rabble-rousing among immigrant Catholics, and he considered the priest's behavior to be unbecoming to his vocation. Privately, Egan chastised William Harold. Publicly, however, he condemned the trustees' behavior, believing that the laity had no right to control a priest's salary in this way.

Egan called a meeting of all of the church's members to discuss what he considered to be "not only an act of injustice, but an invasion of [Father Harold's] right in the government of his church." The gathering quickly deteriorated into a "disorderly" affair, and, according to one observer, "clenched fists were held in the faces of different persons active on the occasion – and one severe blow was given and received." No resolution to William Harold's conflict with the native-born trustees was achieved at this meeting, and in the days that followed, several trustees received anonymous threats, presumably from poor, immigrant Catholics. Charles Johnson, whose father had been the architect that designed St. Mary's Church in 1763, was told to "look out, damn you – you got a great manny Houses, take care of them, fire and faggot is your portion if you dont let the Clergy alone." Johnson responded by resigning from St. Mary's board of trustees.

The disagreement raged on for two more years, and, at one point, the trustees tried, unsuccessfully, to rope Pennsylvania's state lawmakers into the conflict. The arguments took their toll on Bishop Egan, who suffered an "alarming hemorrhage of his lungs" in the summer of 1814 and died two weeks later at the age of fifty-three. As Egan lay dying, his good friend from Ireland, a priest named Peter Kenny, called the bishop "a Martyr of the ... truly Catholic principle: That the laity never had nor ever will acquire by any means the right of nominating and appointing their priests."[58]

CHAPTER CONCLUSION

Egan's successor, Henry Conwell, was in his seventies when he became Philadelphia's second bishop, and he proved to be even less capable than Egan had been when it came to managing the diocese's lay trustees. Conwell was so ill-equipped to handle Philadelphia's fiercely republican Catholics that the Vatican actually stepped in and replaced him in 1829, a full thirteen years before the priest died at the age of 97.[59]

Like Michael Egan, Conwell's replacement, Francis Kenrick, was no fan of lay trusteeism; indeed, he proved to be quite the foe to this thoroughly "American" concept. "In no way can [the laity] claim rights over the temporalities of the church in such a way as to check and control the clergy in the exercise of their spiritual privileges," Kenrick declared – meaning that it was one thing for lay trustees to insist that they had a right to determine when the church's roof needed to be replaced, but quite another for them to insist they had a right to select their priests and determine the priests' salaries. At one point, Kenrick even announced that he'd rather see every parish in the United States fall apart because of poor management by the Church's bishops than "have the authority of the Bishops blocked by the wrong influence of trustees."[60]

The year Francis Kenrick assumed his post in Philadelphia was the same year America's bishops convened in Baltimore for the first of what ended up being ten "provincial councils," or meetings at which the bishops determined how best to implement the mandates of the Catholic Church within an American context. The first council met in 1829, and the last met in 1869. High on the bishops' list of priorities during these councils was the issue of lay trusteeism – or what the bishops called a "scandalous insubordination toward lawful pastors" and an "evil that tends to the ruin of Catholic discipline to schism and heresy."[61]

It would be a "great good," the bishops decided in 1829, if "the system of church trustees [were] entirely abolished." Just fourteen years had passed since Bishop John Carroll's death, and already the republican system that he'd relied upon to build the Catholic Church in America was on the chopping block. America's bishops took steps at the first provincial council to ensure that the property in all new parishes in the United States legally belonged to the bishops who oversaw them, regardless of who had paid for the land or the construction of the church. The council also stipulated that all existing trustees were barred from having any say in the selection or dismissal of their priests.[62]

In the thirty years that followed, America's bishops worked hard to dismantle the system of lay trusteeism in the older parishes where it already existed, gradually convincing trustees in one parish after another to transfer ownership of the parish's properties to the various bishops. The reason America's bishops were able to do this is that the population of Catholics in the United States started changing during these decades, becoming less native-born and more immigrant – specifically, more *Irish* immigrant – with each passing year. For various reasons, Irish immigrants tended to be more deferential than their fiercely republican, American-born counterparts to the authority of their clergy.[63]

Lay trusteeism wasn't the only phenomenon that moved to the wayside, however, as America's Catholic population became increasingly foreign-born. The spirit of ecumenism that characterized the first few decades after the Revolutionary War also began to disappear, at least when it came to Protestant attitudes toward non-Protestants. A new anti-Catholicism began to take root on the political and religious landscape in the United States. This anti-Catholicism was similar in many ways to the older variety, but because it was thoroughly rooted in the American, rather than the British experience, it developed its own set of characteristics and idiosyncrasies. This new, "American" variety of anti-Catholicism became an animating force in some of the most powerful, pan-Protestant reform movements of the nineteenth century – among them, temperance, abolitionism, and the "common school" movement, which led to the creation of our modern-day public education system (and its Catholic corollary, the parochial school system).

NOTES

1. Peter Guilday, *The Life and Times of John Carroll, Archbishop of Baltimore, 1735-1815* (New York, 1922), 2:423; John Adams, "A Dissertation on Canon and Feudal Law," in *The Works of John Adams, Second President of the United States*, Charles Francis Adams, ed. (New York, 2008, rtp.), 3:456.
2. Guilday, *Life and Times of John Carroll*, 425; "Charter of the Military Company of Massachusetts," January 13, 1638, *The Ancient and Honorable Artillery Company Website*, accessed on February 9, 2016: www.ahac.us.com /charter.htm.

3. John Carroll to John Hancock, August 28, 1791, in Guilday, *Life and Times of John Carroll*, 425–426.
4. John Carroll to Charles Plowden, June 11, 1791, quoted in Margaret C. DePalma, *Dialogue on the Frontier: Catholic and Protestant Relations, 1793–1883* (Kent, OH, 2004), 22.
5. Letter of John Carroll, November 10, 1783; rpt. in John Gilmary Shea, *A History of the Catholic Church Within the Limits of the United States* (New York, 1888), 211.
6. DePalma, Dialogue on the Frontier, 22; Timothy Tackett and Claude Langlois, "Ecclesiastical Structures and Clerical Geography on the Eve of the French Revolution," *French Historical Studies* 11(1980), 357; Michael Pasquier, *Fathers on the Frontier: French Missionaries and the Roman Catholic Priesthood in the United States, 1789–1870* (New York, 2010), 15, 27.
7. James S. Sullivan, *One Hundred Years of Progress: A Graphic, Historical and Pictorial Account of the Catholic Church of New England, Archdiocese of Boston* (Boston, 1895), 21; Abbé de Poterie, *To the Publick, on the Fourth of February* (Boston, 1789), 2–4; John Carroll to Claude de la Poterie, April 3, 1789, *The John Carroll Papers*, Thomas O'Brien Hanley, ed. (Notre Dame, IN, 1976), 1:354; Nicholas Pellegrino, "Reviving a Spirit of Controversy: Roman Catholics and the Pursuit of Religious Freedom in Early America," PhD dissertation, University of Nevada, Las Vegas, 2015, 367.
8. John Thayer, *An Account of the Conversion of John Thayer: Formerly a Protestant Minister of Boston* (Boston, 1832), 98.
9. John R. Dichtl, *Frontiers of Faith: Bringing Catholicism to the West in the Early Republic* (Lexington, KY, 2008), 73; Abigail Adams to John Shaw, January 18, 1785, *Letters of Mrs. Adams, the Wife of John Adams*, Charles Francis Adams, ed. (Boston, 1848), 228.
10. John Carroll to John Thayer, February 22, 1791, *The John Carroll Papers*, 1:491; John Thayer, *A Controversy between the Rev. John Thayer, Catholic Missionary of Boston, and the Reverend George Lesslie, Pastor of a Church in Washington, New Hampshire* (Newburyport, NH, 1793), 25.
11. Carroll to Thayer, February 22, 1791, 494; Dichtl, *Frontiers of Faith*, 74.
12. Pauline Maier, "The Pope at Harvard: The Dudleian Lectures, Anti-Catholicism, and the Politics of Protestantism," *Proceedings of the Massachusetts Historical Society* 97 (1986), 17–41.
13. John Lathrop, *A Discourse on the Errors of Popery: Delivered in the Chapel of the University in Cambridge, September 4, 1793* (Boston, 1793), 7, 29.
14. John Thayer, A Controversy, 164; "Book of Members, 1780–2010, Chapter L," American Academy of Arts and Sciences, accessed on March 12, 2016: www.amacad.org/publications/BookofMembers/ChapterL.pdf.
15. Stephen Badin to John Carroll, June 3, 1799, February 4, 1800, and January 29, 1801; and James Twyman to John Carroll, January 11, 1801, quoted in Dichtl, *Frontiers of Faith*, 74–75; Richard J. Purcell, "Father John Thayer of New England and Ireland," *Studies: An Irish Quarterly Review* 31(1942), 171–184.
16. Anonymous, "Observations on the Federal Procession on the Fourth of July, 1788, in the City of Philadelphia; in a Letter from a Gentleman of this City to his Friend in a Neighboring State," *American Museum* 4 (1788), 77. The

gentleman who wrote the letter was Benjamin Rush. See Chris Beneke, *Beyond Toleration: The Religious Origins of American Pluralism* (New York, 2006), 4.

17. Maura Jane Farrelly, *Papist Patriots: The Making of an American Catholic Identity* (Oxford, 2012), 244; Jason K. Duncan, *Citizens or Papists? The Politics of Anti-Catholicism in New York, 1685–1821* (New York, 2005), 22–23.

18. "Resolution of Archbishop and Suffragans," 1829, quoted in Dale B. Light, *Rome and the New Republic: Conflict and Community in Philadelphia Catholicism Between the Revolution and the Civil War* (Notre Dame, IN, 1996), 240.

19. Charles Pinkney, "Observations on the Plan of Government Submitted to the Federal Convention in Philadelphia," in *The Records of the Federal Convention of 1787*, Max Farrand, ed. (New Haven, 1911), 3:122; Daniel L. Dreisbach, "The Constitution's Forgotten Religion Clause: Reflections on the Article VI Religious Test Ban," *Journal of Church and State* 38 (1996), 262.

20. Jonathan Elliot, ed. *The Debates in the Several State Conventions on the Adoption of the Federal Constitution* (Washington, DC, 1836), 2:117, 148; 1:385.

21. John Adams to Zabdiel Adams, June 21, 1776, in *The Works of John Adams, Second President of the United States*, Charles Francis Adams, ed. (Boston, 1856), 9:401; Benjamin Rush, "A Plan for Establishing Public Schools in Pennsylvania" (1786), in Benjamin Rush, *Essays: Literary, Moral, and Philosophical* (Philadelphia, 1806), 8.

22. Gordon Lloyd, "Federalist Anti-Federalist Debates: Biographies of the Key Players," *Teaching American History.org*, accessed on May 14, 2016: http://teachingamericanhistory.org/fed-antifed/biographies/.

23. Thomas Jefferson, *Notes on the State of Virginia*, Query XVII, 1787, *The Avalon Project*, Lilian Goldman Law Library, Yale University, accessed on March 6, 2016: http://avalon.law.yale.edu/18th_century/jeffvir.asp; Thomas Paine, *The Age of Reason: Being an Investigation of True and Fabulous Theology*, Josiah P. Mendum, ed. (Boston, 1874), 6.

24. *New York Evening Post*, June 10, 1809.

25. Vanessa Thorpe, "Aussie Tests on 'Paine's Skull'," *The Guardian*, May 13, 2000, accessed on July 20, 2017: www.theguardian.com/world/2000/may/14/vanessathorpe.theobserver.

26. Northwest Ordinance, July 13, 1787, Article 1 and Article 3, *The Avalon Project*, accessed on March 6, 2016: http://avalon.law.yale.edu/18th_century/nworder.asp.

27. James Madison, "A Memorial and Remonstrance Against Religious Assessments," (1785), *Selected Writings by James Madison*, Ralph Ketcham, ed. (New York, 2006), 22.

28. Kerry S. Walters, *Rational Infidels: The American Deists* (Durango, CO, 1992).

29. For a great discussion of the difficulties involved in determining Madison's religious beliefs, see James Hutson, "James Madison and the Social Utility of Religion: Risks vs. Rewards" (paper presented at the symposium, "James

Madison: Philosopher and Practitioner of Liberal Democracy," *Library of Congress*, Washington, DC, March 2001), accessed on March 11, 2016: www.loc.gov/loc/madison/hutson-paper.html.

30. Madison, "Memorial and Remonstrance," 22; Madison, "Speech in the Virginia Ratifying Convention, June 20, 1788," in *Debates*, Elliot, ed. 3:536.

31. Dreisbach, "The Constitution's Forgotten Religion Clause," 265–267; "Constitution of the Commonwealth of Massachusetts" (1780), Article III, The 189th General Court of the Commonwealth of Massachusetts, accessed on March 17, 2016: https://malegislature.gov/Laws/Constitution.

32. Beneke, *Beyond Toleration*, 4; The Rev. Mr. Bend to the Rev. Mr. (Abraham) Beach, July 9, 1788, in George Morgan Hills, *History of the Church in Burlington, New Jersey* (Trenton, 1885), 715; *Pennsylvania Packet and Daily Advertiser*, July 4, 1788; "George Washington's Letter to the Hebrew Congregation of Newport," Touro Synagogue Foundation, accessed on March 17, 2016: www.tourosynagogue.org/history-learning/tsf-intro-menu /slom-scholarship/86-washington-letter; Ellen Smith and Jonathan Sarna, "The Jews of Rhode Island," in *The Jews of Rhode Island*, George M. Goodwin and Ellen Smith, eds. (Lebanon, NH, 2004), 2.

33. "Washington's Farewell Address, 1796," *The Avalon Project: Documents in Law, History and Diplomacy*, Lillian Goldman Law Library, Yale University, accessed on March 17, 2016: http://avalon.law.yale.edu/18th_century/wash ing.asp; "Letter to the Hebrew Congregation," ibid.

34. John F. Wilson, "The Founding Era (1774–1797) and the Constitutional Provision for Religion," *The Oxford Handbook of Church and State in the United States*, Derek H. Davis, ed. (New York, 2010), 25.

35. Ibid., 24–25; Patrick T. Conley and Robert G. Flanders Jr., *The Oxford Commentaries on State Constitutions: Rhode Island* (New York, 2011), 65.

36. *Maryland Journal and Baltimore Advertiser*, January 21, 1785.

37. J. Hector St. John Crèvcoeur, *Letters from an American Farmer*, 1782, rpt. (New York, 1904), 64–65; Beneke, *Beyond Toleration*, 3–14.

38. Thomas Jefferson, "First Inaugural Address, March 4, 1808," *The Avalon Project*, Yale University Lilian Goldman Law Library, accessed on March 20, 2016: http://avalon.law.yale.edu/19th_century/jefinau1.asp.

39. John Carroll to Pius VI, via John Thorpe, n.d., *John Carroll Papers*, 1:68.

40. John Carroll, "Circular Letter Announcing his Appointment as Prefect" (1784), quoted in Shea, *A History of the Catholic Church*, 249–250.

41. Ibid.

42. Jay P. Dolan, *The American Catholic Experience: A History from Colonial Times to the Present* (Notre Dame, IN, 1992), 105; John Carroll to John Thorpe, February 17, 1785, in *John Carroll Papers*, 1:306.

43. Tricia T. Pyne, "Ritual and Practice in the Maryland Catholic Community, 1634–1776," *US Catholic Historian* 26 (2008), 24; Dolan, The American Catholic Experience: A History from Colonial Times to the Present, 69–97; Maura Jane Farrelly, "Conflict and Community in Early Pennsylvania's Catholic Church," *Pennsylvania Legacies* 15 (Fall, 2015), 7–8.

44. Andrew Nelson, "Restoration work to being at historic Sharon Catholic Church," *Georgia Bulletin*, May 12, 2016; J.F. Regis Canevin, "Loss and

Gain in the Catholic Church in the United States (1800–1916), *Catholic Historical Review*, 2:4 (1917), 380; Farrelly, *Papist Patriots*, 277, n. 5; Ben J. Webb, *Catholicity in Kentucky* (Louisville, 1884), 24–56.

45. Tackett and Langlois, "Ecclesiastical Structures and Clerical Geography," 357; Pasquier, *Fathers on the Frontier*, 15, 27.

46. John Carroll, quoted in Dolan, *American Catholic Experience*, 108.

47. Patrick W. Carey, *People, Priests, and Prelates: Ecclesiastical Democracy and the Tensions of Trusteeism* (Notre Dame, IN, 1987), 4.

48. DePalma, *Dialogue on the Frontier*, 40.

49. Letter of the Trustees of Virginia to Thomas Jefferson and Congress, December, 1818, in Peter Guilday, *The Catholic Church in Virginia, 1815–1822* (New York, 1924), 96, 100.

50. Harriet Martineau, *Society in America* (London, 1839), 237; Charles Carroll to Charles Plowden, February 20, 1782, *John Carroll Papers*, 1:65.

51. Charles Carroll to Charles Plowden, February 20, 1782, *John Carroll Papers*, 1:65; "John Carroll's Letter on Lay Trusteeism in New York City," 1786, in *American Catholic History: A Documentary Reader*, Mark Massa and Catherine Osborne, ed. (New York, 2008), 32.

52. Carey, *People, Priests, and Prelates*, 8.

53. Sarah Barringer Gordon, "The First Disestablishment: Limits on Church Power and Property before the Civil War" (2014), *Penn Law: Legal Scholarship Repository*, Paper 1390, accessed on March 23, 2016: http://sc holarship.law.upenn.edu/cgi/viewcontent.cgi?article=1545&context=penn_law_review, 16–17, 24–30; William Warren Sweet, *Religion in Colonial America* (New York, 1942), 81–88; Thomas Murphy, *Jesuit Slaveholding in Maryland, 1717–1838* (New York, 2001), 15, 48; Ronald A. Binzley, "Ganganellie's Disaffected Children: The Ex-Jesuits and the Shaping of Early American Catholicism, 1773–1790," *US Catholic Historian* 26 (2008), 60.

54. Helen A. Heinz, " 'We Are All as One Fish in the Sea …' Catholicism in Protestant Pennsylvania, 1730–1790," PhD Dissertation, Temple University, 2007, 108, 136, n. 14; Extracts of Letters from William Wappeler and Thomas Schneider, Maryland Province Archives (MPA), Special Collections, Georgetown University, Box 119, Folders 9 and 10; Farrelly, "Conflict and Community," 9.

55. Quoted in Light, *Rome and the New Republic*, 4, 8.

56. "An Act Concerning Aliens," (1798) in *Our Documents: 100 Milestone Documents from the National Archives*, Michael Beschloss, ed. (New York, 2003), 49.

57. William Duane, *A report of the extraordinary transactions which took place at Philadelphia in February, 1799* (Philadelphia, 1799), 2, 4, 32; Kerby A. Miller, *Irish Immigrants in the Land of Canaan: Letters and Memoirs from Colonial and Revolutionary America, 1675–1815* (New York, 2003), 593–594; Farrelly, "Conflict and Community," 7; Porcupine's Gazette, February, 1799, reprinted in *Porcupine's Works, Containing Various Writings and Selections, Exhibiting a Faithful Picture of the United States*, William Cobbett, ed. (London, 1801), 97.

58. Ibid., 52–72; quotes on 61, 62, 72.

59. Carey, *People, Priests, and Prelates*, 264.

60. Quoted in ibid., 226.

61. Quoted in Light, *Rome and the New Republic*, 240.

62. Ibid., 241; Carey, *People, Priests, and Prelates*, 264; Eric Vanden Eykel, "Scripture in the Pastoral Letters of the Provincial Councils of Baltimore," *American Catholic Studies* 121(2010), 61–65.

63. Carey, *People, Priests, and Prelates*, 214–215.

5

"Those Now Pouring in Upon us ... are Wholly of Another Kind in Morals and Intellect"

Anti-Catholicism in the Age of Immigration

In 1834, the celebrated British writer and social critic Harriet Martineau took a two-year-long trip to the United States. Like many European observers,* she was struck by the strong current of freedom that ran through American culture (even as she was appalled by the institution of slavery).[1] She wondered whether all aspects of American society reflected this obsession with freedom. To find out, she undertook a careful examination of American life, focusing on several key components of the country's culture, including its religion. What she discovered when she looked at the religious landscape was that the principle Thomas Jefferson had celebrated in his inaugural address three decades earlier – namely, that "the minority possess their equal rights" in America – was no longer being adhered to by many people living and worshipping in the United States. The American religious landscape had, in fact, become remarkably intolerant when it came to minority beliefs.

This was surprising to Martineau. Given that "the Americans have long taken higher ground, repudiating establishments and professing to leave religion free," she'd fully expected to find an exceedingly tolerant and even polite religious climate in the United States. Instead, what she found was a "bitter oppression exercised by those who view Christianity in one way, over those who regard it in another way." Among the examples of

---

* Many European writers published travel-books and novels about life in the United States in the nineteenth century. Their books included Frances Trollope's *Domestic Manners of the Americans* (1832), Gustave de Beaumont's *Marie: Or, Slavery in the United States* (1835), Alexis de Tocqueville's *On Democracy in America* (1835), Frederick Marryat's *Diary in America, with Remarks on its Institutions* (1839), Charles Dickens' *Martin Chuzzlewit* (1844), and Ferdinand Kürnberger's *Tired of America* (1855).

oppression that Martineau cited were "Quakers (calling themselves 'Friends') excommunicate one another: Presbyterian clergymen preach hatred to Catholics: a convent is burnt and the nuns are banished from the neighborhood: and Episcopalian clergymen claim credit for admitting Unitarians to sit in committees for public objects!"[2]

The burned convent that Martineau referred to was the Ursuline Convent in Charlestown, Massachusetts, a suburb of Boston. It had been rather spectacularly set on fire by an angry Protestant mob just one month before she arrived in the United States. The riot was sparked by an anti-Catholic sermon that a prominent Calvinist minister had delivered in Boston the day before. Reports in several Boston newspapers that the Ursulines were keeping a woman in their convent against her will had also helped to stoke the flames.

The reports were wildly inaccurate, based not on fact or any investigative initiative on the part of the city's journalists, but on a desire to sell papers by capitalizing on the popularity of a fake "autobiography" that was already circulating in the city and alleged a similar story. Gone were the "innumerable favors & civilities" that Protestants in Boston had extended toward Catholics such as John Carroll in the 1790s; instead, Protestant leaders now preached "hatred," "dreadful slanders," and "foul libels against the Catholics," according to Harriet Martineau. The reason for the change, she believed, was that the "vast and rapid spread of the Catholic faith in the United States" had "awakened fear and persecution" in America.[3]

CHAPTER OVERVIEW

The renewed spirit of anti-Catholicism that Martineau observed was a consequence of more than just the "spread" of the Roman Catholic faith. If fact, several legal, cultural, and demographic changes that started in the 1810s and 1820s helped to create the intolerant landscape that Martineau decried. The changes were subtle at first, and some of them actually had nothing to do with Catholics or Catholicism. By 1834, however, when the Charlestown convent was burned, the fact that America was changing was fairly obvious to everyone. And by the 1840s, when thousands of poor and barely literate Irish Catholic immigrants started arriving in the United States – fleeing starvation and clustering in cities such as Philadelphia, New York, and Boston – it was clear that America was no longer the country it had been at the time of the Founding.

The seven Ursuline nuns who moved from Quebec to Massachusetts in 1820 to open a girls' school near Boston joined New England's religious landscape at a sensitive time in the region's development. Congregationalism, the faith that had been dominating the region for nearly 200 years by that point, was losing ground in New England; the arrival of the nuns (not to mention the willingness of some Protestant families in Boston to send their daughters to the nuns' school) was just the latest manifestation of that fact. The nuns' decision to move to Boston during this transitional period in New England's history ultimately played a role in their convent's destruction.

For generations, New Englanders' piety had been solid and monolithic. The part of the United States that is today the least religious part of the country – judging from how often people say they pray or attend worship services, how important they say religion is to them, and whether they profess to believe in God – was actually the region that held onto its state-supported churches for the longest period of time.[4] Decades after lawmakers in every other state had abandoned the idea of financially supporting churches and ministers, four of New England's five states still mandated some form of religious establishment. And Congregationalism was the denomination that benefited the most from this arrangement.

In Connecticut, the Congregational Church was the legal recipient of all of the religious taxes collected in the state, regardless of whether the people who paid those taxes actually attended a Congregational church. In Vermont, New Hampshire, and Massachusetts, non-Congregationalists did have the option of requesting that their taxes be given to their own churches or ministers; the process for making this designation was quite onerous, however, and dissenters often had to prove to state officials that their ministers were "legitimate" before their taxes could be diverted. This requirement was particularly offensive to Baptists, who had long opposed any government involvement in church affairs. Dissenters who didn't get an official dispensation saw their taxes go directly to the Congregational Church.[5]

By the time the first Ursulines arrived in Massachusetts, however, things had started to change in New England. Congregationalists were no longer the demographic force they once had been. The region was home now to a sizable number of Baptists, Methodists, and Episcopalians – and the latter two denominations, unlike the Baptists, didn't even share the Congregationalists' commitment to a Calvinist theology. There were enough dissenting Protestants in New England, in other words, to compel lawmakers to start the process of religious disestablishment, with Vermont's lawmakers making the first move in 1807. Connecticut's lawmakers followed in 1818; New Hampshire's in 1819; and Maine's lawmakers voted not to allow local governments to financially support religious institutions when they broke away from Massachusetts and gained official statehood in 1820. Massachusetts' lawmakers finally voted to disestablish religion in their state in 1833, nine months before the Ursuline convent in Charlestown was burned.[6]

Disestablishment made some of New England's more traditional religious leaders nervous. They saw the demise of state-supported religion as a sign that people in the region were becoming less committed to orthodox Calvinism – and, in many respects, they were right. Calvinism had, in fact, been experiencing a "softening" of sorts for several decades by the time New England's lawmakers decided that the Congregational Church would no longer receive financial support from the government. The theology that the Puritans had brought over to America in the seventeenth century proved to be a hard theology to maintain over the course of several generations, and because of that, people's understanding of it had changed over time, becoming less like the understanding that had animated the Pilgrims' journey to Massachusetts in 1620, and more like the Arminian – that is to say, non-predestinarian – approach to salvation that the Pilgrims had encountered in the Netherlands in 1608, prompting them eventually to leave Europe and travel to North America.

Calvinism taught that the vast majority of human beings were going to Hell and that there was nothing people could do to save their souls if God had decided that damnation was their fate. This was the great rub of predestination– that you could not save yourself. John Calvin's goal had been noble when he'd insisted upon the "arbitrary" nature of God's salvation; in denying human beings any ability to influence the will of God, he was trying to prevent the kind of corruption that had infected the Catholic Church in the sixteenth century. But the prospect of irreversible and likely damnation proved to be too depressing for many people to live with, and because of this, some New England ministers – even very early on – started downplaying the arbitrary nature of God's salvation when exploring the tenets of Calvinism.

These ministers included people like John Davenport, Solomon Stoddard, and Thomas Hooker – whose kinder, gentler approach to Calvinism had prompted him to leave Massachusetts in 1636 and found the colony of Connecticut. Their goal was to prevent people from becoming indifferent toward their faith, or – in the case of Stoddard's son-in-law, Joseph Hawley – so depressed about the fate of their souls that they slit their own throats, rather than delay the inevitable.[7]

Certainly in the decades when Davenport, Stoddard, and Hooker were preaching, most people in New England still had a solid commitment to Calvinism, in spite of the "melancholy humor" that the theology sometimes engendered.[8] Indeed, in the 1740s, Stoddard's grandson, Jonathan Edwards, was able to inspire thousands of people to renew their faith in the orthodox teachings of John Calvin, in a movement that is known to historians today as the "First Great Awakening."

But by the start of the nineteenth century, that Calvinist awakening was solidly over. By the time Vermont's lawmakers voted for disestablishment in 1807, not only was New England home to Episcopalians and Methodists who were not Calvinists, but many people who'd been raised in Calvinist traditions didn't want to hear anymore that they were powerless to save their souls. They still considered themselves to be the heirs to the religious "errand" that the Puritans had started when they came to North America in the seventeenth century, looking to build a model society for the world to emulate; this was why Massachusetts' lawmakers had been concerned in 1788 that Article VI, Clause Three in the US Constitution might have been a "departure from the principles of our forefathers."[9] But a growing number of these Calvinist heirs wanted to hear that the choices they made in their lives had some bearing on the salvation of their souls – that their fates, in other words, were not subject entirely to the whims of an immoveable God. And nothing testified more to the increasing abandonment of traditional, orthodox, Calvinist theology in New England than the decision of Harvard's Board of Overseers in 1805 to appoint Henry Ware, a Unitarian theologian, as the school's Hollis Chair of Divinity.

Unitarianism was a hard nut to crack. It meant different things to different people – but to hardcore Calvinist ministers such as Jedidiah Morse (whose son, Samuel, would help to invent the telegraph in 1836) and Lyman Beecher (whose daughter, Harriet, would publish *Uncle Tom's Cabin* in 1850), Unitarianism was a "downward course ... to the borders of open infidelity." Unitarian ministers preached a theology "totally at variance with the Gospel," according to Morse, because they told their followers that God could be influenced by people's behavior, and they denied the concept of the Trinity (hence, their name), insisting that God was one entity, and that Jesus and the Holy Spirit were separate and distinct from God.[10]

To traditional Calvinists, Unitarianism's repudiation of the Trinity was little better than Deism's denial of God's intercession in worldly events; both belief systems were dangerous because they implied that Christ "was no more than a man" and that "his perfect moral character was formed by his own exertion, vigilance, and fortitude, without supernatural aid." (Most Unitarians in America, it should be said, took exception to this idea, insisting that their faith was fully "Christian" because they believed that Christ preached with a "divine authority," even if he were not actually "God.")[11]

Deists and Unitarians were not common in nineteenth-century America, but their ranks included some of the most prominent leaders on the country's political, intellectual, cultural, and literary landscape, as evidenced by Harvard's decision to have a Unitarian minister direct their divinity school. Charles Bulfinch, Margaret Fuller, Horace Greely, William Lloyd Garrison, Elizabeth Cady Stanton, Louisa May Alcott, Nathaniel Hawthorne, and Ralph Waldo Emerson were just a few of the movers and shakers in the early-to-mid nineteenth century who considered themselves to be Unitarians. Their powerful cultural influence, then, when combined with the decision of New England's lawmakers to disestablish the Congregational Church, made old-school Calvinists like Jedidiah Morse, Lyman Beecher, Timothy Dwight, and Charles Hodge anxious about the nation's future. These religious leaders worried that as the influence of Unitarianism grew, America's citizens would fail to cultivate the virtue that even the Founders had considered to be vital to the success of democracy.

This, then, was the environment in which a small group of Catholic nuns who'd been trained in Quebec chose to establish their convent: one where traditional Calvinist ministers, who were already pre-disposed to feel some degree of discomfort with the very idea of Catholicism, were fighting to retain their claim on New England's soul – and, by extension, the soul of the entire nation.

Explaining why Orthodox Calvinists targeted Catholics – even as Unitarianism and religious disestablishment were the movements that concerned them – is complicated. It becomes even more complicated when we consider that Orthodox Calvinists weren't the only Protestants who didn't have a high opinion of America's Catholics after 1820; Unitarians, too, didn't much care for them.

The distaste that Unitarians had for Catholics was minor at first – and, indeed, some of the greatest defenders of the Ursuline nuns in the aftermath of their school's destruction were Unitarian ministers and lawmakers who considered the power of "the mob" to be a far greater threat to American society than anything the Catholic Church ever could or would do. By the 1850s, however, even Unitarian leaders were delivering sermons and speeches that had strong undercurrents of anti-Catholicism. Theodore

Parker, for example, was a Unitarian minister and staunch abolitionist who believed that the poverty of Irish Catholic immigrants – or what he called "Celtic pauperism" – was rooted in "three bad things – bad habits, bad religion, and worst of all a bad nature." He insisted that Catholicism was inherently incompatible with prosperity and democratic government, since "the Catholic worshiper is not to think, but to believe and obey."[12]

Parker found it particularly concerning that by the mid-nineteenth century, the vast majority of Catholics in the United States were "of the Celtic stock" rather than "the Teutonic population." The Irish, after all, "never much favored ... individual liberty in religion," while Germans "have the strongest ethnological instinct for personal freedom." The massive increase in Irish Catholic immigration that Parker referred to – 838,000 immigrants to the United States from Ireland, just in the latter half of the 1840s – helps to explain both why Calvinist leaders took aim at Catholics when they believed the religious commitment of America's Protestants was getting soft, and why "soft" Protestants such as Theodore Parker (whose approach to Christianity was so liberal that it made even some Unitarians a little uncomfortable) took aim at Catholics, too.[13]

In the case of the hardcore Calvinists, their renewed antipathy toward Catholicism was rooted in a sense that America had become morally vulnerable. If Unitarianism was a virus that had given America a nasty cold and weakened the immune system of the country's soul, then Catholicism was a cancer – a growing cancer, thanks to immigration – that had the potential to capitalize on that weakness and destroy America's soul entirely.

In the case of Unitarians like Theodore Parker, the problem had more to do with the *kind* of Catholics who were coming to the United States than it did with any sense that Catholicism, per se, presented a particular threat to an already-vulnerable nation. Parker's "ethnological" understanding of the differences between German and Irish Catholics was entirely off-base, and it revealed a substantial degree of ignorance about the theological foundations and economic, historical, and cultural contexts of European Catholicism. Yet, the minister was right to observe that Irish and German Catholics were different from one another in some important ways. Not only that, but Catholics born and raised in Europe also tended to be different from Catholics who'd been living in the United States for multiple generations – as some of the lay-trustee tussles of the late-eighteenth and early-nineteenth centuries revealed.

Solidly "American" Catholics, Bishop John Carroll knew, had a contractual, constitutional, and voluntary understanding of freedom that shaped their approach to their clergy and was "nearly in the same manner as the Congregational Presbyterians." In contrast, European Catholics tended to be less "republican" when it came to their Church. They were more deferential to their priests – and Irish Catholics proved to be the most deferential of all. The respect that the Irish laity had for their clergy was a consequence of the fact that the Catholic Church in Ireland had been one of the few institutions that opposed the oppressive policies of the English government and tried to make the lives of Irish peasants better.[14]

The Irish were not the first immigrants to cause a noticeable uptick in America's Catholic population, even if they were the Catholics who most concerned Theodore Parker. The Germans came first, starting in the 1820s, and before that, even, in 1803, America's Catholic population grew by nearly 250 percent – basically overnight – thanks to the Louisiana Purchase, which added around 75,000 Catholics to the American population with the stroke of a pen.[15]

The Germans who came to America were fleeing religious and political violence in Europe, and their ranks were made up of Protestants and Catholics alike. Much like the Syrian refugees who are fleeing religious and political violence in the Middle East today, a sizable number of these immigrants were fairly well-off, financially.[16] That's not to say that there were no poor people among the German immigrants who fled to the United States in the nineteenth century (nor is it to suggest that there is no poverty among the Syrian refugees in modern-day Europe). But many of the Germans who arrived in Philadelphia and New York in the 1820s and 1830s did have financial resources; they simply didn't have the kind of peace and stability in their home provinces that would have allowed them to safely enjoy those resources. And because they were not destitute, then, when they arrived in the ports of the eastern United States, many of these German refugees were able to afford to continue traveling west, on to small but developing cities such as Cleveland, which was founded in 1814; Chicago, which was founded in 1833; and Cincinnati, which was settled in 1788, but didn't really begin to grow until after the completion of the Erie Canal in 1824.[17]

Such was not the case with the Irish, who were already poorer than the German immigrants they joined in the United States, in smaller numbers, in the 1820s and 1830s, and who became increasingly poor – and increasingly Catholic – as their numbers grew in the 1840s. The Irish were fleeing violence *and* poverty. The English government had been working to oppress and control Irish Catholics for more than 200 years by the time the infamous "potato blight" made its presence known on the Emerald Isle in the late 1830s. *Phytophthora infestans* was a fungus-like organism that destroyed potato crops all over Europe in the mid-nineteenth century; the effects of this blight, however, were more devastating in Ireland than they were anywhere else, because English policies and practices in the country had forced the Irish people to rely almost exclusively upon potatoes for their sustenance.

The Irish had this "potato dependency" because the Protestant landlords the British government had placed in the country in the seventeenth century gave their tenants very little land on which to grow crops for their own use.[†] The land that Catholic tenants had was often riddled with stones, since the Irish landscape was (and still is) very rocky, and the first stones that tenants were required to remove on any given day needed to come from the fields that their landlords were using to grow wheat and flax for export. Under such circumstances, Catholics had little time or energy to clear their own plots of rocks – but the nice thing about the potato plant was that it grew well in rocky soil. One plant also yielded a large number of potatoes, making it a good crop for hungry families with tiny gardens.[18]

The estimated 1.5 million people who migrated to the United States from Ireland between 1845 and 1855 were absolutely destitute when they arrived. They'd been able to afford the journey to North America only because the British government helped to finance their trips. Parliament provided subsidies to Samuel Cunard's fleet of North Atlantic steamships because the MPs saw the famine as an opportunity to replace Ireland's inefficient, pre-modern agricultural system with a mechanized one that didn't require as many farmworkers. Under Parliament's famine policies, Ireland's starving Catholics had two choices: they could use the subsidies to leave their country – or they could stay in Ireland and die.[19]

Irish observers understood that the people leaving the country in the 1840s were different from the men and women who'd left even just one decade earlier. "The emigrants this year are not like those of former ones," a reader of the *Cork Examiner* noted in 1847. "They are now actually

---

[†] Irish custom tended to exacerbate this problem. Irish fathers did not practice primogeniture, preferring to distribute their land equally to all of their male descendants, rather than just their oldest sons. This practice, while probably well-intentioned, made already small plots even smaller with each successive generation.

running away from fever, disease, and hunger, with money scarcely sufficient to pay passage for and find food for the voyage."[20]

These emigrants also had "money scarcely sufficient" to pay for their upkeep once they arrived in the United States. They came at a rate of nearly 200,000 per year by the late 1840s, up from just 6,000 per year in the early 1820s, and they settled in dirty and overcrowded neighborhoods in the cities where they first touched American soil. Unlike the Germans, they couldn't afford to continue traveling west.[21]

By 1850, Irish immigrants made up nearly a quarter of all of the inhabitants in Boston, New York, Philadelphia, and Baltimore.[22] They turned for help to their new parish priests, exhibiting a reluctance to question those priests the way their American-born co-religionists did and replicating some of the habits of clerical deference that they had adopted in Ireland. They turned, as well, to the networks of ethnic gangsters and corrupt politicians that sprang up in the mid-nineteenth century to meet the needs (and take advantage) of an extraordinarily poor agricultural population that was ill-equipped to navigate the waters of modern urban life. In so doing, these Irish Catholic immigrants unwittingly revived and fed long-standing Protestant fears about the connections between Catholicism and poverty, ignorance, dependence, and corruption.

These fears, then, were inflamed by orthodox Protestant leaders who believed their status in American society was declining and worried that the cultural changes their still-young country was experiencing threatened the success of American democracy. They were inflamed, as well, by a burgeoning publishing industry that understood the economic potential of any kind of fear. And, finally, they were stoked by a handful of liberal Protestant leaders who weren't threatened by change, per se – indeed, they *wanted* their country's cultural values to change, particularly when it came to issues such as slavery – but who saw Catholic immigration as a mechanism by which oppressive "Old World" values could be exported to the New World, undermining their efforts to advance modern understandings of individual freedom on the political landscape.

UNITARIANS REACT TO THE CONVENT BURNING

Many of New England's more "refined" citizens were embarrassed by the burning of the Ursuline convent in Charlestown, Massachusetts. Caleb Stetson, for instance, a Unitarian minister whose friends included Ralph Waldo Emerson and Bronson Alcott (Louisa May's father), passionately condemned the riot in a sermon he delivered at his church in nearby

Medford about a week after the event. "We are amazed at the delusion, as well as the wickedness of our fellow-citizens," Stetson exclaimed from the pulpit, before going on to announce that "if an exasperated mob is allowed to supersede the laws . . . [and] if unpopular persons or establishments may be destroyed without trial, or jury, or judge, there is an end of our civil and religious freedom."[23]

George Ticknor Curtis, a prominent patent attorney in Boston, agreed with Stetson. Curtis' clients included Cyrus McCormick, inventor of the mechanical reaper; Charles Goodyear, whose vulcanization of rubber led to the creation of our modern-day tires; and Samuel F.B. Morse, the inventor of the telegraph, who had imbibed much of the antipathy toward Catholicism that his father, Jedidiah, often expressed. Morse published several books and pamphlets in the 1830s and 1840s about the "foreign conspiracy" that Catholic immigrants were supposedly hatching in the United States.[24]

Curtis shared his paranoid client's sense that the Catholic Church had gotten it wrong when it came to God's wishes for humanity, stipulating in his own account of the Ursuline convent burning that "with Catholicism, theologically . . . I have not the smallest sympathy" and stating that he was "perfectly willing that they, whose vocation it is to carry on religious controversies, should do whatever battle they please upon that ancient church." He drew the line at harassment and property damage, however. Those who battled Catholicism "ought not to drive [that church's] members beyond the pale of such civil rights, privileges, and equalities as belong to all of us," Curtis insisted. The Harvard-educated attorney believed that "public prejudice against the Roman Catholics" in America "had risen to an extravagant point" and that "the passion that animated the mob [in Charlestown] was religious hatred." If the school being run by the Ursulines "had been a Protestant institution," Curtis was convinced, "no amount of false rumors would have excited a mob to destroy it."[25]

A special committee that Charlestown's mayor convened to investigate the riot concluded that Massachusetts' legislature should compensate both the Diocese of Boston and the students who'd attended the Ursulines' school for the $90,000 in property damage that they'd suffered.[‡] "If property may be thus sacrificed without the possibility of redress," Harrison Gray Otis wrote on behalf of the committee, "who among us is safe?" To think that "the sufferers are entitled to no legal redress from the public for this outrage against their persons and

---

[‡] Adjusting for inflation and using a consumer price index as the gauge, the estimated value of the damage in 2015 dollars was $2,133,000.

destruction of their property is an event of fearful import as well as of the profoundest shame and humiliation."[26]

Otis' uncle, James, had been a leader of the independence movement in Massachusetts, and his aunt, Mercy Otis Warren, wrote one of the first histories of the American Revolution. The Otis family, in other words, was well-known and influential in New England, and Harrison himself had represented Massachusetts in Congress and served as Boston's mayor before the riot. Nevertheless, he was unable to convince the state legislature to compensate the diocese or the students. Unitarians like Otis were prominent in Massachusetts, but they were by no means a majority. Most of the state's lawmakers felt no particular obligation to the Ursuline nuns – who, after all, were just intruders upon the state. The lawmakers seemed, in fact, to agree with the editor of a popular, anti-Catholic newspaper in New York that "any man who ... would vote for the measure, which would rob the treasury of the descendants of the Puritans to build Ursuline Nunneries ... must be a raving lunatic."[27]

Liberal Protestants like Harrison Otis had no particular love or sympathy for the Catholic Church, but they were committed to the rule of law and worried about the precedent that might be set if the nuns and students who'd had their property destroyed were not reimbursed. They believed that the state had the obligation to make the reimbursement because society as a whole bore some responsibility for the riot; the laborers from the Charlestown brickyards who'd burned the Ursuline school had been ginned up by Orthodox Calvinists, and no one with a more "liberal" approach to Protestantism had stepped in to quell the anger. Caleb Steson blamed Lyman Beecher in particular; Beecher had delivered a vehemently anti-Catholic sermon at three different churches in Boston the day before the riot, though he loudly condemned the violence after the damage was done.[28]

The anti-Catholic fears that Beecher expressed in his sermon were numerous – and the environment he delivered them in was already incendiary, since state lawmakers had reluctantly voted to disestablish the Congregational Church in Massachusetts just a few months earlier. High on Beecher's list of concerns was the proliferation of what he called "gratuitous schools," by which he meant Catholic schools like the one the Ursulines operated in Charlestown. Beecher implied that Protestant children were being indoctrinated at these facilities; this allegation, then – when combined with the general belief, already salient in the city, that the Ursuline nuns were doing something unethical behind the closed doors of their convent – resulted in the riot.[29]

THE BIBLE(S) AND THE SCHOOLS

The students who lost their belongings in the convent fire were not all Catholic. Several wealthy and liberal-minded Protestant families actually sent their daughters to the Ursulines' school because they wanted the girls exposed to the classical curriculum – Logic, Chemistry, Philosophy, Arithmetic, Botony, and History – that the Ursuline order had been famous for since the sixteenth century. It didn't bother these families that the curriculum had been designed by Catholics; it also didn't bother them that an Ursuline education cost four times more than an education at a typical New England academy (and was, therefore, something far beyond what any bricklayer from Charlestown could ever hope to afford).[30]

Lyman Beecher's fears about indoctrination aside, there is no evidence that the Ursuline nuns ever tried to convert any of the Protestant girls who attended their school. Indeed, the nuns allowed their students to bring Protestant bibles to the school's daily worship services and to read those bibles while Catholic exercises were taking place, a practice that at least two parents wrote to the nuns about, expressing their gratitude. This policy of allowing Protestant students to read Protestant bibles was also adopted by administrators at several other Catholic boarding schools on the east coast.[31]

A Protestant bible was an un-annotated rendering of Christianity's sacred text. In all likelihood, the Protestant girls who attended the Ursuline school brought the King James Bible with them to their religious services; this English translation of the Hebrew, Aramaic, and Greek versions of the Old and New Testaments was commissioned by King James I in 1604 and completed in 1611. Following James' orders, the translators did not include any pictures or marginal notes with their translations, as such additions were seen by the Church of England's Archbishop of Canterbury as "instructional" – and therefore dangerously papist.[32]

The Vatican did not endorse or sanction the King James Bible. The only bible that English-speaking Catholics were supposed to read was the Douay-Rheims Bible, which was a sixteenth-century English translation of a fourth-century Latin translation that St. Jerome had completed, drawing upon Hebrew, Aramaic, Greek, and Latin sources. The Douay-Rheims Bible was extensively annotated, with a preface that provided insight into the translation process and marginal notes that provided theological and historical context.[33] It was, in many respects, an embodiment of the Catholic understanding of Scripture as something far too complex for any one person to fully access entirely on his or her own.

The issue of which bible was an appropriate one for America's future citizens to be reading became an increasingly contentious issue in the nineteenth century, particularly after the so-called "common school movement" took off in the 1830s. Massachusetts had a long tradition of legally requiring municipal authorities to fund grammar schools, dating back to the founding of the Boston Latin School in 1635 and the passage of the now-famous "Old Deluder Satan Act" in 1647, which required every town having more than fifty families in it to hire a teacher, since illiteracy was "one chief project" of God's most notorious and fallen angel.[34] Most colonies, however – even ones such as Virginia, which had an established church – considered education to be a private matter, the responsibility of parents rather than the government or a state-supported church.

This attitude slowly began to change in some states after the American Revolution, largely through the efforts of people like Thomas Jefferson and Benjamin Rush. Jefferson believed that "if a nation expects to be ignorant and free in a state of civilization, it expects what never was and never will be." Rush suggested that taxpayers – even ones without children – should want to finance public education, since "fewer pillories and whipping posts and smaller jails, with their usual expenses and taxes, will be necessary when our youth are more properly educated than at present."[35]

In spite of these early efforts, the drive to develop a pervasive network of public schools throughout the country was sporadic at first. It wasn't until the late 1830s that state lawmakers finally began to embrace the idea of using tax money to finance grammar and secondary schools for all of the children in their states. Although many factors contributed to this change in attitude – among them, the rise of the factory labor system and the increased mobility made possible by the railroads – the most important factor was the social and cultural upheaval brought about by the massive increase in Catholic immigration.[36]

"Those now pouring in upon us ... are wholly of another kind in morals and intellect," a report commissioned by the Massachusetts state senate observed as thousands of starving Irish Catholic families started arriving in Boston Harbor. The immigrants who'd arrived in Massachusetts from Germany – or even Ireland – just ten years earlier had had some skills, and they'd arrived in the state with the financial means to take care of themselves. These new immigrants, however, were different. Lawmakers worried that "through ignorance and degradation from systematic oppression of bad rulers at home," they would "neither add to the intelligence nor the wealth of this comparatively new country."[37] To avert such a crisis, the lawmakers committed themselves to the creation of a state-wide public education system that would be available to everyone. They established the nation's first state Board of Education in 1837 and appointed one of their own, Horace Mann, to be its head.

Mann believed that education was "the great equalizer of the conditions of men" and "the balance wheel of the social machinery." He wanted to prepare immigrant and native-born children of all faiths and social classes to assume the responsibilities of citizenship; for that reason, he required that churches in the state give up the control that many of them had assumed over the publicly funded schools that already existed in Massachusetts. Mann wanted the curriculum in all of the state's public schools to be "non-sectarian." That did not mean, however, that he wanted the curriculum to be devoid of religion.

By "non-sectarian," Mann meant only that the books being used by schoolchildren in his state should be free of any references to the pedantic bits of theology that separated one Christian denomination from another. The educational reformer did not intend for religion or God to be kept out of the classroom, and indeed he chafed at any insinuation that God-free schools were his goal. "The whole influence of the Board of Education, from the day of its organization to the present time," he angrily wrote to a critic in 1846, "has been to promote and encourage, and, whenever they have had any power ... to *direct* the daily use of the Bible in schools." The bible Horace Mann meant, of course, was the only translation considered legitimate by Orthodox and liberal Protestants alike. That translation was the King James Bible.[38]

Mann's commitment to public schools was shared by educational reformers in other states – among them, Henry Barnard in Connecticut, William Seward in New York, John Pierce in Michigan, and Lyman Beecher's son-in-law, Calvin Stowe, in Ohio. In Pennsylvania, lawmakers passed the Common School Act in 1834 after the Quaker activist Robert Vaux formed the Pennsylvania Society for the Promotion of Public Schools. That group pushed officials in the state to replace Pennsylvania's shoddy collection of "pauper schools" with a vibrant and dynamic system of publicly funded schools that parents of all social classes would want their children to attend. By 1836, more than 17,000 children were enrolled in Philadelphia's public schools – and all of them were required to read the King James Bible.[39]

THE PHILADELPHIA BIBLE RIOTS

In November of 1842, Philadelphia's Catholic bishop, Francis Kenrick, wrote to the Board of Controllers who oversaw Pennsylvania's public schools and asked that Catholic children be allowed to read the Douay-Rheims Bible instead of the King James Bible whenever they were in school. He also asked that Catholic children be excused from any classes where the religious instruction involved prayers, the singing of hymns, or oral recitations of passages from the King James Bible. The Controllers reluctantly agreed to his request, instructing administrators in all of the state's schools to allow children to bring their own versions of the bible to class with them and to honor any parental requests that children be exempted from religious instruction.[40]

Not long after the Board honored Kenrick's request, Hugh Clark, a native-born Catholic and School Director in the Kensington neighborhood of Philadelphia, visited one of the schools in his district. There he observed several Catholic girls leave their classroom after their principal announced she would be reading to the students from a King James Bible. Distressed by the situation and seeing it as needlessly discriminatory, Clark later remarked to a Protestant colleague that "if the Bible caused such confusion," perhaps it "ought not to be read" in the public schools. Before long, rumors were circulating that Clark had "peremptorily commanded" the principal to stop reading from the bible and that he'd threatened to demote her if she didn't follow his orders.[41]

Philadelphia was a tinder box by the mid-1840s. Just one month before Hugh Clarke made his remarks, a prominent publisher in the city had released a book that accused Catholic priests (erroneously) of burning Protestant bibles. Wages were extremely low – driven down by the increased labor supply that immigrants provided – and several local politicians had leveraged the growing resentment against immigrants to get themselves elected. One of the most virulently anti-Catholic social groups in the country had also been founded in Philadelphia one year earlier, in 1842. The American Protestant Association (APA) regularly hosted public lectures that called for the country's naturalization laws to be changed. The Association's speakers claimed that Catholic immigrants were being sent to the United States by the pope so that they could vote for corrupt politicians who would help the pope take over the United States. Conveniently, these speakers also claimed that early Christian theologians had predicted that the Anti-Christ, when he came to Earth, would be supported by a group of men who were celibate and abstained from eating meat on Fridays.[42]

The APA called for Hugh Clark's resignation, insisting that if he did not resign, it would "put us on a level with the age before the Reformation." On the night of May 3, 1844, more than a dozen Irish immigrants showed up at an APA meeting and attacked the group's speakers before tearing down the platform the speakers had been using. Four days later, someone set fire to thirty houses in Kensington that were occupied by Irish Catholic families.[43]

According to one contemporary Protestant observer, Kensington was "the least religious section of the city," and most of the rioters, whether they were Protestant or Catholic, "would not have known the difference between the Protestant and Catholic Bible if it had been placed in their hands." None of that mattered, however, once the violence started. The Kensington Bible Riots lasted for a week, with the violence escalating on both sides, as immigrant Catholics shot at native-born Protestants and native-born Protestants ransacked and burned Catholic churches and seminaries. In July, then, similar riots broke out in the nearby neighborhood of Southwark. By the time the fighting was over, at least fourteen people were dead and the estimated property damage amounted to $150,000 – or $3,800,000, in 2015 terms.[44]

Following the riots, Catholic bishops in the United States abandoned any hope that the public school system would be able to offer Catholic children a proper education. They focused instead on the creation of a vibrant and well-funded system of Catholic schools, ultimately decreeing that "no parish is complete till it has schools adequate to the needs of its children." Priests across the country started regularly instructing Catholic parents to "send their children to Catholic schools whenever practicable" and to avoid any situation where "Protestants, Jews, and Infidels meet promiscuously." "Watchful Catholic parents," the bishop of Rochester, New York, warned, "would never allow their children to associate with such [people] ... justly fearing contamination."[45]

Philadelphia was the city where the school issue deteriorated into the worst violence, but other cities also saw fights break out between Protestants and Catholics over the question of religion's place in the public schools. One city that saw such fighting was New York, where the newly appointed Catholic bishop, John Hughes, quickly gained a reputation among lawmakers for tolerating no encroachment on the civil rights of the Catholic laity. Hughes placed armed guards in front of every Catholic church in New York after he learned of the riots in Philadelphia – and then rather famously (though perhaps apocryphally) warned the city's mayor that if anyone tried to burn down one of his churches, New York would "become a second Moscow," a then-obvious reference to the 'scorched-earth' tactic utilized by the Russians during Napoleon's invasion of their country thirty years earlier.[46]

Bishop Hughes had been battling with school officials in Albany and New York City even before the riots broke out in Philadelphia, publicly debating ministers about the Protestant religious content in the curricula of the public schools and offering a $1,000 reward to anyone who could prove that the Douay-Rheims Bible sanctioned the burning of heretics, as Methodists in New York contended. Hughes also tried to secure government funding for all Catholic schools in the state, joining forces with several Jewish leaders in New York who were equally unhappy with the religious tone of the instruction in the city's public schools. The Catholic–Jewish coalition failed to secure any funding from the state, but they did manage to convince the legislature to pass a law banning all forms of religious instruction from the public schools in New York state.[47]

THE IMPACT OF THE PUBLISHING INDUSTRY

The anti-Catholic book that helped to spark the Philadelphia Bible Riots was called *The Burning of the Bibles,* and it was printed and distributed in 1843 by a prominent Philadelphia publisher named Nathan Moore.[48] The book was part of the growing supply of anti-Catholic literature that Americans had at their fingertips, particularly after 1820, as publishers like Moore slowly began to re-discover the economic potential of anti-popery.

The decades that followed the conclusion of the American Revolution saw an explosion of publishing in the United States. From 1790 to 1835, the population of the country quadrupled, while the number of newspapers increased by a factor of twelve, from 106 to 1,258. European observers like Harriet Martineau and Alexis de Tocqueville marveled at the sheer number of newspapers in America – even as they were occasionally horrified by the inflammatory rumor and innuendo that those newspapers published. Tocqueville believed that the reason America had so many newspapers was that the country had adopted an extraordinarily individualistic (dare we say "Protestant"?) understanding of freedom – and that such fierce individualism could stymie any effort to accomplish big, collective projects "unless you can persuade every man whose help you require that his private interest obliges him voluntarily to unite his exertions to the exertions of all the others." "Nothing but a newspaper,"

Tocqueville noted in 1835, "can drop the same thought into a thousand minds at the same moment."[49]

As Tocqueville's observations implied, the impulse behind much of the growth in early America's print culture was political. Newspapers like the *Boston Democrat* (1808) and the *Richmond Whig and Public Advertiser* (1822) were founded and operated unabashedly by men who had political agendas. They knew how they wanted their country or state to be a run and what they wanted their lawmakers to do. And a newspaper, they believed, was a good way to "drop the same thought" into the minds of other voters.[50]

Politics, however, was not the only source feeding America's publishing industry. In a country that had eschewed religious establishments and embraced religious freedom, Protestant ministers understood that they needed to market their ideas if they were going to get people into the pews. Much like the leaders of America's political parties, therefore, they turned to the media for help, eventually touching off a massive religious revival in the United States known today as the "Second Great Awakening."

Protestant leaders – both those who subscribed to the kind of Calvinist Orthodoxy that was becoming less popular in the United States, and those who embraced a "softer" approach to Protestantism that didn't necessarily amount to Unitarianism – formed bible societies, tract societies, and Sunday school unions that hired printers to produce thousands of pamphlets featuring hymns, words of wisdom from the bible, and personal stories of conversion. They also founded their own newspapers, starting with the *Boston Recorder*, which was launched in 1816 by leaders of the Presbyterian Church in that city. Other religious groups soon followed the Presbyterians' lead. Baptists started publishing the *Christian Watchman* in Boston in 1819, and Samuel F.B. Morse's Congregational brothers, Sydney and Richard, started publishing the *New York Observer* in 1823.[51]

By 1827, more than thirty Protestant newspapers were being published in the United States – and all of them had weekly sections that were devoted to fighting the idolatry, cruelty, and blasphemy of the Church of Rome. "Not only do they assail us and our institutions ... misrepresent our tenets, [and] vilify our practices," America's bishops wrote to the Catholic laity about these Protestant newspapers in 1829, "but they have even denounced you and us as enemies to the liberties of the republic."[52]

Some Catholic bishops attempted to fight fire with fire. Bishop John England of Charleston, for instance, started his own newspaper in 1822, the *United States Catholic Miscellany*. "Almost every division of Christians here has its peculiar publication, for the exposition of its doctrines," the bishop explained in the *Miscellany*'s inaugural edition. Many of these publications, however, had done much more than simply articulate the basic tenets of their sponsoring denominations; they'd published articles and editorials that perpetuated Protestant misperceptions about the Catholic faith. It was "only natural," therefore, that the nation's growing Catholic population "should be desirous of having a similar publication" that would correct these misperceptions and allow "those persons who have been misled into erroneous opinions of the principles of their [Catholic] neighbors . . . to judge correctly of their tenets, and to form rational opinions of their practices."

England intended for his paper to be more than just a diocesan newsletter. He wanted Catholics up and down the eastern seaboard –"from Maine to Florida," in his words – to read the paper and use it to formulate an understanding of the cultural and political issues that had implications for the Catholic Church in the United States. As his note to the paper's readers in the *Miscellany*'s inaugural edition made clear, however, Charleston's Irish-born bishop hoped his publication would be read by Protestants, as well.[53]

England's newspaper *was* read by many Protestants – in the South, where anti-Catholicism was not nearly as vitriolic or pervasive as it was in the North, thanks in no small part to the fact that the social hierarchy in the region had been determined long before Irish Catholic immigrants started arriving in the United States. That hierarchy made it clear that whites could never be at the bottom, not even if they were immigrant Catholics.[54] In states like Pennsylvania, New York, and Massachusetts, however, the publishing landscape was too riddled with anti-Catholic literature for John England's newspaper to have much impact.

Newspapers were only part of the problem for Catholics in the North. There was also the fact that nineteenth-century publishers such as Nathan Moore had re-discovered a truth that was well-known in the seventeenth and eighteenth centuries, but had been forgotten during the brief period of religious tolerance that followed the American Revolution. That truth, of course, was that people would pay good money to read salacious stories about secretive nuns and lying priests who used the veil of celibacy to shroud their promiscuity. This interest in the hypocrisy of the Catholic clergy was what had made *The French Convert* such a publishing success when it first came out in 1696, and this same interest made *Six Months in a Convent*, published in Boston in 1835, and *Awful Disclosures of the Hôtel Dieu Nunnery of Montreal*, published in New York in 1836, literary sensations.

Six Months in a Convent purported to tell the true story of Rebecca
Reed, a young, Episcopalian woman from Boston who briefly attended the
school the Ursulines ran in Charlestown as a charity case from 1831 to
1832. Reed's story was completely made up, although Reed herself did
actually exist. The story was not formally released by its publisher until
after the Ursuline convent had been burned. Versions of it were available,
however, to ministers and newspaper editors in the area for several
months before the riot happened – and because Reed claimed in her
story to have been imprisoned by the Ursulines after she decided she no
longer wanted to attend the school, her story colored the way people in
Boston interpreted the story of Sister Mary St. John, a young nun who
truly did leave the Ursuline convent on the night of July 28, 1834, but then
returned to the facility the following day.

It's not clear why Sr. Mary (who had been born Elizabeth Harrison in
Cambridge, Massachusetts) left the school. Following the riot, the convent's Mother Superior suggested that the young woman may have been
feeling a little overworked, noting that such complaints were not uncommon among the newer nuns and that Sr. Mary had been acting "queerly"
for several days before she left. In any event, Elizabeth Harrison seems to
have gone back to the convent willingly, as evidenced by a conversation
she had with her brother when he visited her at the school a week and a
half after she had returned.

Her brother's account of that conversation was published in the *Boston
Morning Post* on August 11, 1834. By that point, however, several newspapers in the area had already reprinted a story that another paper, the
Mercantile Journal, had run a few days earlier, on August 8; that story
claimed that Harrison's friends had recently "called for her" at the convent, "but she was not found, and much alarm is excited in consequence."
The story from the *Mercantile Journal* quickly became the popular narrative in Boston. When it was combined with Lyman Beecher's fulminations
against Catholic schools, the result was a riot.[55]

The first printing of Rebecca Reed's story sold out in just two hours. By
the end of the first month, more than 200,000 copies of the novel had been
sold, and the book threatened to break records in England and the United
States.[56] As popular as *Six Months in a Convent* was, however, its reception paled in comparison to that of *Awful Disclosures*, which was published by a Canadian woman named Maria Monk the following year.

Monk claimed to be a Protestant who entered a convent in Montreal in
order to be educated. She eventually converted to Catholicism and took
the veil, but then fled not long after she learned that the nuns were

MOTHER ABBESS STRANGLING THE INFANT.—Part II, p. 62.

FIGURE 5.1 Maria Monk's allegations about the Hôtel Dieu Nunnery were copied by other authors. William Hogan's *Popery, As it Is and As it Was* claimed in 1845 that "if the nunneries in the United States were dug open, hundreds of the bodies of strangled infants, the offspring of nuns and Popish priests, may be found in them." Credit: American Antiquarian Society.

expected "to live in the practice of criminal intercourse" with the priests who said Mass in the convent. These priests, Monk claimed she was instructed, were to "be considered our saviors, as without their services we could not obtain the pardon of sin, and must go to hell."[57]

Monk told stories of pregnant nuns who baptized their babies immediately after giving birth to them and then strangled them, throwing the bodies into a lime pit that the nuns kept in the basement for that very purpose (Figure 5.1). These women, Monk claimed, comforted themselves with the knowledge that the babies' souls would go straight to heaven, since the baptism had purified them, and they'd been "'sent out of the world before they had time to do anything wrong.'"[58]

It was when she herself became pregnant that Monk knew she had to leave. Her story nicely explained the birth of her illegitimate son in New York in August of 1835, though the story was quickly undermined by a sworn affidavit that her mother, Isabella Mills, released in October of that same year. Mills claimed that Monk had never actually entered the convent in Montreal – and that she'd been prone to melancholy and "deranged in the head" ever since "about the age of seven years, [when] she broke a slate pencil in her head." Mills testified that she had tried at one point to get Monk admitted to a nunnery, "even though ... I was a Protestant and did not like the Catholic religion." Monk, she stated, was a wild and unruly child, and Mills believed the convent would be able to provide her daughter with some necessary discipline, since "the nuns of Montreal" (even though she did not like their faith) were "the most pious and charitable persons I ever knew." Mills' efforts, however, were "without success."[59]

In spite of the compelling reasons to doubt Maria Monk's story – reasons that were made more compelling in 1838, when she gave birth to a second illegitimate son, this time having clearly spent no time in a nunnery – *Awful Disclosures* was a huge success, selling more copies than any other book in American history until the publication of *Uncle Tom's Cabin* in 1850.[60] Mira Sharpless Townsend, a prominent Quaker philanthropist from Philadelphia, was so struck by the book that in 1839, when she and her husband visited Niagara Falls, she insisted that they continue on to Montreal, so that she could visit the Hôtel Dieu nunnery that Monk claimed to have spent time in. The nuns, alas, did not open their doors to Townsend. "We were told that since [Monk's] disclosures, they keep themselves much secluded," the Quaker wrote in her diary, expressing some sympathy for the nuns' reservations. Townsend could not understand, however, why the Ursuline nuns in nearby Trois Rivières – who had trained the first sisters to open a convent in Boston – were similarly unwilling to let her visit their convent. "So much privacy is a bad design," Townsend concluded judgmentally in her diary.[61]

The success of *Awful Disclosures* inspired several printers in Boston and New York to resurrect old, anti-Catholic literature that had been printed in England and Ireland in the eighteenth century, issuing new editions of books such as Anthony Gavin's *The Great Red Dragon; or, the Master-key to Popery*, which was first published in Dublin in 1724. The book's American publisher, Samuel Jones, marketed Gavin's story as a "new publication" that was "just published," even though the story was more than one hundred years old by the time Jones discovered it. A reviewer for the *Boston Bee* concluded that "this book comes at a good time. Everyone should read it. Historically, it is of the greatest interest. It gives much light on a very dark subject."[62]

CHAPTER CONCLUSION

Horace Mann was a Unitarian who explicitly rejected the fire-and-brimstone approach to salvation that was advocated by the orthodox Calvinists who'd raised him.[63] When he joined with Massachusetts' lawmakers in expressing concern about Boston's immigrants, therefore, worrying that these immigrants would not contribute to the "intellect" or "wealth" of the United States, Mann was not expressing the status anxiety that animated hardcore Calvinists like Lyman Beecher, who believed that America's commitment to God was growing soft. Instead, Horace Mann was expressing a fundamental belief about Catholicism and the nature of American freedom.

Catholics, he and other liberal thinkers like him deeply believed, had been ill-prepared by their faith to assume the responsibilities of citizenship in American society. Irish immigrants were little better than slaves in the estimation of reformers such as Mann. They were utterly incapable of the kind of autonomous thought that American democracy required. Certainly the oppressive policies of the British government had played a role in making the Irish this way – but so, too, had the Catholic Church. And while the iron fist of Britain had not followed these immigrants to America, the iron fist of the pope had.

Orthodox Calvinists – and even some Protestants who were less hardcore – believed that the pope had sent the Irish to America so that they could vote for corrupt politicians who would then allow the Vatican to take over the country. More liberal-minded Protestants rarely expressed their fears in such paranoid terms, but they, too, worried that Catholics would vote the way their priests told them to vote, putting little-to-no independent thought into the process. The reason this was problematic was that most liberal Protestants desperately wanted the United States to outlaw slavery, and America's Catholic bishops had consistently failed to condemn the institution. Indeed, when Pope Gregory XVI criticized slavery in 1839, America's bishops had quickly scrambled to explain to the country's politicians that the slavery the pope was condemning was not the kind of slavery that existed in the United States.

Under such circumstances, liberal reformers felt that they had just two options for saving the nation: They could change the country's immigration laws so that Catholics would not be allowed to come to the United States – or not be allowed to become voting citizens if they did; or they could properly educate the children of immigrants, making those children more like Protestants. The latter option was the one adopted by reformers such as Horace Mann at first. After the Philadelphia Bible Riots of 1844, however, it seemed unlikely that reformers were going to be able to utilize Mann's tactic, since Catholic priests were insisting that Catholic parents had to send their children to Catholic schools. And so liberal Protestants turned, increasingly, to the tactic of immigration reform.

NOTES

1. Harriet Martineau, *Society in America* (New York, 1837), 2:343; Thomas Jefferson, "First Inaugural Address, March 4th, 1808," *The Avalon Project*, Yale University, Lilian Goldman Law Library, accessed on March 20, 2016: http://avalon.law.yale.edu/19th_century/jefinau1.asp.
2. Martineau, Society in America, 2:222.
3. John Carroll to John Hancock, August 28, 1791, in Peter Guilday, *The Life and Times of John Carroll, Archbishop of Baltimore, 1735–1815* (New York, 1922), 425–426; Martineau, *Society in America*, 2:323.
4. Michael Lipka and Benjamin Wormald, "How Religious Is Your State?" *Pew Research Center Fact Tank: News in the Numbers*, February 29, 2016, accessed on April 4, 2016: www.pewresearch.org/fact-tank/2016/02/29/how-religious-is-your-state/?state=alabama.
5. Steven K. Green, *The Second Disestablishment: Church and State in Nineteenth-Century America* (New York, 2010), 120–121; Wesley W. Horton, *The Connecticut State Constitution: A Reference Guide* (Westport, CT, 1993), 142.
6. Green, The Second Disestablishment; Carl H. Esbeck, "Dissent and Disestablishment: The Church-State Settlement in the Early American Republic," *Brigham Young University Law Review*, 4 (2004), 1458. Ronald P. Formisano, *For the People: American Populist Movements from the Revolution to the 1850s* (Chapel Hill, NC, 2008), 45.
7. Ola Elizabeth Winslow, *Jonathan Edwards, 1703–1758* (New York, 1961), 154–155; George M. Marsden, *A Short Life of Jonathan Edwards* (Grand Rapids, MI, 2008), 48–49.
8. Jonathan Edwards to Benjamin Colman, November 6, 1736, quoted in Leonard I. Sweet, "The Laughter of One: Sweetness and Light in Franklin and Edwards," in *Benjamin Franklin, Jonathan Edwards, and the Representation of American Culture* Barbara B. Oberg and Harry S. Stout, eds. (New York, 1993), 118.
9. Jonathan Elliot, ed. *The Debates in the Several State Conventions on the Adoption of the Federal Constitution* (Washington, DC, 1836), 2:117.
10. Jedidiah Morse, "Review of American Unitarianism," *The Panoplist* (Boston, 1815), 1.
11. Ibid., 7; William E. Channing, "Unitarian Christianity" (1819), in *The Works of William E. Channing, D.D.* (Boston, 1888), 367.
12. Theodore Parker to F.E. Parker, April 15, 1858, in *Life and Correspondence of Theodore Parker*, John Weiss, ed. (New York, 1864), 1:397; Parker, "A Sermon on the Dangers Which Threaten the Rights of Man in America," 1854, in *The Collected Works of Theodore Parker*, Frances Power Cobbe, ed. (London, 1864), 6:127; D.A.E. Harkness, "Irish Emigration," in *International Migrations: Interpretations*, Walter F. Willcox, ed. (Cambridge, MA, 1931), 2:265.
13. Theodore Parker to F.E. Parker, ibid; Harkness, "Irish Emigration," 2:265.
14. "John Carroll's Letter on Lay Trusteeism in New York City," 1786, in *American Catholic History: A Documentary Reader*, Mark Massa and

Catherine Osborne, eds. (New York, 2008), 32; John T. McGreevy, *Catholicism and American Freedom* (New York, 2003), 19–37; John Jordan, "Irish Catholicism," *The Crane Bag* 7 (1983), 106–116.

15. J.F. Regis Canevin, "Loss and Gain in the Catholic Church in the United States (1800–1916), *Catholic Historical Review*, 2:4 (1917), 380.

16. Jess McHugh, "Europe Refugee Crisis Facts: Wealthy, Educated Syrians Risking Lives to Leave War," International Business Times, September 9, 2015.

17. Albert Bernhardt Faust, *The German Element in the United States* (Boston, 1909), 391–468.

18. Susan Campbell Bartaletti, *Black Potatoes: The Story of the Great Irish Famine, 1845–1850* (Boston, 2001), 7; Kerby Miller, *Emigrants and Exiles: Ireland and the Irish Exodus to North America* (New York, 1985), 33, 49–54; 286–291.

19. Oscar Handlin, *Boston's Immigrants: A Study in Acculturation, 1790–1880* (Boston, 1941), 49.

20. The *Cork Examiner* quote is in Handlin, Boston's Immigrants, 51.

21. Miller, *Emigrants and Exiles*, 291–292.

22. Kevin Kenny, "New Directions in Irish-American History," in *New Directions in Irish-American History*, Kenny, ed. (Madison, WI, 2003), 5.

23. Caleb Stetson, *A Discourse on the Duty of Sustaining the Laws, Occasioned by the Burning of the Ursuline Convent* (Boston, 1834), 7; Tiffany K. Wayne, *Encyclopedia of Transcendentalism* (New York, 2006), 266.

24. Samuel F.B. Morse, *Foreign Conspiracy Against the Liberties of the United States* (New York, 1841); Chandler B. Beach, ed. *The New Student's Reference Work for Teachers, Students, and Families* (Chicago, 1914), 1:489.

25. George Ticknor Curtis, *The Rights of Conscience and of Property; Or, the True Issue of the Convent Question* (Boston, 1842), 7–8, 19.

26. Nancy Lusignan Schultz, *Fire and Roses: The Burning of the Charlestown Convent* (Boston, 2000), 201; *Report of the Committee Relating to the Destruction of the Ursuline Convent* (Boston, 1834), 13, 12; Ray Allen Billington, *The Protestant Crusade, 1800–1860* (New York, 1938), 85; "Seven Ways to Compute the Relative Value of a US Dollar Amount, 1774–the Present," *Measuringworth.com*, accessed on May 14, 2016: https://www.measuringworth.com/uscompare/result.php?year_source=1834&amount=100&year_result=2014#.

27. *American Protestant Vindicator*, January 21, 1835; also Billington, The Protestant Crusade, 89.

28. Ray Allen Billington, "The Burning of the Charlestown Convent," *New England Quarterly* 10 (1937), 18–19.

29. Schultz, Fire and Roses, 165–166.

30. Ibid., 14, 80–88; "Ursuline Convent: Mount Benedict, Charlestown, Massachusetts," pamphlet, n.d., The Ursuline Convent, Charlestown, Mass., Collection, *The Catholic University of America Digital Collections, University Libraries*, accessed on April 4, 2016: http://cuislandora.wrlc.org/islandora/object/achc-ursuline%3A771#page/1/mode/1up; B.B. Edwards, "Education and Education Institutions—1832," *Barnard's American Journal of Education* (April, 1877), 6:305.

31. Schultz, *Fire and Roses*, 92–94; Catherine Clinton and Christine Lunardini, *The Columbia Guide to American Women in the Nineteenth Century* (New York, 2000), 45.

32. David Daniell, *The Bible in English: Its History and Influence* (New Haven, 2003), 431, 439, 458, 488.

33. Ibid., 283.

34. Nathaniel B. Shurtleff, ed. *Records of the Governor and the Company of the Massachusetts Bay in New England, 1642–1649* (Boston, 1853), 2:203; William J. Reese, *The Origins of the American High School* (New Haven, 1995), 3.

35. Thomas Jefferson, quoted in Merrill D. Peterson, *Thomas Jefferson and the New Nation* (New York, 1970), 145; Benjamin Rush, A Plan for Establishing Public Schools in Pennsylvania (1786), in Harry G. Good, *Benjamin Rush and His Services to American Education* (Berne, IN, 1918), 218.

36. Reese, *Origins of the American High School*, 2–3, 91, 117.

37. "Extract from an 1848 Report by the Massachusetts State Senate" in Stephen A. Brighton, *Historical Archaeology of the Irish Diaspora: A Transnational Approach* (Knoxville, TN, 2009), 73.

38. Horace Mann, "Twelfth Annual Report to the Board of Education of the State of Massachusetts (1848)," in Lawrence A. Cremin, *The Republic and the School: Horace Mann and the Education of Free Men* (New York, 1957), 86–87; Mann to Matthew Hale Smith, October 19, 1846, in Horace Mann, William Bentley Fowle, and Matthew Hale Smith, *The Bible, the Rod, and Religion in Common Schools* (Boston, 1847), 24; William H. Jeynes, *American Educational History: School. Society, and the Common Good* (Thousand Oaks, CA, 2007), 145–150.

39. Audrey Thompson, "Surrogate Family Values: The Refeminization of Teaching," *Educational Theory* 47 (1997), 315; William W. Cutler, "Public Education: The School District of Philadelphia," The Encyclopedia of Greater Philadelphia, accessed on May 28, 2016: http://philadelphiaencyclopedia.org/archive/public-educationthe-school-district-of-philadelphia/.

40. Elizabeth M. Geffen, "Industrial Development and Social Crisis, 1841–1854," in *Philadelphia: A 300-Year History*, Russell F. Weigley, ed. (New York, 1982), 357; John Back McMaster, *A History of the People of the United States from the Revolution to the Civil War* (New York, 1916), 7:376.

41. McMaster, A History of the People of the United States; Katie Oxx, *The Nativist Movement in America: Religious Conflict in the Nineteenth Century* (New York, 2013), 57.

42. "Oxx, The Nativistist Movement, 57–58." Her work is what directed me to the APA's claim that the Anti-Christ would be supported by men who didn't eat meat on Fridays; it's important, therefore, that I credit her for that.

43. McMaster, *A History of the People of the United States*, 377; Geffen, "Industrial Development and Social Crisis," 357.

44. Geffen, "Industrial Development and Social Crisis"; "Consumer Price Index Estimate (1800–), *Federal Reserve Bank of Minneapolis*, accessed on May 28, 2016: www.minneapolisfed.org/community/teaching-aids/cpi-calculator-information/consumer-price-index-1800.

45. "Pastoral Letter of the Archbishops and Bishops of the United States, Assembled in the Third Plenary Council of Baltimore," in *Memorial Volume: A History of the Third Plenary Council of Baltimore* (Baltimore, 1884), 17; "Editorial Notes – The German Catholic Benevolent Union," in *The Catholic Record: A Miscellany of Catholic Knowledge and General Literature* (Philadelphia, 1875), 124; Bishop Bernard McQuaid to Pope Leo XIII, January 16, 1893, in Frederick J. Zwierlein, "Bishop McQuaid of Rochester," *Catholic Historical Review* 5 (1920), 340–341.

46. Timothy L. Hall, *American Religious Leaders* (New York, 2003), 177; David A. Wilson, *Thomas D'Arcy McGee: Passion, Reason, and Politics, 1825–1857* (Montreal, 2008), 79.

47. Billington, *Protestant Crusade*, 160, n. 27; William J. Stern, "How Dagger John Saved New York's Irish," Wall Street Journal, March 17, 1997.

48. John Dowling, *The Burning of the Bibles: Defence of the Protestant Version of the Scriptures Against the Attacks of Popish Apologists for the Champlain Bible Burners* (Philadelphia, 1843).

49. Paul Starr, *The Creation of the Media: Political Origins of Modern Communications* (New York, 2004), 86; Alexis de Tocqueville, *Democracy in America*, Henry Reeve, trans. (New York, 1899), 2:119.

50. Jeffrey L. Pasley, *The Tyranny of Printers: Newspaper Politics in the Early Republic* (Charlottesville, VA, 2001), 1–23.

51. Starr, *Creation of the Media*, 128–129; Billington, *Protestant Crusade*, 43.

52. The First Provincial Council of Baltimore, 1829, quoted in Billington, *Protestant Crusade*, 44.

53. *United States Catholic Miscellany*, June 5, 1822.

54. Andrew H.M. Stern, *Southern Crucifix, Southern Cross: Catholic-Protestant Relations in the Old South* (Tuscaloosa, AL, 2012).

55. Billington, *Protestant Crusade*, 82, n. 104, 72, 74–75.

56. Ibid., 90.

57. Maria Monk, *Awful Disclosures of the Hôtel Dieu Nunnery in Montreal*, 3rd edn. (New York, 1855), 37.

58. Ibid., 11, 88.

59. "Appendix," in ibid., 238.

60. Billington, *Protestant Crusade*, 108.

61. Quoted in Kara Maureen French, "The Politics of Sexual Restraint: Debates Over Chastity in America, 1780-1860," PhD dissertation, University of Michigan (2013), 220. Townsend's library is located in the Schlesinger Library at Harvard University.

62. *Christian Inquirer*, September 2, 1854; Joan R. Gunderson, "Anthony Gavin's A Master-Key to Popery: A Virginia Parson's Best Seller," *Virginia Magazine of History and Biography* 82 (1974), 39–46.

63. Horace Mann to Austin Craig, January 1856, in Mary Mann, *Life of Horace Mann: By His Wife* (Boston, 1865), 79–80.

6

"The Benumbing and Paralyzing Influence of Romanism is such, as to Disqualify a Person for the Relish and Enjoyment of Liberty"

Anti-Catholicism and American Politics

Orestes Brownson was not a fan of Catholic education, though he deeply loved the Catholic Church. Raised in Vermont by orthodox Congregationalists, Brownson turned to Catholicism when he was in his late thirties. He started studying Catholic theology because he believed the highly individualistic impulses inherent within Protestantism had facilitated some of the gross economic inequalities wrought by capitalism. In October of 1844, at the age of thirty-nine, Orestes Brownson formally became a member of the Roman Catholic Church.[1]

For the rest of his life, Brownson remained committed to the idea that Catholicism was the best faith for Americans to adopt. He was a prominent figure on the intellectual landscape of antebellum New England, and he wrote frequently about the beauty and fragility of American democracy. He believed that all democracies had the potential to become dangerous, since human beings are "governed by their passions and interests ... which not unfrequently lead them astray, and produce much mischief." It was a "joke" and a "humbug" to think that the natural "virtue and intelligence of the American people" would always prompt them to elect leaders who "promote justice and equality ... and the equal rights of all classes and interests." "Our free institutions cannot be sustained without an augmentation of popular virtue and intelligence," Brownson wrote in 1845, sounding a bit like John Adams and Benjamin Rush fifty years earlier. The difference was that Brownson – unlike Adams or Rush – believed the Catholic Church was the only institution that could make the American people virtuous.

"Without the Roman Catholic religion, it is impossible to preserve a democratic government," Brownson insisted. Protestant denominations couldn't augment Americans' virtue or serve as a check on their passions

because all forms of Protestantism were built on a foundation of unwa-
vering faith in the ability of individual people, on their own, to discern the
will of God. "Was it not for this reason that ... [Protestants] separated
themselves from what had been the Church," he asked rhetorically, "and
attempted, with such materials as they could command, to reconstruct the
Church on its primitive foundation?"[2]

Brownson's concerns, ironically, were similar to the concerns that had
animated John Calvin three hundred years earlier. Both men believed that
human beings were extraordinarily flawed – vulnerable to forces such as
greed and arrogance, and capable, therefore, of really messing things up.
Calvin's concerns had led him to adopt a deeply suspicious posture
toward human institutions such as the Church – formulating a theology
that attempted to avoid systemic corruption by insisting upon the obligation that each individual had to engage in an unmediated confrontation
with the Word of God. Brownson's concerns, however, led him to adopt a
deeply suspicious posture toward the idea of individual autonomy; he
placed his faith in the "wisdom of the crowd," so to speak, insisting that
all people needed to be guided by something greater than themselves and
that the collective, divine, and oftentimes centuries-old wisdom found in
the Church's doctrines was that greater thing.

Yet, even as he called upon America's citizens to be guided by the teachings of the Catholic Church, Brownson could not help but express dismay at
the condition of Catholic education in the United States. The problem, as he
saw it, was that the instructors at Catholic schools refused to embrace the
modern condition, and, in so refusing, they failed to prepare America's future
Catholic citizens to live in the contemporary world. "They who are educated
in our schools seem misplaced and mistimed in the world," Brownson wrote.
"They come out ignorant of contemporary ideas, contemporary habits of
mind ... and large numbers of them sink into obscurity, and do nothing for
their religion or their country."

Catholic schools were too obsessed with teaching children about the
errors of the Protestant Reformation, Brownson believed; they prepared
students "not for the present or the future, but for a past which can never
be restored." Catholic education, therefore, was "a gross anachronism."

America's future Catholic citizens needed to become comfortable with
modern American ideas about progress, justice, equality, and freedom if
they were going to leave their mark on the country. This imperative was
particularly important in light of the fact that the overwhelming majority
of America's Catholics were Old World peasants who'd arrived in the
country with outdated understandings of what freedom and justice looked

like – understandings that did not recognize certain rights as inherent or "unalienable." Brownson feared the impact that immigration might have on American culture if Catholic schools didn't embrace modern ideas. "Our Catholic population, to a great extent, is practically a foreign body," he observed, "and brings with it a civilization foreign to the American, and in some respects inferior to it."[3]

CHAPTER OVERVIEW

Orestes Brownson's opinions reflected a Nativist impulse – even as they were also the embodiment of everything Nativists feared. "Nativism" is the term used to describe a complex cluster of ideas, principles, rhetorical devices, and legislative proposals that characterized the American political landscape in the mid-to-late nineteenth century.* At the core of the Nativist movement were the ardent beliefs that immigrants were ill-equipped to handle the responsibilities of American citizenship, that their habits and values were different from and inferior to those of native-born Americans, and that they would – through the power of their sheer numbers – alter, corrupt, and eventually destroy America's unique and highly advanced civilization.

Many Nativists also believed that the pope was using immigrants to destroy the United States – which is why Orestes Brownson confused them. They agreed with him that immigrants came from cultures that were less sophisticated and enlightened than that of the United States, and they, too, believed that teaching the children of immigrants to embrace American notions of freedom was essential to the nation's security. They were horrified, however, by Brownson's musings on the influence that the Catholic Church ought to have on American voters. Indeed, voters who did what their priests told them to do were what Nativists feared the most.

Catholics, it should be said, were not the Nativists' only targets. German Protestants also experienced hostility from anti-immigrant groups, since they tended to congregate in towns and neighborhoods where they would run schools, publish newspapers, and manage shops entirely in the German language. Writers and politicians attempted to

---

* Nativism has found a new incarnation in twenty-first century America in the Tea Party's calls for "real immigration reform," the vigilante border control efforts of the Minuteman Project, and the deportation rhetoric of Donald Trump's 2016 presidential campaign. It has also found modern expression in the opposition to Muslim immigrants from North Africa and the Middle East being articulated by European politicians such as Marine Le Pen of France and Geert Wilders of the Netherlands.

prevent Mormon converts from immigrating to the United States from Europe, seeing the Church of Jesus Christ of Latter Day Saints as "a foreign kingdom ... guided and controlled by foreigners" (even though it had been founded in the United States in the 1830s by a man from upstate New York). Asian immigrants, too, were targeted by Nativist politicians, who advanced their careers by capitalizing on the tensions that developed after Chinese workers began flowing into the Pacific Northwest following the discovery of gold in California in the 1850s.[4]

Nativists such as Simon Schmucker feared that immigrants were part of a grand, European conspiracy to take down America. "The monarchists and statesmen of Europe well know the fruitlessness of any attempt to destroy our republic by open invasion," Schmucker told a group of Lutheran seminarians in Gettysburg, Pennsylvania, in 1838. "The only mode of reaching us is by indirect action." Some of that indirect action involved shipping Europe's poorest, least educated, and most criminally inclined residents to America; Old World leaders, in other words, were not "sending their best."[†] The *New York Observer* claimed in 1845 that "the people or governments of Europe" were "sending off their paupers and criminals to the United States." The US State Department, according to the paper, had recently launched an investigation into whether a German duke had emptied Saxony's "jails and workhouses" of the region's most "notorious criminals" and then paid ship captains seventy dollars a head to transport the miscreants to New York.[5]

Criminals, however, weren't the only people Nativists believed were being shipped to the United States as part of a plan to destroy everything that made America great. "As Popery, which is a *system of politico-religious despotism*, is well understood to be hostile to liberty," Simon Schmucker explained, "we see hundreds of societies organized in Catholic Europe ... to propagate popery in America." One of those societies was the Association for the Propagation of the Faith, a private Catholic charity group that was founded in France in 1822 to support the Vatican's global conversion efforts. Nativists believed that the Association was sending Catholics to the United States to destroy the country with a secret plan – a plan so secret, in fact, that lay Catholics themselves did not even know about it. "We are met by the objection that papists, when interrogated, deny every intention hostile to our liberties," Schmucker told his audience

---

[†] When he declared his candidacy for the Republican presidential nomination in June of 2015, Donald Trump told advocates of immigration reform that "when Mexico sends their people, they're not sending their best."

of seminarians: "We answer, the mass of common papists we have already exonerated from the charge of being privy to such designs. The secret has not been confided to them. They have only been taught implicitly to obey the priest and pope and councils, at the hazard of eternal ruin, and thus, in due time, as common soldiers, to obey their commanders."[6]

Not all Nativists were conspiracy theorists like Simon Schmucker. Many people who worried about the impact that immigration would have on the political landscape in the United States felt that the pope didn't need to have an actual "plan" in order for the Catholic Church to destroy democracy. Catholic voters would ruin things in America simply by failing to think for themselves as they cast their votes; they would ruin things simply by failing to be free.

There was, therefore, no room for reconciliation between American and Catholic identity. Americans, after all, were great lovers of freedom, and because the Catholic Church had presented itself as "infallible and insusceptible of reformation," it was "opposed to the genius of all free institutions," according to Alexander Campbell, a Protestant minister (and Scots-Irish immigrant) whose efforts to unite all Protestant denominations under the rubric of a single "Christian" faith made him an early leader of the Second Great Awakening in Ohio and Kentucky.[7]

In reality, the question of whether anything about the Catholic Church ever was or could be "infallible" was a source of much debate within the Church's own hierarchy. The subject of papal infallibility was not settled until 1870, when the First Vatican Council presented the infallibility of the Church as dogma, even as it separated the Church's infallibility from that of the pope and placed limits upon the circumstances under which either could be seen as being beyond reproach.[8]

Still, that the Church did not err in its teachings was certainly a premise that many Catholic leaders in the nineteenth century had adopted, and Alexander Campbell was not wrong to suggest that this posture might present some problems for American democracy, given that the country's system of government had been designed, quite deliberately, *not* to be theocratic. Even Orestes Brownson did not believe that what Catholic educators were teaching in the schools was wrong, per se; he just felt that there was much the Church needed to be teaching students, yet wasn't.

What Brownson saw as the solution to democracy's shortcomings – namely, the fact that the Catholic Church's moral authority was perfect and unassailable – Protestant leaders such as Alexander Campbell saw as "essentially anti-American." People who'd been taught that their Church could do no wrong were incapable of "freedom of thought," Campbell asserted in 1837 during a public debate that he had with Cincinnati's bishop, John Baptist Purcell. Such people "rarely or ever can be emancipated or invigorated," and "the benumbing and paralyzing influence of Romanism is such, as to disqualify a person for the relish and enjoyment of political liberty."[9]

Beginning in the 1840s, politicians and activists who believed that immigrants constituted a dire threat to America's future came together and formed political alliances – local ones at first, primarily in states such as New York, Pennsylvania, and Massachusetts. By 1852, however, what became known as the Native American[‡] or "Know Nothing" Party had grown strong enough, nationally, to nominate a candidate for president. That candidate, Secretary of State Daniel Webster, died a week before the election, and the replacement that the Know Nothings found for him failed to garner more than a few thousand votes.

In 1856, however, the Know Nothings tried again – having enough political legitimacy this time to float a candidate who was already familiar with the White House and well-known to the American people. Millard Fillmore had spent the bulk of his political career as a Whig, serving as Zachary Taylor's vice-president from 1850 until 1853, when Taylor died of an intestinal illness and Fillmore became president. In 1856, Fillmore ran as the American Party's nominee against the Democrats' James Buchanan and the Republicans' John C. Fremont. He garnered nearly 23 percent of the popular vote, making him the second-most successful third-party presidential candidate in American history after Theodore Roosevelt, who garnered 27 percent of the popular vote as a Progressive Party candidate in 1912.[10]

Some Know Nothings were like Simon Schmucker, in that they were convinced the pope was using Catholic immigrants to destroy America; for that reason alone, they fought to bar immigrants from ever holding office, restrict the number of immigrants who could come into the country in any given year, and extend the amount of time that it took before an immigrant could become a voting American citizen.[11] Other Know Nothings, however, had concerns that were more specific – perhaps even more real – than just a nebulous and undefined "papal conspiracy." These Know Nothings were opposed to slavery. They wanted to keep it from expanding into the Western territories that the United States acquired in 1848 and 1850 as a consequence of the Mexican War, and they believed – not without reason – that immigrant Catholic voters would not help them

---

[‡] In the nineteenth century, "Native American" referred to people born in the United States, not Native American Indians.

in that fight. They tried, therefore, to keep Catholics from being able to vote.

CATHOLICS, ABOLITIONISTS, AND SLAVERY

In the summer of 1854, Bostonians were up in arms. A twenty-year-old black man named Anthony Burns had been arrested in May while walking to his job at a clothing shop on Brattle Street. The year before, Burns had run away from his master in Virginia. Under the provisions of the Fugitive Slave Act, passed by Congress in 1850, all local law enforcement officials – indeed, all American citizens – were obliged to report known runaway slaves to the appropriate authorities and arrange for their transport back to their owners. The sworn testimony of a supposed owner was enough "proof" to confirm the runaway status of a black man or woman; those accused of being runaway slaves could not even request a more detailed investigation under the provisions of the federal law.[12]

New England was a hotbed of abolitionist sentiment by this point, and not long after the passage of the Fugitive Slave Act, lawmakers in several cities and towns across the region passed "nullification laws" that required that accused runaways be given jury trials before they could be deported. In Vermont, lawmakers went so far as to require that all state law enforcement officials ignore the mandates of the federal law and actually *assist* runaway slaves in finding sanctuary and retaining their freedom. In Boston, the local law mandated that Anthony Burns be allowed to defend himself in court, but the proceeding was a mere formality since the young man really was a runaway slave. A judge ruled that Burns had to be returned to his owner, and, in early June, the slave whose story had become a cause célèbre among anti-slavery activists was loaded onto a ship in Boston Harbor and sent south.[13]

Theodore Parker – the extremely liberal Unitarian minister who fretted frequently about the growing number of Irish Catholic immigrants in his city – was among the loudest critics of the situation. At a meeting that abolitionists held in Faneuil Hall before Anthony Burns was deported, Parker sarcastically referred to the people of Boston as his "fellow subjects of Virginia" and vowed not to stop calling them that until they "accomplished deeds worthy of freemen" and found a way to save Anthony Burns.[14]

Parker's bitterness at the failure of Boston's residents to protect the young slave (a vigilante assault on the courthouse had managed only to kill a part-time bailiff) flavored his sermons and speeches for the rest of the summer. In

July, he celebrated America's independence by delivering a sermon on "the Dangers which threaten the Rights of Man in America." There were four of them, according to Parker: 1) the nation's "exclusive devotion to riches"; 2) the belief that "there is no Higher Law above the Statutes which Men make"; 3) "the institution of Slavery"; and 4) "the Roman Catholic Church, established in the midst of us."[15]

Theodore Parker placed Catholicism on his list because like many other abolitionists, including Elijah Lovejoy, George Bourne, and George Cheever, he believed that the Catholic Church stood in the way of slavery's destruction. "The Catholic Church ... is the natural ally of tyrants and the irreconcilable enemy of freedom," Parker told the hundreds of people who had turned out to hear him in Boston's recently opened Music Hall. Catholic immigrants, therefore, could not be relied upon to fight slavery when they went to the polls. Certainly there were "individual Catholics" who "favor the progress of Mankind"; Parker was, perhaps, thinking of people such as Orestes Brownson, who traveled in many of the same intellectual circles as Parker. Such Catholics, however, were "exceptional; the Catholic Church has an iron logic, and consistently hates liberty in all its forms."[16]

While it was hyperbolic for Theodore Parker to insist that the Catholic Church hated liberty, he was right to observe that the Catholic understanding of liberty was very different from the Protestant one – and that that understanding did not require Catholics to condemn the institution of slavery. That American Catholics did condemn slavery, at least as it was practiced in the United States, is irrefutable. Orestes Brownson, for instance, pointed to the fact that slaves were not legally allowed to marry as a sign that Christianity was "incompatible with chattel slavery." Father Edward Purcell, brother to the Cincinnati bishop who debated Alexander Campbell, believed that slavery should be abolished because it hindered the work of religion. "Religion flourishes in a slave state only in proportion to its intimacy with a free state," Purcell claimed in an 1863 editorial that he wrote for the *Cincinnati Catholic Telegraph*. "It is the hard-working laboring man who builds the church, the school house, the orphan asylum, not the slaveholder, as a general rule."[17]

Yet, neither Brownson's nor Purcell's condemnation really touched upon what was actually wrong with the system of hereditary, race-based slavery in the United States – namely, that it denied a host of basic human rights to an entire race of people. The *Cincinnati Catholic Telegraph* was also the only Catholic newspaper in the country to call for the emancipation of slaves. Most Catholic papers, if they commented on slavery at all, echoed the sentiments of Courtney Jenkins, editor of the *Baltimore Catholic Mirror*, who wrote in 1860 that "it is fanaticism or hypocrisy to condemn slavery as itself criminal, or opposed to the laws of God."[18]

The problem with slavery, as Jenkins and other Catholic leaders articulated it, was not that it was a hierarchical institution that limited human rights and insisted that some men were born to govern, while others were born to be governed. It was that many governors were refusing to recognize that slavery was a system of reciprocal duties – and that slaveholders, therefore, had certain obligations to their bondsmen. In a perfect Catholic world, Savannah's bishop Augustin Verot proclaimed, all slaveholders would understand that they needed to feed and clothe their slaves, respect the integrity of those slaves' families,[§] abstain from the "frequent occasions of immorality, which the subservient and degraded position of the slave offers to the lewd," and provide slaves with the moral guidance of the Church (something most Protestant slaveholders had been reluctant to do prior to the 1830s, since they worried they would be morally obliged to free their slaves once those slaves became Christian).[19] A perfect Catholic world, however, did not require the abolition of slavery.

Historians have traditionally pointed to the job and wage competition that newly freed slaves would have presented (and indeed did present) to immigrant Catholic workers when explaining why so few Catholics in the United States called for the abolition of slavery.[20] Certainly this explanation has many merits. But it is also true that Catholicism is a faith that prides itself on its conservatism and points proudly to the unbroken, historical and theological connections it has to the earliest propagators of global Christianity – many of whom condoned or accepted the institution of slavery.

Peter and Paul, for instance, spoke of the mutually beneficial relationship between a master and his slave; Augustine of Hippo insisted that slavery, while not a requirement of Natural Law, was a natural consequence of Original Sin; Thomas Aquinas believed that slavery brought order to a fallen world where some people were born without an ability to govern themselves; and St. Ignatius of Loyola, the founder of the Jesuit order that served the Catholic population in colonial and early-national

---

[§] The Jesuits in colonial and early-national Maryland owned hundreds of slaves, and they regularly exhorted Catholic slaveholders to keep slave families together and allow slaves to marry (in spite of the mandates of Maryland's law). In 1838, however, when the Society of Jesus decided to sell all of its slaves, the Jesuits made little effort to keep the families they owned together, separating husbands from wives and selling several children to planters who were different from the planters their parents were sold to.

America and was responsible for the Church's early institutional and intellectual development in the United States, believed that slavery could be a powerful tool in the Church's fight against the spread of Protestantism.[21]

Several Catholic leaders in the nineteenth century did condemn the international slave trade and speak of race-based slavery as unfortunate, if necessary. Until the twentieth century, however, no Catholic leaders insisted, as Protestants such as William Ellery Channing did in 1835, that slavery was wrong because "man has rights from his nature ... gifts of the Creator, bound up indissolubly with our moral constitution."[22] Rights-talk, after all, was a Protestant way of framing things. Properly ordered societies were not ones that focused on individual rights, according to the Catholic Church. Properly ordered societies were hierarchical organizations that, like the Church itself, stressed the importance of reciprocal prerogatives and duties.[23]

In 1839, when Pope Gregory XVI condemned the international slave trade in his letter, *In supemo apostolatus*, America's bishops scrambled to explain to Protestants and Catholics alike that the pope had not been commenting on slavery as it was practiced in the United States. Bishop John England of Charleston pointed out that Gregory had said it was wrong to "unjustly ... reduce to slavery Indians, blacks, and other such peoples," and no one in America was "reducing those who were previously free into slavery" anymore. Writing to Secretary of State John Forsyth, a slaveholder from Georgia, England, noted that the United States had outlawed the international slave trade in 1808, such that by 1839, the only people becoming slaves in America were those who had been born to it – not "reduced" to it. "I also see the impossibility of abolishing [slavery] here," England helpfully added.[24]

THE REGIONAL NATURE OF ANTI-CATHOLICISM: THE SOUTH

One year after an angry Protestant mob stormed the Ursuline convent in Charlestown, Massachusetts, burning it to the ground, dozens of Protestants in central North Carolina, including the state's governor, David L. Swain, turned out for a fund-raiser that was meant to finance the construction of a new Catholic church in Raleigh. North Carolina's Catholics didn't have a chapel of their own, and for several years they'd been renting space in a Presbyterian church. The Presbyterians were more than happy to continue providing Raleigh's Catholics with that space, but John England, whose diocese included both of the Carolinas and the state of Georgia, had decided it was time for the city's Catholics to have their own chapel.

Two years earlier, in 1833, William Gaston, a wealthy Catholic attorney from the coastal town of New Bern, had been appointed to the state's Supreme Court by Governor Swain. Gaston quickly used his influence on the court to arrange for a new constitutional convention so that a provision in the state's original constitution, dating back to 1776, could be removed. That provision had restricted office-holding in the state to Protestants. North Carolina's coastal residents had been flagrantly ignoring it since at least 1812, however, when they first sent William Gaston to the state Senate to represent them.[25]

The experiences that North Carolina's Catholics had with their Protestant neighbors highlight the reality that anti-Catholicism was not an evenly distributed sentiment in antebellum American culture; it varied according to the region Catholics lived in. While not non-existent, animosity toward Catholics in the antebellum South was quite low. The Catholic Church was comfortable with slavery, after all – and pro- and anti-slavery advocates both knew this. Catholics were also white – an extremely important distinction. The South, of course, was not the only part of the country that had embraced a racial hierarchy; the antebellum North was hardly a racial utopia. But in the Northeast, African Americans were less than 2 percent of the overall population in 1850, while they were nearly 40 percent of the population in the South at that time.[26] The mere presence of black people in southern states gave institutional and cultural racism greater power in the South – and provided all people who were white with certain advantages that they simply did not have in areas where there were few black people for them to compare themselves to.

Additionally, the number of immigrants from Europe who settled in cities such as Charleston, Savannah, and New Orleans paled in comparison to the number who moved to Baltimore, Philadelphia, New York, Boston, Cincinnati, and Chicago. Eighty-eight percent of the immigrants in the United States in 1850 lived in the Northeast and the Midwest, while less than 10 percent of them lived in the South.[27] The South, therefore, did not experience the kind of social and cultural upheaval that the North experienced in the 1840s and 1850s as a consequence of immigration.

No southern city had a neighborhood like "Dutch Hill," for instance, which the *New York Times* described as a huge collection of "board or mud shanties" in the middle of Manhattan where "thousands of Irish and German squatters" picked through garbage and lived in filth with their children and farm animals on land that didn't belong to them. Southern cities also didn't have street fights like the Astor Place Riot of 1849 or the Dead Rabbits Riot of 1857, during which networks of immigrant and ethnic gangs fought with one another over territory and political influence, destroying property and filling New York's hospitals, morgues, and prisons in the process.[28] Native-born Southerners did not experience the difficult cultural transformations that come with any mass migration – and this, in turn, rendered them less inclined than their northern counterparts to resent the immigrant Catholics among them.

Finally, the Catholic Church was a primary contributor to the development and management of the social-services infrastructure in the South. The region had few hospitals, almshouses, or schools – but the few it had were often run by priests or nuns. The first orphanage in Kentucky was opened by the Sisters of Nazareth in 1832. In Mobile, Alabama, the only hospital in town was managed by the Sisters of Charity from 1837 until after the Civil War. One European observer noted in 1845 that priests were teaching the sons of many of St. Louis' most prominent citizens. "The Jesuits have seized ... on the education of the future statesmen and legislators of Missouri," the traveler proclaimed. Jefferson Davis, future president of the Confederate States of America, spent three years at a school run by Dominican priests in Kentucky and even expressed an interest in converting to Catholicism while he was there. He was dissuaded from doing so by one of the school's more politic priests – someone who recognized, no doubt, that the toleration southern Protestants extended toward their Catholic neighbors probably had its limits.[29]

Fears of immigrants did occasionally find expression on the South's political landscape. Henry Johnson was a Whig senator from Louisiana who became involved with the American Republican Party, a precursor to the Know Nothing Party, in the mid-1840s. The American Republicans wanted to increase the number of years that immigrants had to spend in the country before they could apply for citizenship. Johnson, in particular, believed that the naturalization process was riddled with fraud, and, in 1844, he called for the Senate's Judiciary Committee to investigate the situation. That investigation confirmed much of what Senator Johnson feared; the Democratic party in several cities across the country was paying judges to issue naturalization papers to immigrants who were not yet eligible for them even under the existing naturalization laws, which the American Republicans believed were already too lenient. To Johnson's dismay, fraudulently naturalized "citizens" were also found to be patrolling the polling stations in his own state and turning native-born American citizens away.[30]

But Henry Johnson's fears of immigrants never involved a fear of Catholicism. He was a Louisianan, after all; while not Catholic himself, he was quite comfortable around Catholics, as the Church of Rome had been the dominant faith in the Mississippi delta since before Louisiana had even become an American state. In the 1830s, when Johnson was living in Washington, DC, and serving in the House of Representatives, he dined frequently with the Jesuits who ran Georgetown University. Indeed, in 1838, Johnson helped Thomas Mulledy, the president of Georgetown, sell the Society of Jesus' slaves to planters in the deep South as part of an effort to save the school from financial ruin.[31]

THE REGIONAL NATURE OF ANTI-CATHOLICISM: THE WEST

The start of the Mexican War in 1846 – at the height of the Catholic exodus from Ireland – exacerbated fears, even in the South, and convinced many Protestants that Catholics would soon outnumber them. The war was extremely controversial, since the United States had essentially invaded Mexico in order to acquire more land for the expansion of slavery. Abolitionists hated it; Henry David Thoreau famously refused to pay his taxes to support it. But even people who staunchly favored slavery weren't sure they wanted to acquire territory that was already populated with Catholic Mexicans. South Carolina Senator John C. Calhoun – who considered slavery to be a "good where a civilized race and a race of a different description are brought together" – worried specifically about the "violent religious conflict" that could result if "we bring into our Union eight millions of people, all professing one religion – and all concentrated under a powerful and wealthy priesthood."[32]

But if anti-Catholicism was a reason to be wary of the war, it was also a reason to be supportive of it. In spite of what abolitionists such as Henry David Thoreau believed, the expansion of slavery wasn't the only reason Congress had voted to go to war with Mexico. The annexation of Texas, which was the war's declared objective, also wasn't Congress' only goal. This point became clear at the end of the war, when the peace treaty the United States forced Mexico to sign gave the territory that is now California, Nevada, Utah, Arizona, New Mexico, Colorado, and Wyoming to the United States, as well.[33]

By 1846, many Americans had come to believe that they had what the journalist John O'Sullivan called a "manifest destiny," and that this destiny was "to possess the whole of the continent which Providence has given us for the development of the great experiment of liberty and federated self-government entrusted to us." Americans believed they had a divinely prescribed duty to spread their individualistic, rights-oriented understanding of freedom across the entirety of North America. Mexico, as a "Romish" country with "slavish" citizens, stood in the way of that (as did the Sioux, Navajo, and Cheyenne Indians). "There are already rumors of sending 5 or 6 thousand Yankees to Mexico to civilize the country, that is to say, to Protestantize it," Bishop Joseph Crétin of St. Paul, Minnesota, sarcastically wrote to a friend in 1846. "The Americans are becoming proud, more and more," he warned his friend, who ministered to Catholics in Iowa and was, like the bishop himself, an immigrant from France. "They are people whom one must handle very delicately like puffed-up persons."[34]

Bishop Crétin recognized that the idea of "manifest destiny" was a contemporary incarnation of the same spirit that had prompted the Puritans to travel across the Atlantic and establish a "city upon a hill" for the people back home in England to learn from and follow. The same anxieties that fueled the Puritans' "errand into the wilderness" throughout the seventeenth century also fueled the collective sense that Americans had in the nineteenth century that it was their duty, as God's people, to spread the light of Protestant freedom across the entire continent.[35] Those anxieties were about more than just a fear of Catholicism, as important as that fear was. The anxieties were also about a fear of irrelevance – a fear that what each group of Americans was doing in the New World might ultimately be superfluous, and that in the end, none of it would matter.

Recall that not long after John Winthrop and his fellow Congregationalists established the city of Boston in 1630, the Calvinists who'd stayed home in England stopped paying attention to what they were doing. They took over Parliament, executed their king, and established their own Commonwealth, all without any help or guidance from John Winthrop and his band of intrepid colonists. New England *had* to work under such circumstances; the Puritans had to build a society that was perfectly in accord with the will of God. Anything less than a complete and total success would suggest that the trip across the ocean had been entirely unnecessary.

Two hundred years later, the heirs to the Puritans' experiment faced a similar threat of irrelevance, thanks to religious disestablishment, the growth of Unitarianism and other varieties of experimental religion (such as Mormonism), and a surge in Catholic immigration. As they did before, Protestants looked west, formulating what they called a "Plea for the West," which became the foundation, then, for the idea of Manifest Destiny, the war with Mexico that that idea sparked, and the political careers of numerous mayors, governors, and state and national lawmakers.[36] "The West" – by which politicians and religious leaders meant everything from Ohio and Kentucky to California and Oregon – became a region of the United States where fears of Catholicism that had their roots in the English colonial experience found a unique, "American" voice.

In 1832, while Massachusetts' lawmakers debated religious disestablishment, Lyman Beecher agreed to be the first president of Lane Theological Seminary in Cincinnati, Ohio. The school had been established earlier that year by two Orthodox Presbyterians who worried that Ohio's residents were not being served by adequately trained ministers – that is to say, men who understood and accepted the full stakes of Calvinism. Beecher moved his family out to Cincinnati, which had seen its population increase by a factor of ten in the previous two decades.[37] Although he did not abandon all hope of saving his native New England from the forces of disestablishment, Unitarianism, and Catholicism, Lyman Beecher chose to devote himself thoroughly to the project of protecting the West from the moral decay he had witnessed in Massachusetts and Connecticut.**

Beecher was not alone in thinking that the West needed to be saved. Even many of the "soft" Protestants Beecher fretted about – Baptists who deemphasized the limited nature of salvation, even if they hadn't actually deteriorated into Unitarianism; Methodists who'd evolved out of the Episcopal Church and had therefore never even embraced Calvinist theology – were worried about Catholic influence in the West. Several Protestant newspapers on the east coast, in fact, warned their readers that 15,000 priests were working in the territory west of the Appalachian Mountains – a statistic that the editor of the *Cincinnati Catholic Telegraph* found particularly hilarious, given that the actual number of priests in the region was closer to just 700. Baptists in New York worried about the impact that "infidelity" and the "Romish hierarchy" might be having on the Mississippi Valley (primarily Illinois, Missouri, and Iowa); both forces, they believed, had been brought to the region by German immigrants.[39] These Baptists eventually joined with other east-coast Protestant denominations to form the American Home Missionary Society, the purpose of which was to meet the "pressing and urgent call from the west" for "not Bibles nor tracts merely – but MEN."[40]

** Beecher did eventually reconcile himself to the reality of disestablishment, calling it "the best thing that ever happened to the State of Connecticut," thanks to the spirit of religious voluntarism that it unleashed. But for many years, he insisted that the day Connecticut disestablished the Congregational Church was "as dark a day as I ever saw."[38]

Alluding to the old, familiar understanding of Catholics as people who slavishly followed the directives of their priests, the Society insisted that its missionaries needed to have "warm hearts and sound heads, that can think and act for themselves, that have never called any man master on earth, that have not studied theological systems till they have almost forgotten the Bible." More than a decade before John O'Sullivan coined the term "Manifest Destiny," the American Home Missionary Society's magazine proclaimed that "the Western part of our country is destined to exert a powerful influence on the destinies of the whole nation."[41]

Some Protestants who actually lived in the West resented the idea that they needed to be "missioned" to. "Nothing can be more false than the idea that the Valley of the Mississippi is peopled with irreligious characters . . . who are perishing from want of missionary preaching," one angry Presbyterian wrote from Illinois in the 1840s.[42] Other frontier Protestants felt that their east-coast co-religionists had an exaggerated sense of the dangers posed by Catholicism. In Kentucky, for instance, Presbyterians understood that being around Catholics didn't threaten their commitment to Calvinism. Dozens of them turned out in 1830 to hear Bishop John England preach for an hour and a half – during which time the bishop even made the Catholic "sign of the Cross" over the King James Bible. "What a sight for a Catholic," England's clerical colleague, Benedict Joseph Flaget, remarked, "to find himself in a meeting house of Calvinists . . . when a Roman Catholic was preaching the words of truth in the presence of three other bishops, 5 or 6 ministers of different sects, and an audience of which two-thirds were Protestants."[43]

But regardless of how Protestants in the West felt about Catholics or the status of their own religiosity, Protestants on the east coast were convinced that the frontier needed to be protected from the effects of Catholicism and irreligion. This impulse animated a host of mission-based reform movements, centered in the Northeast, that were founded in the midst of the Second Great Awakening. East-coast Protestants believed the West needed "colleges and academies, day schools and Sabbath schools." It needed temperance laws that would combat the whiskey-drinking of the Irish and the beer-guzzling of the Germans. It needed Sabbatarian laws that would shut down the post offices on Sundays, since post offices – interestingly enough – were where immigrants gathered on the frontier to drink and socialize (rather than worship). The region needed blasphemy laws that would make it illegal for anyone to "deny human accountability and moral obligation, and, of course, a future state of retribution." It needed strong, Protestant families to migrate to Ohio, Indiana, Illinois, and Missouri. And it needed trained ministers who knew how to get people to accept "the more objectionable parts of Christianity, such as total depravity, the necessity of an atonement, and regeneration."[44]

All that cost money. Lyman Beecher's greatest contribution to the effort, then, was a fund-raising pamphlet that he used as the basis for lectures that he delivered throughout the northeast, where most of the money was located. Published in 1835, *A Plea for the West* railed against the evils of popery and warned of the dire consequences that would result if immigrants who had been "educated under the despotic governments of Catholic Europe" were allowed to "settle down upon the unoccupied territory of the West." Full of shocking (and not entirely inaccurate) statistics about the growth of Catholic immigration in the United States, particularly along the frontier, Beecher's pamphlet claimed that "American travelers" in Europe had discovered maps in the Catholic capitals of Vienna and Rome that were "explanatory of the capacious West, and pointing out the most fertile soils and the most favored locations, and inviting to emigration." Through "the medium of their religion and priesthood," Beecher proclaimed, "the foreign emigrants whose accumulating tide is rolling in on us" constituted "an army of soldiers, enlisted and officered, spreading over the land."[45]

Ten years after Beecher published *A Plea for the West*, a different group of soldiers – these ones enlisted and officered in the United States Army – started spreading over the land in an effort to save the West from the stultifying effects of Catholicism. Several hundred of the American soldiers who invaded Mexico in 1846 were immigrant Catholics who'd enlisted in the regular army to prove their loyalty to the United States. By 1847, however, many of these Catholics – including the members of a mostly Irish-born battalion known as the "San Patricios" – had deserted to the Mexican Army, disgusted by the US military's habit of looting Catholic churches and desecrating Catholic shrines.[46]

President James Polk, a Democrat, had intentionally appointed two Jesuit priests to serve as chaplains in the United States Army, hoping to prove to the Mexicans – and to Catholics who lived in the United States – that America did not intend to "destroy their churches and make war upon their religion."[47] The Democratic party had been making a concerted effort to reach out to immigrant Catholic voters since the early 1830s, seeing great potential in the power of their numbers; Polk, therefore, wanted these voters to know that, officially, the war with Mexico was to be no Protestant "crusade."

Nevertheless, churches *were* looted. Long after the war was over, a man from Ohio told a Mexican newspaper that his father was responsible for the "valuable stones and huge golden images" that were found buried beneath some flagstones in Mexico City in 1902. The man's father and several other soldiers had apparently stolen the treasure from a number of cathedrals and buried it, planning to come back for it at some later date. The soldiers never did return; instead, in the 1860s, one of them wrote to the Mexican government, asking "if there would be any chance of a division of the spoils if he should tell the government where it could find the sacred and valuable altar decorations that had been stolen." The Mexican government responded by warning the man that if he knew anything at all about the rampant looting of the country's churches that had occurred during the war "he would do well ... to keep quiet, lest his life be sacrificed in revenge for the desecration of the cathedrals."[48]

NATIVISM AND POLITICS

Lyman Beecher's efforts to save the West may have helped to launch a war, but they failed to stem the tide of Catholic immigration to the United States. By 1850, Catholicism was the largest single religious denomination in the country, and it has maintained that status ever since.[49] Beecher's efforts to save orthodox Protestant Christianity from the deteriorating influences of liberalism, however – embodied most treacherously in the phenomenon of Unitarianism – did bear some fruit. His preaching tours in the 1830s and 1840s played a vital role in fomenting the Second Great Awakening. That revival – while not always as traditional or orthodox as old-school Calvinists such as Beecher would have liked – did ensure that America remained a culturally Protestant nation, in spite of the immigrants and Unitarians.

Lyman Beecher's articulation of the threat represented by Catholic immigration also served as the foundation for a paranoid and loud-mouthed political movement in the 1840s and 1850s that might have had more of an impact on America's laws, had its concerns about the pope's plans to "invade the territory of the United States, or assail the rights of our country" not been eclipsed by secession and Civil War.[50] The Know Nothings were a secretive movement at first; politicians who subscribed to the movement's anti-immigrant beliefs were instructed to claim they knew "nothing" of the movement's goals – and then work quietly to implement those goals as members of one of the country's more traditional political parties.

The Whig party was a particularly fecund breeding ground for secretive Nativist activity in the 1840s. Party leaders regularly exhorted Americans to "support candidates for office who have independence enough to come out against the secret plots of Romanism." This Whig antipathy toward Catholicism was one of the reasons Catholics voted overwhelmingly to put the Democratic candidate, Franklin Pierce, in the White House in 1852. The overtly Nativist third-party candidate in that campaign, Daniel Webster, had died right before the election, but Catholics still knew that the Whig's man, Winfield Scott, could not be trusted. "Has not the outcome of the last presidential election been the outcome of the foreign vote," the abolitionist Anna Ella Carroll[††] asked with dismay. "Did not the Romish church contract and bargain to sell its influence at the ballot box to cause that result?"[51]

By the mid-1850s, the Whig Party was falling apart, undermined by disagreements over whether slavery should be allowed to expand into the territory the United States had acquired from Mexico. Nativists responded by coming thoroughly out into the open, forming their own political party and cultivating the anger of working-class, native-born Protestants who – thanks to innovations such as the railroads and the telegraph – were now vulnerable to national and international economic forces that had never touched the lives of their parents before them. In 1854 and 1855, the members of the Native American or Know Nothing Party captured the mayor's offices in Philadelphia, Boston, Washington, DC, and San Francisco; most of the seats in the Massachusetts state legislature; and nearly 20 percent of the seats in the US Congress.[52]

The prominence that the Know Nothings have enjoyed in America's historical narrative belies the limited impact that they actually had on the country's network of laws. The Native American Party was rhetorically powerful, but legislatively ineffective. Its members were a "busy, talking, agitating, fanatical, proscribing" group of people, according to one New York Congressman, but once in office, they did little more than "stain [the political discourse] with indelible disgrace."[53] The Know Nothings offend our ideals today, which is why they are remembered so vigorously; but they also offended the ideals of many Americans even in their own times, which is why they tended not to be very good at passing legislation, even as they were quite good at getting themselves elected.

[††] Carroll, an Episcopalian, was a political activist who worried about corruption in politics and wrote frequently about what she called "the contest between Christianity and Political Roman-ism." She was also, interestingly enough, the granddaughter of Charles Carroll of Carrollton, the Catholic signer of the Declaration of Independence.

The Democratic Party also proved to be good at frustrating Know Nothing aspirations. Local party leaders in many of America's cities operated like finely tuned machines, reaching out to newly naturalized immigrants and providing them with job opportunities and even cash payments in exchange for votes. In an age before Social Security, Food Stamps, and Unemployment Insurance (none of which existed in the United States until the twentieth century), these payments went a long way toward securing the partisan loyalty of voters who were poor.[54]

Democrats worked hard, then, at the state and national levels to oppose Nativist legislation and protect the immigrants whose votes they relied upon. In 1860, the party even went so far as to nominate for president a man who was raising his children within the Catholic Church. Stephen Douglas was married to Adele Cutts, who came from an old Catholic family that traced its roots in the United States to colonial Maryland. Although Douglas never converted to his wife's faith, he did allow Adele to baptize his sons from a previous marriage as Catholics. Some supporters of his opponent, Abraham Lincoln, seized on this as proof that Douglas was, himself, a secret Catholic and used it against him in the campaign.[55]

The Know Nothings' primary legislative agenda was the reformation of America's naturalization laws. The Constitution gives Congress the power to decide the parameters of American citizenship, and, in 1795, Congress passed the Naturalization Act, defining non-native citizens as "free, white persons" (meaning men) who had been living in the country for at least five years. With the exception of a brief period in the late 1790s when that wait-time was extended to fourteen years, the probationary period on naturalization has always been five years, even as the race and gender limits on naturalized citizenship have slowly been lifted.[56]

The Know Nothings wanted to extend the wait-time to twenty-one years. Their argument was that native-born citizens had to live in the country for twenty-one years before they were allowed to vote;[‡‡] immigrants, therefore, should be required to do the same. This logic failed to move enough Congressmen to change the country's naturalization laws, even after more than a decade of trying; in January of 1855, therefore, Know Nothing lawmakers adopted a different tactic, putting forward a bill that would have barred "foreign paupers, criminals, idiots, lunatics, the insane, and blind persons" from entering the United States. "I

---

‡‡ The voting age was not lowered to eighteen until 1971, with the passage of the 26th Amendment.

sympathize with the poor and unfortunate in every country," Senator Stephen Adams of Mississippi insisted when announcing his support for the bill, "But [I] am Native American enough to prefer that the tyrannical Governments which produce these paupers should take care of them."[57]

The foreign pauper bill never made it out of committee. Democrats – and even some Whigs and Republicans in Congress – insisted that the law would violate the Constitution, since the federal government didn't have the power to tell the individual states that they couldn't let certain kinds of people past their borders. The committee reviewing the proposed bill suggested that the states themselves ought to pass laws against the admission of foreign paupers if they didn't want to assume the costs of caring for them. No state did pass such a law, however – not even New York, where poor relief efforts were costing taxpayers as much as $800,000 a year, or $20,240,000 in 2015 terms.[58]

Indeed, much of what the Know Nothings put forward – on both the national and the state levels – failed to become law. Nativists in Massachusetts did manage to convince their lawmakers to create a "Nunnery Committee" within the ranks of the state legislature in 1855, when Know Nothings occupied most of the seats in that governing body. The committee was tasked with looking into whether women in the state were being kept in convents against their will. When, after the law was passed, a non-Nativist lawmaker from Roxbury pointed out that Massachusetts didn't actually have any convents, since the Ursulines had returned to Quebec after their convent was burned in 1834 and no other nuns had been scrappy enough to replace them, lawmakers told the committee to investigate Catholic schools in the state instead.[59]

Nationally, the Know Nothings were hindered by an inability to agree with one another about how much of a role anti-Catholicism should play in their movement. In the North and West, Know Nothing candidates frequently spoke of the threat that Catholicism represented; in the South, however – especially in Maryland and Louisiana, where there were large populations of native-born Catholics – concerns about immigrants tended not to touch upon the immigrants' religious beliefs. Indeed, in 1855, when the Know Nothing Party captured its largest number of national seats, the party committees in Maryland, Virginia, South Carolina, Missouri, Louisiana, and California had no calls for a religious test on voting or office-holding in their platforms, even as a constitutional amendment allowing such a test was a primary goal for Know Nothing chapters in New York and Massachusetts.[60]

Disagreements about slavery also kept the Know Nothings from coalescing into a strong, national movement. Northern Know Nothings opposed slavery – and frequently linked their opposition to the concerns they had about the influence of Catholicism in the United States. "Roman Catholicism and slavery . . . [are] alike founded and supported on the basis of ignorance and tyranny," a Know Nothing chapter in Massachusetts resolved in 1854. The two institutions were "natural allies in every warfare against liberty and enlightenment."[61]

Southern Know Nothings, naturally, had no problem with slavery, and their disagreement with northern Know Nothings about this issue became far more important – and far more capable of upending the Know Nothings' anti-immigrant agenda in Congress – after the spring of 1856. That was when John Brown, an abolitionist who believed violence was the only way to end slavery in the United States, traveled to Kansas, where voters had not yet decided whether to ask for admission to the union as a slave or a free state. On the night of May 24, Brown and his supporters hacked five pro-slavery settlers to death along Pottawatomie Creek. After that, Southern lawmakers had no interest in cooperating with northern lawmakers on any agenda – most especially one that might threaten a religious group that had proven to be very accommodating toward slavery.

CHAPTER CONCLUSION

The Know Nothings were very good at whipping up fear and then using that fear to get people to the polls. They were not very good at bargaining, compromising, or deal-making, however – that is to say, the art of politics – which is why most of the time they failed to implement the promises they'd made to the voters who put them in office.

More so than their own incompetence, however, the Know Nothings had the Civil War to thank for their demise. Much of the success they'd been having at winning elections in the 1850s relied upon disagreements among Whigs and former Whigs over the question of whether slavery should be allowed to expand into the West. Once South Carolina seceded from the union in December of 1860, that question was no longer relevant or politically useful.

Anti-Catholicism certainly didn't disappear from the American landscape after the war, even if the Know Nothing Party did. Indeed, one of the ironies of our modern-day understanding of Church–State separation, particularly when it comes to the nation's public schools, is that that understanding was originally a reaction against the growing popularity and strength of the Catholic school system in the United States in the 1860s and 1870s. Much like the first act of religious toleration in the English-speaking world – initiated by Cecilius Calvert in Maryland in 1649 – our contemporary approach to religious toleration in the United States has its roots in an anti-Catholic impulse.

In 1869, when education officials in Cincinnati contemplated banning "all religious books, including the Holy Bible" from the city's public schools, it was because nearly half of Cincinnati's school children were enrolled in Catholic schools, rather than public schools. Ohio's parochial school system had grown by leaps and bounds in the 1860s, as priests and parents sought to protect their children from the embarrassment of having to leave a public school classroom because a teacher had initiated a lesson using the King James Bible.

Education officials worried about the long-term impact that all this exposure to priests and nuns might have on the city's future citizens. They wanted to convince Catholic parents to send their children back to the public schools, and Henry Ward Beecher, Lyman Beecher's son, thought that the best way to do that was to remove religious instruction entirely from the public schools. It was a controversial idea – one that Beecher's father would have condemned, had Lyman still been alive to hear it. To soften the blow, the younger Beecher presented his proposal as a thoroughly "American" initiative. "Compulsory Bible [instruction] in schools is not in accordance with [the] American doctrine of liberty of conscience," he insisted. It was not proper for the state "to show partiality to one or another sect in religion."[62]

Reformers pointed out that removing the Bible from the schools had the added benefit of making it more difficult for Catholic leaders to argue that some of the money available to the public school system should be diverted to the parochial school system. Bishop John Hughes of New York had tried in the 1840s to argue that tax money should be used to fund Catholic instruction because it was being used to fund Protestant instruction in the public schools. His efforts were unsuccessful, but that didn't stop Catholic leaders in other states from making the same argument. Education officials should "free the schools of everything against which this kind of opposition may be fairly urged," the editors of *Harper's Weekly* magazine advised in 1870. Why continue to "furnish a weapon for the enemy?"[63]

Some lawmakers worried that it wasn't enough just to remove the weapon of public-school Bible instruction from their Catholic "enemy." Catholic leaders, after all, might still succeed at getting the courts to order the individual states to finance Catholic education. Beginning in the 1870s, therefore, lawmakers in dozens of states proposed what were known as "Blaine

Amendments" to their states' constitutions. These amendments banned the use of tax money by any religious group or denomination. The amendments took their name from James G. Blaine, a congressman from Maine who had proposed a similar amendment to the US Constitution in 1875.

By the time Blaine ran for president in 1884, all but ten states in the Union had incorporated Blaine amendments into their constitutions, indicating that fears of Catholic influence were still running high in the United States. Those fears, however, weren't high enough to counter the power of the Catholic vote and win the election for James G. Blaine. Even at the time, many observers believed that the reason Blaine lost to Grover Cleveland was that he'd been unwilling to condemn an alliterative chant that had been picked up by many of his supporters. That chant predicted that a Cleveland victory would lead to "Rum, Romanism, and Ruin," and the nation's ever-growing mass of immigrant Catholic voters, many of whom were now coming not from Ireland, but from Italy, decided that they could not vote for a man who was unwilling to divorce himself from that prediction.[64]

NOTES

1. Arthur M. Schlesinger Jr., *Orestes Brownson: A Pilgrim's Progress* (Boston, 1959), 3–112; Patrick W. Carey, *Orestes A. Brownson: American Religious Weathervane* (Grand Rapids, MI, 2004), 55–154; Stewart Davenport, *Friends of the Unrighteous Mammon: Northern Christians and Market Capitalism, 1815–1860* (Chicago, 2008), 123–154; Orestes Brownson, "The Primeval Man Not a Savage" and "The Democratic Principle, *Brownson's Quarterly Review* 2 (April, 1873), 205–259.

2. Orestes Brownson, "Catholicity Necessary to Sustain Popular Liberty," *Brownson's Quarterly Review* 4 (October, 1845), 516–519.

3. Orestes Brownson, "Catholic Schools and Education," *Brownson's Quarterly Review* 1 (January, 1862), 71–73, 76–81.

4. Christian B. Keller, *Chancellorsville and the Germans: Nativism, Ethnicity, and Civil War Memory* (New York, 2007), 10–23; Christine Talbot, *A Foreign Kingdom: Mormons and Polygamy in American Political Culture, 1852–1890* (Urbana, IL, 2013), 136–146, the C.C. Goodwin quote is on 136; Mark Kanazawa, "Immigration, Exclusion, and Taxation: Anti-Chinese Legislation in Gold Rush California," *Journal of Economic History* 3 (2005), 779–805.

5. S.S. Schmucker, *Discourse in Commemoration of the Glorious Reformation of the Sixteenth Century* (Philadelphia, 1838), 123; "Importation of Paupers and Criminals," New York Observer, January 4, 1845; "Full Text: Donald Trump Announces a Presidential Bid," Washington Post, June 16, 2015.

6. Ray Allen Billington, *The Protestant Crusade, 1800–1860: A Study in the Origins of American Nativism* (New York, 1938), 121; Schmucker, *Discourse*, 123–125.

7. Alexander Campbell and John B. Purcell, *A Debate on the Roman Catholic Religion, Held in the Sycamore-Street Meeting House, Cincinnati, from the 13th to the 21st of January, 1837* (Cincinnati, 1837), 311; Alexander Campbell, *Alexander Campbell and Christian Liberty: In His Own Words*, James Egbert, ed. (St. Louis, 1909); Campbell, *Delusions: An Analysis of the Book of Mormon* (Boston, 1832).

8. Howard Bromberg, "Infallibility," in *Encyclopedia of Catholic Social Thought, Social Science, and Social Policy*, Michael L. Coulter, Stephen M. Krason, Richard S. Myers, and Joseph A. Varacalli, eds. (Toronto, 2012), 3: 150–151.

9. Campbell, *Debate on the Roman Catholic Religion*, 311.

10. "Election of 1856," *The American Presidency Project*, accessed on June 10, 2016: www.presidency.ucsb.edu/showelection.php?year=1856.

11. John P. Sanderson, *The Views and Opinions of American Statesmen on Foreign Immigration* (Philadelphia, 1856), 199–200.

12. "Fugitive Slave Act of 1850," *The Avalon Project*, Lillian Goldman Law Library, Yale University Law School, accessed on June 11, 2016: http://avalon.law.yale.edu/19th_century/fugitive.asp; Irene E. Williams, "The Operation of the Fugitive Slave Law in Western Pennsylvania from 1850–1860," *Western Pennsylvania Historical Magazine* 4 (1921), 150.

13. Horace K. Houston Jr., "Another Nullification Crisis: Vermont's 1850 Habeas Corpus Law," *New England Quarterly* 2 (2004), 252–277; *Boston Slave Riot and Trial of Anthony Burns* (Boston, 1854), 13–15.

14. Ibid., 9.

15. Ibid., 35; Theodore Parker, "A Sermon on the Dangers to the Rights of Man in America," July 2, 1854, in Parker, *Additional Addresses, Speeches, and Occasional Sermons* (Boston, 1859), 2:228–229.

16. Ibid., 242; John T. McGreevy, "Catholicism and Abolition: A Historical (and Theological) Problem," in *Figures in the Carpet: Finding the Human Person in the American Past*, Wilfred M. McClay, ed. (Grand Rapids, MI, 2007), 405–427.

17. Orestes Brownson, "Slavery and the Church," *Brownson Quarterly Review* 4 (October, 1862), 467; Edward Purcell, "The Church and Slavery," *The Catholic Telegraph*, April 8, 1863, in *Documents in American Catholic History*, John Tracy Ellis, ed. (Milwaukee, 1962), 380.

18. Ibid., 379; The *Mirror* quote is in H. Shelton Smith, *In His Image, But . . . : Racism in Southern Religion, 1780–1910* (Durham, NC, 1972), 200.

19. A. Verot, "Slavery and Abolitionism: Being the Substance of a Sermon Preached in the Church of St. Augustine, Florida, on the 4th Day of January, 1861," *New York Freeman's Journal*, June 18 and July 9, 1864; Charles Colcock Jones, *The Religious Instruction of the Negroes in the United States* (Savannah, GA, 1842), 197; Charles F. Irons, *The Origins of Proslavery Christianity* (Chapel Hill, 2008), 23–30; Albert J. Raboteau, *Slave Religion: The "Invisible Institution" in the Antebellum South* (New York, 1978), 99–107, 126–127, 132

20. David Roediger, *The Wages of Whiteness: Race and the Making of the American Working Class* (London, 1991), 133–186; John T. McGreevy, *Catholicism and American Freedom: A History* (New York, 2003), 51.

21. Thomas J. Murphy, *Jesuit Slaveholding in Maryland, 1717–1838* (New York, 2001), 131, 147–149.
22. William Ellery Channing, "Slavery," in *The Complete Works of W.E. Channing* (London, 1892), 577; John Thomas Noonan, *A Church that Can and Cannot Change: The Development of Catholic Moral Teaching* (Notre Dame, IN, 2005), 17–61; Avery Dulles, "Development of Reversal?," *First Things* (October, 2005), 53–61; Rodney Stark, "The Truth About the Catholic Church and Slavery," *Christianity Today*, July 2003, web only, accessed on November 20, 2014: www.christianitytoday.com/ct/2003/july web-only/7-14-53.0.html
23. Maura Jane Farrelly, "American Slavery, American Freedom, American Catholicism," *Early American Studies* 1 (2012), 69–100.
24. Gregory XVI, *In Supremo Apostolatus*, December 3, 1839, *Papal Encyclicals Online*, accessed December 1, 2014: www.papalencyclicals.net/Greg16/g16 sup.htm; Bishop John England to Secretary of State John Forsyth, September 29, 1840, in *Letters of the Late Bishop England to the Hon. John Forsyth*, rpt. (Gale, Sabin Americana: Independence, KY, 2012), 17–18.
25. Stephen C. Worsley, "Catholicism in Antebellum North Carolina," *North Carolina Historical Review* 4 (1984), 422; William S. Powell, ed. *Dictionary of North Carolina Biography* (Chapel Hill, 1986), 283.
26. Joseph Adna Hill, ed., *Negro Population in the United States, 1790–1915* (New York, 1968), 56.
27. "Foreign-born Population by Historical Section and Subsection in the United States: 1850–1990," *US Bureau of the Census*, March 9, 1999, accessed on October 25, 2016: https://www.census.gov/population/www/documenta tion/twps0029/tab14.html.
28. "New-York City. Dutch Hill," *New York Times*, March 21, 1855; Tyler Anbinder, *Five Points: The 19th Century New York City Neighborhood that Invented Tap Dance, Stole Elections, and became the World's Most Notorious Slum* (New York, 2001), 274–296.
29. Andrew H.M. Stern, *Southern Crucifix, Southern Cross: Catholic-Protestant Relations in the Old South* (Tuscaloosa, AL, 2012), 38–108; G. Lewis, *Impressions of America and the American Churches* (Ediburgh, 1845), 252.
30. Billington, *The Protestant Crusade*, 203–207.
31. Rachel L. Swarns, "272 Slaves Were Sold to Save Georgetown. What Does It Owe Their Descendants?," *New York Times*, April 16, 2016.
32. Henry David Thoreau, *Resistance to Civil Government* (Boston, 1849); John C. Calhoun, "Slavery a Positive Good," February 6, 1837, in *Selection Orations Illustrating American Political History*, Samuel Bannister Harding, ed. (New York, 1919), 248; Calhoun, "Speech on the War with Mexico," February 9, 1847, in *The Papers of John C. Calhoun*, Clyde N. Wilson and Shirley Bright Cook, eds. (Columbia, SC, 1998), 24:131.
33. John C. Pinheiro, *Missionaries of Republicanism: A Religious History of the Mexican-American War* (New York, 2014), 1–2; "Treaty of Guadalupe Hidalgo," February 2, 1848, *The Avalon Project*, Lillian Goldman Law Library, Yale University Law School, accessed on June 15, 2016: http://ava lon.law.yale.edu/19th_century/guadhida.asp.

34. John L. O'Sullivan, "The True Title," *New York Morning News*, December 27, 1845; reprinted in Julius W. Pratt, "The Origin of 'Manifest Destiny,'" *The American Historical Review* 4 (1927), 796; Joseph Crétin to Mathias Loras, August 17, 1846, quoted in Jon Gjerde and S. Deborah Kang (ed.), *Catholicism and the Shaping of Nineteenth Century America* (New York, 2012), 134.

35. John Winthrop, "A Model of Christian Charity," 1630, *The Winthrop Society*, accessed on June 15, 2016: http://winthropsociety.com/doc_charity.php; Samuel Danforth, *Recognition of New Englands Errand into the Wilderness* (Cambridge, MA, 1671).

36. Pinheiro, *Missionaries of Republicanism*, 1–34; 53–66.

37. Elliott Smith, "Historical Background of the Cincinnati Observatory," *Popular Astronomy* 7 (1941), 347. In 1810, the population of Cincinnati was 2,840; by 1830, it was slightly more than 25,000.

38. Lyman Beecher, *Autobiography, Correspondence, Etc. of Lyman Beecher*, Charles Beecher, ed. (New York, 1864), 344.

39. *Cincinnati Catholic Telegraph*, December 11, 1845; "Eight Annual Report," *The Home Missionary* 2 (1834), 19–20.

40. *Cincinnati Catholic Telegraph*, December 11, 1845; "Eight Annual Report," *The Home Missionary* 2 (1834), 19–20; "Letter from a Gentlemen after having traveled in the west," *The Home Missionary* 3 (1834), 44.

41. Ray A. Billington, "Anti-Catholic Propaganda and the Home Missionary Movement, 1800–1860," *The Mississippi Valley Historical Review* 3 (1935), 361–384; "Letter from a Gentlemen," ibid.

42. Quoted in John R. Bodo, *The Protestant Clergy and Public Issues, 1812–1848* (Princeton, 1954),

43. Quoted in Bodo, The Protestant Clergy and Public Issues, 1812–1848; quoted in John R. Dichtl, *Frontiers of Faith: Bringing Catholicism to the West in the Early Republic* (Lexington, KY, 2008), 161.

44. "Letter from a Gentleman," 44; Steven Green, *The Second Disestablishment: Church and State in Nineteenth-Century America* (New York, 2010), 110–118; Susan Juster, "Heretics, Blasphemers, and Sabbath Breakers: The Prosecution of Religious Crime in Early America," in *The First Prejudice: Religious Tolerance and Intolerance in Early America*, Chris Beneke and Christopher S. Grenda, eds. (Philadelphia, 2011), 123–142.

45. Lyman Beecher, *A Plea for the West* (Cincinnati, 1835), 57, 51, 55–56.

46. Pinheiro, *Missionaries of Republicanism*, 122–124; Robert Fantina, *Desertion and the American Soldier, 1776–2006* (New York, 2006), 54–62.

47. James Polk, *The Diary of James K. Polk During His Presidency, 1845–1849*, Milo M. Quaife, ed. (Chicago, 1919), 3:104.

48. "Tells of Loot of Cathedrals in Old Mexico," *San Francisco Call*, December 26, 1902.

49. Jay Dolan, *In Search of American Catholicism: A History of Religion and Culture in Tension* (New York, 2002), 58.

50. Quoted in John R. Mulkern, *The Know Nothing Party in Massachusetts: The Rise and Fall of a People's Movement* (Boston, 1990), 108.

51. William G. Brownlow, *A Political Register, Setting Forth the Principles of the Whig and Locofoco Parties in the United States* (Jonesboro, TN, 1844), 78; Carroll, quoted in William B. Predergast, *The Catholic Voter in American Politics: The Passing of the Democratic Monolith* (Washington, DC, 1999), 78.

52. Michael F. Holt, "The Politics of Impatience: The Origins of Know Nothingism," *Journal of American History*, 60 (1973), 309–331; Billington, *Protestant Crusade*, 408–409, 412; "Diary and Memoranda of William L. Macy," *American Historical Review* 3 (1919), 643, n. 7; J. Michael Gallman, *Receiving Erin's Children: Philadelphia, Liverpool, and the Irish Famine Migration, 1845–1855* (Chapel Hill, NC, 2000), 158; Darcy G. Richardson, *Others: Third-Party Politics from the Nation's Founding to the Rise and Fall of the Greenback-Labor Movement* (New York, 2004), 206.

53. *The Congressional Globe*, 29th Congress (Washington, DC, 1845–1846), 80.

54. Terry Golway, *Machine Made: Tammany Hall and the Creation of Modern American Politics* (New York, 2014).

55. Anne C. Rose, Beloved Strangers: Interfaith Families in Nineteenth-Century America (Cambridge, MA, 2001), 84.

56. Rogers M. Smith, *Civic Ideals: Conflicting Visions of Citizenship in US History* (New Haven, 1997).

57. Billington, *Protestant Crusade*, 203; the Adams quote is on 410.

58. Ibid., 193–200; 411–412; 324; "Consumer Price Index Estimate (1800–), *Federal Reserve Bank of Minneapolis*, accessed on May 28, 2016: www.minneapolisfed.org/community/teaching-aids/cpi-calculator-information/consumer-price-index-1800.

59. Billington, *Protestant Crusade*, 414.

60. Ibid., 422.

61. Quoted in ibid., 425.

62. Green, The Second Disestablishment, 276, 278; *New York Tribune*, December 3, 1869

63. Quoted in Green, The Second Disestablishment, 278–279.

64. Jay S. Bybee and David W. Newton, "Of Orphans and Vouchers: Nevada's 'Little Blaine Amendment' and the Future of Religious Participation in Public Programs," *Nevada Law Journal* 2 (2002), 551–552; Mark Wahlgren Summers, *Rum, Romanism, and Rebellion: The Making of a President, 1884* (Chapel Hill, 2000), 282–303.

Epilogue

In his 1873 novel satirizing the greed and political corruption of what he calls the "Gilded Age," Mark Twain has one of his minor characters, a newspaper editor in Washington, DC, publish an editorial defending the honor of an unscrupulous lobbyist who's on trial for having killed her lover. "History never repeats itself," the editorial begins, "but the kaleidoscopic combinations of the pictured present often seem to be constructed out of the broken fragments of antique legends."[1]

It's a beautifully melodic quote – but hardly a memorable one. It has morphed, therefore, into a far less poetic, though no less insightful aphorism, utilized by writers and pundits, teachers and politicians, contrarians and arm-chair activists across America: "History never repeats itself," a simple Google search will tell you, "but it rhymes."[2]

While writing this book, there were times when I felt as if I were being haunted by rhyme schemes. When I wrote about the Acadians who were forced out of Nova Scotia and the security risk that Protestants in colonial Maryland believed they represented, I could not help but think of the recent opposition among state and national lawmakers to Barak Obama's plan to relocate 10,000 Syrian refugees to the United States. When I wrote about Congress' recommendation in 1855 that the states pass their own laws to keep "foreign paupers" from crossing their borders, I was reminded of then-Governor Mike Pence's effort in 2015 to stop Syrian refugees from settling in his state. Pence tried to prohibit state agencies in Indiana from providing financial assistance to housing and medical groups that were helping the refugees relocate.[3]

While writing about the Bible Riots in antebellum Philadelphia, I thought of the more peaceful, but no less angry protests against the building of an Islamic cultural center in downtown Manhattan in 2010. In 1844, Protestants in Philadelphia believed they were being "put on a level with the age before the Reformation" because officials there had not banned the Douay-Rheims Bible from the city's public schools. In 2011 and 2012, lawmakers in thirty-one states took steps to ban Sharia law from their states' courts. The steps were legally redundant, but rhetorically powerful. According to one state representative from South Carolina, excluding Islam's laws from the country's judicial system was about "preserving and protecting the American way of life."[4]

The constancy of human nature can be as frustrating as it is gratifying. There is a thread, I think, that ties our contemporary debates about the place of Muslims in American society to the country's history of anti-Catholicism. That thread is the idea of 'freedom.'

This is not to suggest that the violence of September 11, 2001, and the bloodshed that ISIS has more recently orchestrated are irrelevant to the debate. After all, "remember, remember, the fifth of November." It is to suggest, however, that the main reason Muslims – the vast majority of whom are not violent Jihadists – don't seem to many Americans to be a good 'fit' for American culture is that the understanding of freedom that dominates the Islamic world is different from the understanding that dominates life in the United States.

The status of women, for instance, in predominantly Muslim countries that define freedom as 'submission' to the will of God is repugnant to people who understand freedom to be the exercise of certain individual rights, such as the right to personal expression or a jury of one's peers. And as an American, I am certainly not going to defend the legal and cultural status of women in countries like Afghanistan and Pakistan. That being said, repugnant, too, has been the condition of some women in Western countries such as the United States and Austria, where an overweening respect for the individual's right to privacy and personal property recently enabled men like Ariel Castro and Josef Fritzl to keep women imprisoned in their basements for decades, even though both men were visited by police officers and had next-door neighbors.[5]

Human nature may be constant, but our understanding of what freedom is most certainly is not. It changes with time, culture, and circumstance. The different meaning that freedom has to different people is the source of some of our most basic cultural disagreements. Yet, the fact that freedom's meaning can change also offers us a promise that those disagreements don't always have to be with us.

The biggest reason Americans no longer consider Catholicism to be a threat is that our cultural understanding of what freedom is has changed; it has become a bit more compatible with the corporate approach to freedom that the Catholic Church has always insisted upon. That corporate approach was outlined by Pope Leo XIII in 1899 in a letter that he wrote to an American bishop about American culture. The country's culture, Pope Leo believed, distorted freedom and turned liberty into selfishness and isolation by telling people that they had an "assumed right to hold whatever opinions one pleases upon any subject and to set them forth in print to the world." America's preoccupation with individual rights had caused the American people (and remember – Leo was expressing these concerns in an age well before Facebook and Twitter) to develop a "passion for discussing and pouring contempt upon any possible subject." That passion, then, had fueled a climate of anger, disrespect, and indifference that made America's people "unmindful of both conscience and duty."

Godwin's Law* aside, Leo's disdain for the idea that a person might actually have a right to hold and express his own opinions is as odious to Americans today as it was in 1899. But his concern that America's highly individualistic approach to freedom could cause people to forget their communal responsibilities – to forget their obligation to "be solicitous for the salvation of one's neighbor," in Leo's words – does sound a bit different to a twenty-first-century audience that has accepted (to varying degrees) the premise behind Teddy Roosevelt's trust-busting, his cousin Franklin's "New Deal" reforms, and the programs that came out of Lyndon Johnson's "Great Society."[6]

In a broad sense, the history of the twentieth century was the history of how Americans came to terms with the reality that individual rights, on their own, were not enough to produce a society that was both free and industrialized. In an age of massive, multi-national corporate conglomerates (and the wealth polarization that such conglomerates produced), lawmakers came to understand that American freedom needed more support than the mere exercise of individual rights was able to provide.

In his 1964 State of the Union address, Lyndon Johnson declared a "war on poverty" that gave good government the obligation of protecting not just an individual's rights, but also her potential. The housing, food, and educational assistance programs that he put forward were designed to

---

* This is the idea put forward in the 1990s by Mike Godwin of the Electronic Frontier Foundation; it posits, somewhat tongue-in-cheek, that any internet-based discussion, if it goes on long enough, will deteriorate into insults about Nazis and Hitler.

"give our fellow citizens a fair chance to develop their own capabilities." Drawing upon FDR's "four freedoms" address of 1941, Johnson called for America to be "a nation free from want," expanding the conditions of freedom well beyond the individual rights to property and political representation outlined by Anglo-American jurists like such as William Blackstone in the eighteenth century.[7]

Just as the Catholic Church has always taught that Scripture alone cannot help an individual access truth, American policies and institutions (even many of the more conservative ones) now teach to varying degrees that rights alone cannot help individuals access the freedom that is available to them as human beings. This shift in Americans' understanding of what makes freedom possible is one of the reasons they no longer view Catholicism as an existential threat.

The Catholic Church has also changed its understanding of freedom – specifically religious freedom. Until 1965, the Church–State separation enshrined in America's Bill of Rights was anathema to the Catholic Church. "Error has no rights" was the phrase that animated the Vatican's relations with secular authorities, and as the only earthly institution that contained the fullness of divine truth, the Catholic Church was believed to be the only proper partner for any state.[8]

But in the midst of the Cold War, Pope John XXIII worried that the world was being threatened by "a temporal order which some have wished to reorganize excluding God." Under such circumstances, any belief in God became preferable to Communism. The Pope convened the Second Vatican Council, therefore, to consider several modern questions, including the questions of religious liberty and ecumenism. The result was *Dignitatis Humanae*, which recognizes religious freedom as a "social and civil right," grounded in "the dignity of the human person as this dignity is known through the revealed word of God and by reason itself."[9]

Traditionalist Catholics resist the idea, but the fact of the matter is that the Catholic Church embraced a Protestant understanding of religious freedom in 1965 when it adopted *Dignitatis Humanae*.[10] That embrace was in response to a perceived threat – the threat of godless Communism. Today, some Protestants in the United States are turning to an older, pre-Vatican II understanding of Catholic religious freedom in response to another perceived threat – in this case, the Supreme Court's insistence that gays and lesbians have a fundamental and constitutional right to marry.

The growing support in American culture for gay and lesbian rights is the reason evangelical voters turned out in droves in 2012 to support Rick

Santorum's effort to become the Republican Party's presidential nominee. A self-proclaimed traditionalist Catholic who attends a Latin Mass, Santorum told voters that he didn't "believe in an America where the separation of church and state is absolute." Support for Santorum was strong among evangelical Protestants even before he announced his presidential candidacy – so strong, in fact, that in 2005, *Time* magazine named him one of the "25 Most Influential Evangelicals in America," in spite of his Catholicism.[11]

The idea that religion should have "no influence or no involvement in the operation of the state is absolutely antithetical to the objectives and vision of our country," Rick Santorum told a reporter for ABC News in 2012, before admitting that John F. Kennedy's speech to the Greater Houston Ministerial Association made him want to "throw up." On this point, the Republican from Pennsylvania actually had something in common with many of the world's Muslims – though naturally, Santorum would have disagreed with those Muslims about which religion ought to be involved in the operations of the state. A survey conducted in 2012 by the Pew Research Center's Global Attitudes Project found that 98 percent of the Muslims in Jordan, 97 percent of the Muslims in Pakistan, and 92 percent of the Muslims in Egypt believed that the teachings of Islam should "hold sway" over the laws in their countries.[12]

Interestingly, in the United States, Muslim immigrants seem to hold different views. In 2007, 60 percent of them told Pew researchers that they thought mosque leaders should "keep out of political matters" when they were asked about the relationship between religion and government.[13] Much like Catholics in colonial America, American Muslims today seem to have adopted an understanding of freedom that is different from the understanding held by their co-religionists in other countries. This suggests that cultural understandings of freedom are protean and dependent on more than just a person's religious beliefs – as important as those religious beliefs are.

NOTES

1. Mark Twain (Samuel L. Clemens) and Charles Dudley Warner, *The Gilded Age: A Tale of To-day*, rpt. (New York, 1901), 2:178.
2. Charles C. Doyle, Wolfgang Mieder, and Fred Shapiro, eds., *The Dictionary of Modern Proverbs* (New Haven, 2012), 121.
3. Patrick Healy and Julie Bosman, "GOP Governors Vow to Close Doors to Syrian Refugees," *New York Times*, November 16, 2015; "Judge blocks Indiana's order barring state agencies from helping Syrian refugees," *Chicago Tribune*, February 29, 2016.

4. Michael Barbaro and Marjorie Connelly, "New York Poll Find Wariness for Muslim Site," *New York Times*, September 2, 2010; Paul Vitello, "In Fierce Opposition to a Muslim Center, Echoes of an Old Fight," *New York Times*, October 7, 2010; John Back McMaster, *A History of the People of the United States from the Revolution to the Civil War* (New York, 1916), 7:377; Council of American Islamic Relations (2013). *A Brief overview of the Pervasiveness of anti-Islam legislation* [press release]. Accessed on July 10, 2016: www.cair.com/images/pdf/Pervasiveness-of-anti-Islam-legislation.pdf; Jordan Schachtel, "South Carolina House Passes Bill Excluding Sharia Law from State Courts," *Breitbart News*, January 28, 2016, accessed on July 10, 2016: www.breitbart.com/big-government/2016/01/28/exclusive-south-carolina-house-passes-bill-banning-sharia-law/.

5. Rachel Dissell, "Police Visited Ariel Castro's Section of Seymour Avenue Often While Women Were Captives," *Cleveland Plain Dealer*, May 18, 2013; Mark Landler, "Austria Stunned by Case of Imprisoned Woman," *New York Times*, April 29, 2008.

6. Tom Chivers, "Internet rules and laws: the top 10, from Godwin to Poe," *The Telegraph* (London), October 23, 2009; Leo, XIII, *Testem Benevolentiae Nostrae* (Letter on Americanism), January 22, 1899, Papal Encyclicals Online, accessed on July 15, 2016: www.papalencyclicals.net/Leo13/l13teste.htm.

7. Lyndon Johnson, "State of the Union Address," January 8, 1964, quoted in Earl Johnson, Jr., *To Establish Justice for All: The Past and Future of Civil Legal Aid in the United States* (Denver, 2014), 62; Franklin Delano Roosevelt, "Address to Congress," January 6, 1941, in *The Four Freedoms: Franklin D. Roosevelt and the Evolution of an American Idea*, Jeffrey A. Engel, ed. (New York, 2016), xi–xiii.

8. Pius IX, "The Syllabus of Errors Condemned by Pius IX," December 8, 1864, Papal Encyclicals Online, accessed on July 10, 2016: www.papalencyclicals.net/Pius09/p9syll.htm.

9. John XXIII, *Humanae Salutis* (Convocation of the Second Vatican Council), December 25, 1961, in Ann Michele Nolan, ed., *A Privileged Moment: Dialogue in the Second Vatican Council, 1962–1965* (New York, 2006), 65; Paul VI, *Dignitatis Humanae* (Declaration of Religious Freedom), December 7, 1965, *Archives of the Holy See*, accessed on July 10, 2016: www.vatican.va/archive/hist_councils/ii_vatican_council/documents/vat-ii_decl_19651207_dignitatis-humanae_en.html.

10. For a sense of the contours of this debate, see Robert B. George and William L. Saunders, Jr., "Dignitatis Humanae: The Freedom of the Church and the Responsibilities of the State"; Avery Cardinal Dulles, "Dignitatis Humanae and the Development of Catholic Doctrine"; Thomas Heilke, "The Promised Time of Dignitatis Humanae: A Radical Protestant Perspective"; and David T. Koyzis, "Persuaded, Not Commanded: Neo-Calvinism, Dignitatis Humane, and Religion Freedom," in *Catholicism and Religious Freedom: Contemporary Reflections of Vatican II's Declaration on Religious Liberty*, Kenneth Grasso and Robert P. Hunt, eds. (New York, 2006), 1–18; 43–68; 87–114; and 115–134.

11. Samuel G. Freedman, "Santorum's Catholicism Proves a Draw to Evangelicals," *New York Times*, March 23, 2012; Molly Redden, "Rick Santorum's Virginia Church and Opus Dei," *New Republic*, March 6, 2012; George Stephanopolous, "Rick Santorum: JFK's 1960 Speech Made Me Want to Throw Up," *ABC News*, February 26, 2012, accessed on July 10, 2016: http://abcnews.go.com/blogs/politics/2012/02/rick-santorum-jfks-1960-speech-made-me-want-to-throw-up/; "The 25 Most Influential Evangelicals in America: Rick Santorum," *Time*, February 7, 2005, accessed on July 10, 2016: http://content.time.com/time/specials/packages/article/0,28804,1993235_1993243_1993316,00.html.

12. Stephanopolous, "Rick Santorum"; Richard Wike, Juliana Menasce Horowitz, Katie Simmons, Jacob Poushter, and Cathy Barker, "Most Muslims Want Democracy, Personal Freedoms, and Islam in Public Life," *Pew Research Center Global Attitudes Project* (Washington, D.C., July 10, 2012), 18–20, accessed on July 10, 2016: www.pewglobal.org/2012/07/10/chapter-3-role-of-islam-in-politics/.

13. Andrew Kohut, "Muslim Americans: Middle Class and Mostly Mainstream," Pew Research Center (Washington, DC, May 22, 2007), 46, accessed on July 22, 2017: www.cie.ugent.be/documenten/muslim-americans.pdf.

Index

Printed in the USA
CPSIA information can be obtained
at www.ICGtesting.com
CBHW060317240724
12043CB00007B/462